ROCK GARDENS

HOW TO MAKE AND MAINTAIN

BY

LEWIS B. MEREDITH

WITH AN INTRODUCTION BY

SIR FREDERICK W. MOORE

M.A., A.L.S.

THIRD EDITION

LONDON

WILLIAMS & NORGATE

14 HENRIETTA STREET, COVENT GARDEN

1923

First Edition . . . *June* 1910
Second Impression . . *March* 1914
Third   ,,   . . *May* 1923

Printed in Great Britain by
NEILL & CO., LTD., EDINBURGH.

THE IRIS VALLEY
(In the Author's Garden)

I DEDICATE THIS, MY FIRST BOOK,

TO

MY MOTHER,

MY MOST INDULGENT CRITIC

PREFACE TO SECOND EDITION

I AM glad to have an opportunity of rectifying an omission that occurred in the Preface to the First Edition of this book—namely, to acknowledge, when writing Chapter XI., the great help I received from the valuable paper by Mr Clutton Brock in the Royal Horticultural Society's *Journal*, vol. xxxv., part 2, page 167 *et seq.*, to which I would refer my readers.

Since the First Edition rock gardening has become increasingly popular, and to meet the growing demand many new plants have been put on the market. Some of them are acquisitions, while others, though new to horticulture, are of little value. I have endeavoured to select those likely to prove worthy additions to the already long list of plants for the rock garden.

My best thanks are due to Mr Clarence Elliot for the list of plants he has found suitable for the moraine, and also for the description and cultural directions of the novelties he has introduced.

LEWIS B. MEREDITH.

November 1913.

PREFACE

A WORD of introduction seems needed to explain the purpose of this book. No branch of horticulture at the present time occupies so much general attention as rock-gardening. Yet not a single book deals with the subject of the cost, which I have attempted to estimate, basing it on my own practical experience. It is superfluous to observe that I have not aspired to any literary graces, but merely to tell simply what I believe to be needed.

My aim has been to provide a practical volume which will enable anyone to make and plant a rock garden. When making my own, I know what I had to find out for myself, and in the following pages my endeavour has been to save others the trouble. If I may occasionally seem to repeat myself, it is because I wish to emphasise more clearly the salient points of my subject. A rock garden is one of the most fascinating of possessions. It is an inexhaustible mine of pleasure; it entails no heavy labour, and is within the most modest means. If others derive half the enjoyment from their rock gardens that I have from mine, they will be abundantly repaid for any trouble they may take. Should I be of use to any unknown reader, I trust he will not hesitate to write to me, as I shall be delighted to reply to any questions he may care to put.

My warmest thanks are due to Mr Frederick W. Moore, Curator of the Royal Botanic Gardens, Glasnevin, who not only assisted me throughout by his kind advice, but also for ushering in my book. A preface from an acknowledged authority of his renown dignifies my own modest effort and gives it an importance to which it could not otherwise aspire. I am also deeply indebted to Mr W. Irving, of the Royal Botanical Gardens at Kew, for so kindly checking the lists of plants at the end of the book. Passed by him, they can be safely commended both to the novice and to the more experienced owners of rock gardens.   Grateful acknowledgments must also be made to Mr F. W. Moore and Mrs Delves - Broughton, who have so graciously given me photographs, and to the Editor of the *Ladies' Field* for kind permission to reproduce some of them.

LEWIS B. MEREDITH.

GRAIGUECONNA,
BRAY, CO. WICKLOW.

INTRODUCTION

LITERATURE treating of gardens and of gardening has been offered in plenty to garden lovers in recent years. It may fairly be said that much of it had better have been left unwritten, as it really has served no useful purpose, and has only tended to confuse rather than to assist novices, or even those with some experience of plants and their requirements. Such strictures cannot apply to this volume. It is a practical work, written by a practical man about a subject which he thoroughly understands, and by one who has experienced all the joys and sorrows connected with the cultivation of rock plants and alpines. The rock garden is no longer a feature to be found only in large establishments or in Botanical Gardens. The pleasure which is derived from the successful cultivation of miniature gems and of dwarf alpine plants is now fully recognised, and rock gardens have become a popular feature in gardening of to-day. In a properly constructed rock garden many little plants which refuse to grow and live under the ordinary conditions of an herbaceous border, and which resent the aggressive attentions of their more robust neighbours, generally demonstrating their resentment by dying, can be cultivated and kept in health and vigour for many years, protected by stones, sheltered from drying winds, and from shade or sunshine, dryness or moisture, according to their requirements. They can, owing to their raised position, be seen and tended in a manner more conducive to the comfort of the observer and cultivator than would be possible if they were grown on the flat.

To ensure even moderate success in rock gardening two main points are essential: a properly constructed rock garden, and a reliable guide to the nature and requirements of plants to be grown on it. There existed a demand for a sound practical work, giving explicit and detailed information on these points, and this volume meets it. Mr Meredith writes with practical experience. His own rock garden, constructed by himself, is artistic in conception, covers a considerable area, and suits the requirements of a large and varied collection of all classes of alpines. In it many difficult subjects, such as *Edrianthus Pumilio, Morisia, Androsace Sarmentose, Carnea, Villosa, Saxifraga retusa, aretioides, cæsia, Diapensoides, Daphne cneorum* and *Blagayana,* flourish and grow into good-sized tufts.

The details of how this success has been achieved are fully explained, concisely but clearly, and all necessary information is given.

F. W. MOORE, M.A., A.L.S.

ROYAL BOTANIC GARDENS,
GLASNEVIN, DUBLIN.

CONTENTS

PART I

CHAPTER I

THE SITE

CHAPTER II

THE TYPES OF ROCK GARDEN

CHAPTER III

THE NATURAL ROCK GARDEN

CHAPTER IV

THE ARTIFICIAL ROCK GARDEN

CHAPTER V

THE ROCKWORK

CHAPTER VI

THE SOIL

CHAPTER VII

THE BOG GARDEN

CHAPTER VIII

THE WILD AND WATER GARDENS

CHAPTER IX

THE WALL GARDEN

CHAPTER X

PROPAGATION

CHAPTER XI

CULTIVATION

CHAPTER XII

PLANTING THE ROCK GARDEN

CHAPTER XIII

COST

PART II

LIST OF ILLUSTRATIONS

PART I

CHAPTER I

THE SITE

Surroundings — What to avoid — Objections to trees—
Aspect—Contour—Nature of soil—Chief points to
be noted—Typical site.

"Where shall I lay it out?" This is the
first of the many problems to confront one
who intends to become the happy possessor of
a rock garden. In some cases this unfortunately presents but few difficulties—unfortunately, I say, for then the ground that is available, frequently not of the most suitable, is so
limited that there is little, if any, choice in
the matter. But others, who have a greater
variety of positions to select from, will need
to give the question more careful consideration. Therefore it would be a mistake to
lay down any hard and fast rule as to where
the site should or should not be, for this

must obviously greatly depend on what choice of positions there is.

A rock garden can be made almost anywhere —almost, be it emphasised ; for under certain conditions, which I shall point out later on, the chances of success would be but small.

But no matter what the position is, whether the spot selected be the most ideal, or the most unpromising, it will require considerable thought and no little skill to lay out the garden to the best advantage.

The object of this book is to help the reader to approach as near as circumstances will allow to the ideal rock garden : that earthly Paradise, which, alas ! the skill of mortal man has not yet achieved, nor ever will, I fear.

Though there is a great difference of opinion as to what this lovely spot should be like, at the same time there are many points on which all agree. Some indeed are absolutely essential to the well-being of those alpine gems, which one hopes to see grow and thrive as they do in their natural home, though too often one is doomed to disappointment. Yet be not discouraged, for there are many and lovely plants which are not in the least difficult to cultivate, and which will amply repay the care devoted to them. But two conditions they do require, light and pure air, which, as with all plants, are essential to success, and indeed I may add a third, sufficient drainage. One has only to remember where most of these treasures make their home in order to realise how important these factors are.

Let us for a moment imagine ourselves on some mountain slope where the alpines are in their natural state ; where the Androsaces and Saxifrages carpet the boulder-strewn ground, or beautify the weather-beaten rock with their dainty loveliness ; where by the tiny stream can be seen the lovely Soldanellas and Ranunculus and a thousand other plants to delight the heart of man. Standing there, gazing around, what a picture meets the eye ! The craggy height above ; below, the wind-swept pines ; and, far as the eye can reach, range upon range of mountains with their eternal snow-capped peaks glistening in the sunshine. Here is no jarring note ; all is peace and quiet. Nowhere has the hand of man marred the beauty of the landscape. We see Nature as she is.

With this picture in our minds let us see how best to apply the lesson it has taught us.

First we learn that the rock garden should, where possible, be out of sight of all stiff surroundings ; out of sight of the formal garden, with its trim beds and smooth lawn, its close-clipped hedges and rose-clad walls, in some quiet and secluded spot merging from the shrubbery or wild garden. At the same time let it not be so far from the house as to prevent us snatching odd moments amongst our treasures to see what flower has at last bloomed out, or what special plant was raided by the slugs last night.

As variety of outline is one of the keystones of success, endeavour to select a spot that will afford this with the minimum amount of labour.

As the spots to choose from are so many and varied, perhaps it would be best, first of all, to find out what should be avoided and what conditions would militate against success.

The worst and perhaps really the only hopeless site is one with large overhanging trees; for the drip from their branches would all too soon prove fatal to the plants underneath. Although there are some plants that will live and even thrive beneath trees, they are not sufficiently attractive to cultivate exclusively. So to choose such a spot would be but to court disaster; and in addition to the damage caused by the drip from the branches, the roots of the trees would very soon exhaust the soil that had been so carefully prepared for the alpine treasures. It would surprise many to find to what a distance these roots extend. So, above all, let there be no trees overhead, and, if possible, none within at least 15 yards—this is the minimum,—and then only to the north and west. On the other points, south and east, they should be still further away—at least 30 yards,—and even at that distance, as few of them as possible. For if they are closer, the air, which all plants so urgently require, will be shut out, and part at least of the garden will be in constant shade during the winter, with fatal results to many of the plants. Therefore, when feasible, choose a position where there is no chance of trees intercepting the low winter sun, for this is more valuable when the days are short than during the summer months.

In cases where, owing to unavoidable circumstances, the trees on the north and west are rather close, provided there is no drip on the garden from their branches, much may be done to overcome the root trouble. A narrow trench sunk rather deeper than the roots of the trees descend, and filled with rough concrete, will form an effectual barrier.

Now, having decided that the site must not be overshadowed nor shut in by trees, the next point to be considered is the aspect.

This is all-important. The problem is to find out at what point sufficient, but not too much, sunshine can be obtained with due regard to shelter from cold winds. A spot should be selected having an aspect as nearly as possible south-east; and if there be a wood or a belt of trees some distance off on the north-west, so much the better. This aspect will give the maximum amount of the winter's sun, and, as south-west is theoretically the hottest point, the rock garden will not be so liable to be burnt up during the summer.

The next point to be investigated is the contour of the land, and on this will depend to a great extent the type of rock garden to be constructed.

Sloping ground, undulating if possible, is undoubtedly the best, for thus more pleasing effects can be obtained, with less labour and expense, than can be expected on level ground, and the fact that the drainage can be made more effective is by no means the least important consideration. Hollows should at all times be avoided when there are any difficulties in the way of draining them effectively. Nothing is more fatal to alpines, and indeed to all plant life, than stagnant moisture, which so quickly makes the ground sour.

The nature of the soil should be also taken into account. It is a great mistake to imagine that rock plants do not require good soil ; the very best fibrous loam, the deeper the better, with a light sandy subsoil, is what they delight and revel in. Therefore, in the selection of a site, avoid as far as possible anything in the nature of a heavy clay soil in which it will be found difficult if not impossible to grow many of the choicer plants, and which will require more drainage and be always hard to work, whether in very dry or wet weather. A stream should be brought through the garden, if it can be obtained by fair means or foul. The merest trickle will suffice, so long as it is constant, but constant it must be, and it will add tenfold to the charm of the garden and afford unlimited possibilities.

Having fully described the chief conditions favourable and unfavourable in selecting a site, I briefly recapitulate them as follows :— The garden, when circumstances will permit, should be away from and out of sight of anything formal, approached through the wild garden or shrubbery, but still within reasonable distance of the house ; the ground should be undulating, with good light fibrous loam, facing south-east, with, when possible, a stream ; but, most important of all, it must be free from encroaching or overshadowing trees and have plenty of air and sunshine.

Bearing these points in mind, a typical

ROCK GARDEN AND STREAM, MOUNT USHER.
(From a Photo. by Mrs Delves Broughton.)

position for this would-be garden of delights may be considered. Perhaps at the foot of a nicely wooded hill facing south-east, with undergrowth around, there may be some open spot, the extent of which is not altogether important; by removing some shrubs and perhaps a few trees, it can be enlarged, if too small, and, on the other hand, if too big, it will afford scope for judicious planting. This open ground may be in the form of a little valley sloping up the hill, or, again, a small prominence thrust out from the surrounding and gradually rising ground, or undulating with natural hills and hollows. Or, perhaps, the site could be a miniature gorge with wooded heights on either side and a stream flowing through it. These are indeed ideal positions from which to select, provided always that they afford sufficient air and sunshine.

But with far less promising material—for instance, a sloping field, or even a level one —much can be done. The former is by far the better of the two, for on level ground the question of drainage would probably arise and cause serious difficulties.

Sunken ground in the form of a large hollow, such as an old sandpit, can be utilised to some advantage, as can also an old quarry. These, if wooded above, will make charming sites; but here again attention must be given to the essential necessity of obtaining sufficient fall for the drains. On that point let there be no uncertainty, for, if the drains prove defective, but a poor return will be made for time and money expended.

The foregoing are, I think, a few of the most usual sites to select, and their description will, I hope, suggest to the reader how to make the best choice of the ground he has at his disposal. What form the garden will eventually take, and how it can most advantageously be laid out, will in a great measure depend on such details as soil, locality, contour of ground, money to be expended, etc. All these will be dealt with in the following chapters.

CHAPTER II

THE TYPES OF ROCK GARDEN

The natural — The artificial — Types of the natural —
The old quarry — The amphitheatre — The horseshoe—The valley—The cliff—The rocky bank—
The rocky knoll — Points to be noted — Types of
the artificial—The sunken—The gravel-pit—Bank
and knoll types — The rocky bed — The very
large rock garden — Advantages and disadvantages
of the natural — Advantages and disadvantages of
the artificial.

THE different types of rock garden may be
divided into two sections, which can be called
the natural and the artificial.

In the Natural garden the rocks are already
placed there by Nature, and all that is required
is to utilise them to the best advantage.

In the Artificial garden—the name speaks
for itself—the rocks have to be placed, and in
some cases even the banks on which to lay
them have to be formed.

In the first section, the Natural, there are three types—the old quarry, the rocky bank, and the rocky knoll.

The second section is more varied, and in it may be included the sunken garden, the old gravel-pit, the bank, the knoll, the rocky bed, and the very large rock garden.

The *old quarry*, a favourite and very charming site for a rock garden, and one that has many points to recommend it, is hard to deal with owing to the difficulty of adorning the large masses of perpendicular rocks, which, although capable of giving very striking effects with their cataract of flower and foliage, require years of growth even under the most favourable conditions. It usually takes one of four forms, which may be called the amphitheatre, the horseshoe, the cliff, and the valley.

First let us note the *amphitheatre*, a very uncommon type. This formation, as the name would imply, is a hollow almost or entirely surrounded by rocky sides, and will seldom be a really suitable site. Most probably it will be found very difficult to drain thoroughly, and even were this done, there would still be that

VALLEY TYPE.

VALLEY TYPE. PORTION OF AUTHOR'S GARDEN.
(*Veronica Lavaudiana* and *Aubrietia Dr Mules* in foreground.)

want of air which causes plants to damp off, especially during the winter. The only occasion on which this form of quarry is admissible is when it is on a very large scale, at least 25 yards across, and even then it will generally prove but a doubtful success.

The next and perhaps the commonest form is the semicircle or *horseshoe*, usually an excavation into the side of a hill, giving bold rocky places for planting. This is an excellent form to choose, provided it fulfils certain conditions. It should not open towards the north, for then it would be exposed to the cold winds and the greater part of the rocks would constantly be in shade, and although some shady corners will be found useful, the majority of plants like the sun. In fact, any point but this will do, for so long as the entrance is sheltered from the north it is a matter of no great importance where it may be; but the southeast is preferable, for it gives greater variety of position, both for sun- and shade-loving plants.

The *valley* or defile form can be made very effective. The best way for it to lie is east

and west, but this is not so important provided
that its course winds sufficiently. The more
it winds the better, for it then provides the
greatest variety of aspects and sheltered and
shady nooks, the advantage of which will be
duly appreciated when the time comes for
planting. It will also be beneficial if the
bottom of the valley slopes gradually from
one end to the other, thereby ensuring more
efficient drainage. A stream down the centre,
when it can be obtained, greatly enhances the
charm and considerably enlarges the scope
for variety in plants that can be cultivated,
because those preferring moisture can be
planted on its banks, and those requiring a dry
soil will find a home on the heights above.

The *cliff* type, as the name implies, is of
abrupt formation, rising from comparatively
level ground, and is one of the best and most
effective forms, provided the aspect is suitable.
South-south-east is the best, but any other
point will do so long as it does not face towards
the north, for with a northern aspect the
garden would get but little sun, certainly not
the amount all alpines so imperatively require.

In this type the surroundings should be carefully noted, so that they may be in keeping with the proposed rock garden.   The ideal approach is through some open and undulating stony ground, with occasional patches of stunted gorse and heather, dotted here and there with oak, holly, or birch trees ; then a stretch of grassy sward, with occasional rocks, which become more numerous as the slope gently rises towards the foot of the cliff.   Even this is a delightful scene ; but picture the face of the rock, now bare, clothed with sheets of Aubrietias, Rock Roses, Dianthus, and innumerable other equally lovely plants, the Silver Saxifrages springing from some almost invisible chink or cranny, and nestling close to the rock, with their airy blooms waving in the breeze, while from some shady nook the Ramondias peep forth.   This is indeed a delightful picture, therefore care should be taken to see that the frame is worthy of it.

There are now a few points to be noted which apply equally to all the foregoing forms of garden made from an old quarry.

The first and most important is to observe

the state of the quarried face of the rock. By this is meant, whether it is much broken in outline or presents a sheer, perpendicular face. It should be rough and jagged, so as to give a number of ledges—the more numerous they are and the greater their variety the better—forming steps or terraces, by which easy access can be had to all parts. Otherwise it will probably be necessary to plant the alpines and examine them from the steps of a ladder, which, to say the least, is not desirable. But, bad as a too smooth surface may be, an overhanging rock face is even worse. An odd protruding ledge here and there does not so much matter, in fact they may prove of service, but even they should not be of sufficient size to prevent the rain from reaching the plants below. The whole tendency of the rock should be to slope back from the ground at the foot, for it is necessary that rain should have access to every part. Though it is wonderful in what apparently dry and arid spots alpines will thrive, it is certain that their roots must find moisture somewhere. Few people realise to what an extent rocks retain moisture even during a dry season, so it is important that the slope should be sufficient to catch and store the rain. If it is intended to conduct a stream through the garden, make sure the outlet will be such as to prevent any risk of the garden suffering from flood.

The next type is the *rocky bank*. This, as its name would imply, is a bank of natural rock, and may be the face of a small hill, or form part of a large one.

It is, in fact, rather similar to the quarry cliff, already described, except that the rock, being as nature left it, will probably have a more gradual slope, and therefore possess the advantage of being easier to clothe.

The advice as regards surroundings applies equally here. The rock garden should be approached through shrubbery or wild garden, and situated in some open, though not too exposed, spot facing south-east, with a background of suitable trees, such as oak, holly, or birch, or any of the Conifer family.

The *rocky knoll* is the next and the last of the natural types. It may be a small eminence of rocky ground standing out by itself, or a sort of promontory on the side of a hill, or on sloping ground.

This type is practically identical with the last described, except that in this case the whole or the greater part of the hill is dealt with, whereas in the former only one face of it was. The knoll is undoubtedly the better of the two, for with it a much greater variety of aspects can be obtained, and also more scope for developing the different natural undulations of the ground. The aspect is, of course, unimportant, for a hill standing by itself will be open to all points of the compass ; and even if it be part of a larger hill, it will be shaded only on one side, which will not so greatly matter. With this type, also, care should be taken that the surroundings are suitable.

As this concludes the types of the natural rock gardens, a few points in connection with them may be mentioned before proceeding to the artificial.

In the first place, large masses of rock have to be dealt with as placed by Nature's all-powerful hand, and we must therefore adapt ourselves to whatever conditions we may find.

KNOLL TYPE.

BANK TYPE.
(In course of construction.)

Since the chief object is to provide as many spots as possible to plant in, select the type of rock that will give the greatest variety of pockets, remembering at the same time that all pockets, no matter of what size, must be able to be drained. The necessity of draining having already been emphasised in the first chapter, it is superfluous to dwell further on it here.

The quality of the rock should be carefully observed, and if there be any choice in the matter, select a soft and porous stone, such as sandstone, in preference to hard rock. The former has the double advantage of absorbing the moisture essential to plants, and minimising labour when it comes to making drains.

Examination of the different types of artificial rock gardens reveals that they are, as one would naturally expect, more difficult and probably more expensive to make, demanding more thought and skill to engineer successfully than do the natural gardens. On the other hand, they possess the great advantage of extreme adaptability, for they can be made almost anywhere, from a level field to the side of a mountain.

The first and perhaps the most usual is that
type which, for the want of a better name, I
shall call the *sunken garden*. One form of
this is a sunken path, the centre of a little
valley. The other is represented by a large
hollow with banks surrounding level ground,
rather similar to what was called the *horseshoe*
in the quarry type.

Of these two, the former is the more usual
and indeed the most attractive ; nor is the reason
far to seek, for in this type every aspect can
be obtained by making the paths wind sufficiently ; this at the same time has the advantage of providing, in a limited area, more surface
whereon to plant. This form can be made
on the level ; but sloping ground is to be preferred, for the effect is better, and, what is more,
or at least equally, important, the drainage can
thereby be assured. The surroundings, as in
all other cases, should be as wild and natural
as possible, though much may be accomplished
by judicious planting. As the latter, however,
takes years to become really effective, it is best,
whenever practicable, to have the surroundings
provided by natural means.

BANK TYPE.
(Site being cleared.)

BANK TYPE.
(Rocks in place.)

The large hollow is not a form which re-commends itself very much, for it is apt to look too artificial and also entails considerable labour to make.   But in cases where there is only a very limited extent of ground it is useful, for in this form the maximum amount of surface available for planting can be obtained. It must be on sloping ground, for to dig a large hollow in the level will usually result in the formation of a small lake.   The lower side should be open and at least level with the surrounding ground, above it if possible.   This entrance should face either east or south ; the north is the least desirable aspect, because then so little of the garden would get any sun.

The *gravel-pit* is practically identical with the foregoing, except that the hollow is already made.   The lie of the ground here must also be such as to ensure the drainage being efficacious, and the open side should face any point except the north, preferably south or east.

The *bank* and *knoll* types are exactly the same as the rocky bank and rocky knoll already described, except that in the former the natural rock is already there, while in the latter cases we have only the soil, and the rock will have to be placed.

Both these types are attractive, but in a great measure dependent on the natural contour of the ground, which should lend itself to their several requirements.   The bank form can be made in a gently sloping field, but the labour entailed would be great.   In the case of the knoll, so great would it be that I would not advise the reader to embark on it, not at least on a large scale, for I doubt if the result would sufficiently repay him.

Next we will deal with the *rocky bed* or very small rock garden.   This is a most delightful and useful way of growing alpines for those who can only spare a few square yards, or who do not wish to attempt anything larger.   The surroundings in a garden of this kind are not, of course, of such importance as in the case of the larger gardens, but all the same it is as well to select as sunny and open a spot as can be obtained, and removed as far as possible from the shade or drip of trees.   There is no garden, no matter how small, that cannot have a rocky bed, tiny though it may have to be ; and it is surprising with what success some of the most difficult alpines can thus be cultivated, creating no small amount of envy amongst the possessors of larger rock gardens.

The best and most usual form is a raised bed, the outline of which may be as varied as fancy dictates. It can also be made on the sunken principle, but would then occupy more space and not prove as satisfactory in many ways, whilst it would also entail more labour and greater cost. For all that is aimed at in a garden of the rocky bed type is to have some spot in which to grow the choicest treasures. It is useless to endeavour to imitate larger gardens, because the result would be only disappointing and would look puny and out of keeping. Therefore I most strongly recommend those who cannot, owing to circumstances, have any of the foregoing types, to try the rocky bed, and I feel sure they will never regret the experiment.

We will now go to the other extreme and describe the *very large rock garden*. This garden is diametrically opposed to all other

types hitherto dealt with, in which the alpines
are grown on the lower banks or slopes, with
shrubs and trees above; for in this case the
shrubs are planted in the valleys and the alpines
on the heights.   Without doubt this is copying nature more closely; but to be effective
the plan must be on a large scale, and cover
at least two or three acres, composed of naturally very broken ground, with hills and hollows
well defined and as varied as possible.

The rockwork must correspondingly be of a
bolder formation and its lines more generous.
If this is not the case, the result will be but
a poor and insignificant imitation of Nature's
handiwork, and consequently be far from
pleasing.   As, however, bold rockwork entails
larger rocks, with cost and labour increased
proportionately, I should not advise anybody
to whom expense is a matter of importance
to embark on a garden of this type.   But
those who are fortunate enough to be indifferent to cost, and who possess suitable ground,
may well be urged to make this style of garden,
and I feel sure that they will never have cause
for regret, provided it is skilfully laid out.

ROCKY BED.

HABERLEA RHODOPENSIS.

The surroundings are, if possible, even more important than in any of the foregoing types, for here ugly spots cannot be planted out with banks of shrubs, and, as the paths and rockwork are on the heights, there is every opportunity of seeing those walls and hedges which we fain would imagine to be miles away. For these reasons, therefore, the site should be some distance from any of those blots which mar the view, and the approach should be through some wood, or ground of a similar and uncultivated character.

A spot such as the following would be ideal : a large open stretch of very undulating and broken ground at the foot of a wooded hill—with perhaps a stream running through it into a piece of marshy ground at its lower side —which in turn merges into scrub and stunted trees, fully exposed to all points except, perhaps, the north, where it is sheltered by a belt of ancient and majestic pines. This would indeed be a spot worthy of the bestowal of every care and trouble, in order to develop it to the best advantage. The ground for a garden of this sort must be very undulating ; by undulating I do not mean merely uneven ground, but a spot with well-defined hills and hollows—the bolder and more marked they are the better.

This concludes a terse survey of the various types of rock gardens, and some consideration of the various advantages offered by each may assist in deciding which of them shall be adopted. As a rule, though, the choice is but " Hobson's choice," for the site in most cases decides the type that will have to be adopted.

The advantages of all rock gardens belonging to the natural section, quarry, rocky bank, or knoll, are that the rock is there ready placed by nature in masses far larger and bolder than could ever artificially be put into position, and that, for this reason, more striking effects can be obtained, both as regards height and boldness of outline. It may also be a very cheap garden to make. But this is a very uncertain quantity, and is difficult to ascertain at first. It may ultimately turn out to be both expensive and troublesome, because so much depends on the formation and description of the rock. One of the disadvantages is that it is often very difficult, and, in fact, at times almost impossible to get as much soil into the pockets as the plants that are to inhabit them require. Often, indeed, it is hard to find pockets or ledges of any description where they are wanted, and although rocks are attractive in conjunction with flowers, still they are only the means to an end, and that end the cultivation of the plants. Effective drainage may at times be found difficult and expensive to carry out successfully, but as this depends enormously on the texture of the rock and other circumstances, it would be a mistake to lay down any hard and fast rules regarding it.

It is a great fallacy to imagine that alpines, because they are dwarf-growing, do not require a deep rooting medium, for there is no class of plants whose roots penetrate so deeply in comparison to their height. In addition, as all the rockwork has to be artificial, every description of pocket and ledge can be made, as varied and numerous as the needs of the plants demand, the benefit of which will be found when the time comes for putting the alpines into their home.

The chief disadvantage is purely a matter of cost, though this is often a rather important point. The labour of digging out the garden and, in all probability, of having to cart the rocks some distance means expense. Those people are fortunate indeed who have the rocks close at hand, and only those who have had to draw their supplies of stones from a distance can fully realise how great a saving it is.

The merits of the sloping bank and knoll types are, that if the ground has the necessary conformation, the only labour entailed is to clear the surface of scrub and weeds, and to place the rocks in position ; therefore, unless any unforeseen difficulty should arise, they are probably the least costly types to make, but at the same time they are not so effective as are some of the other forms.

As regards the old sand- or gravel-pit, pretty well the same remarks apply to them as the foregoing, except that in these cases soil may have to be procured in addition to rocks, and perhaps, the outline being bolder, better effects may be obtained.

The small rocky bed (we can scarcely call

VALLEY TYPE.

VALLEY TYPE.

it a rock garden) has this advantage over all the other types, that it can be made in a very limited space ; but it does not give scope for the effective massing of plants ; its purpose is merely to satisfy those who wish to grow alpines, but do not desire to embark on any large undertaking.

We now come to the last, namely, the large rock garden with its shrub-filled valleys. This form, provided that the space is large enough and its undulations sufficiently well and boldly defined, can be made most effective ; but it is, without doubt, the most difficult to lay out really well, and the cost, owing to its size, must be considerable, for in order to get the proper effect it must be made on very generous lines. Big, bold masses of rockwork are essential to success, and these should so combine with the undulations of the ground as to give it that natural appearance which should be the characteristic feature of all rock gardens.

CHAPTER III

First preparations—Cleaning ground—Exposing and preparing the rock—Pockets natural and artificial.

THIS chapter will be devoted to the development of the natural rock garden, the various types of which have been dealt with in the previous chapter.

As may be expected, very similar treatment will be required for all types, in order to convert them from rocks, either bare or covered with rank vegetation, into gardens in which the choicest flowers can be grown. The following directions will therefore equally apply to all natural rock gardens, irrespective of their various forms.

When the scene of operations has been decided on, the first thing to be done is, if necessary, to expose the surface of the rocks and clean out every nook and cranny, removing all weeds or other vegetation growing there. This will at times be found no light task, for it is surprising how roots, especially those of weeds, penetrate into almost invisible fissures. It is difficult to oust such a plant as a dandelion when it gets its long and fleshy tap-root down several inches into some crack in solid rock, for it will not be sufficient merely to cut off its crown—its severed crown will promptly reappear worse than before.

All overhanging trees should be cut down which are likely to cause a drip on to the plants below, or which would in any way shut out light and air from the garden. It is, however, advisable, in the initial stages at least, to leave any small stunted trees or shrubs springing from fissures in the face of the rock, or clinging to its summit, especially if these include such kinds as mountain ash, oak, holly, or any of the Conifer family. They are characteristic of and in keeping with mountain plants, and can easily be removed later, if it be deemed advisable.

3

When the work of clearing and exposing
the rock has been done, the next operation is
to prepare receptacles for the soil in which
to grow the plants. These may be obtained
by opening up and developing natural fissures,
by making new ones, or by forming pockets
among the rocks.

The only means of accomplishing this is
with the crowbar or cold chisel, assisted at
times with some explosive, such as dynamite
or gunpowder ; but this latter method is
dangerous in every sense. Besides requiring
very careful manipulation, it is very apt to do
more harm than good by removing rocks that
would have been better left, or by imperceptibly loosening others, the first intimation
of whose unstable condition is finding them
one morning at the foot of the cliff burying
some of our choicest plants in their *débris*.
It is well to remember, when splitting rocks,
whether it be for the purpose of making or
enlarging some crevice, or opening up some
pocket, to first find out how the " grain "
of the rock runs, and split the rocks with, not
across it. For rock, like wood, has a regular

and defined dip or grain, though perhaps not as well marked as the latter.

As it is obviously impossible that any definite rules can be laid down as to how such pocket or fissure is to be formed, the reader must exercise his own judgment in the matter, and utilise the grain of the rock to the best advantage. In no case should a pocket or a crevice, whether perpendicular or horizontal, be made in an overhanging rock face. Of even greater importance is the necessity of ensuring that the bottom of each pocket can be drained thoroughly, even should this entail cutting through solid rock. If this, however, be found impossible owing to position, or other circumstances, in order to prevent water lodging, fill up the pocket with rough concrete to the point where the draining becomes effective.

When there is a difficulty in getting a sufficient number of natural pockets in the rock a good deal may be accomplished with the assistance of cement, yet it should never appear in the completed work, but always be most carefully hidden by either plants or soil.

Examples of this kind of work are the building of a small terrace of stones along the front of some ledge, incapable of holding any or a sufficient depth of soil, or the fixing of wedge-shaped pieces of stone with their thin ends up in some large vertical fissure to keep in the soil, which otherwise it would be found difficult, if not impossible, to prevent being washed out by heavy rain.

Bare rocky ledges which slope outwards in such a way that the rain is thrown off, instead of being directed back towards the soil behind, can have this fault remedied by raising the front with a layer of concrete.

Steps may also have to be cut to give access to the plants. These should never be formal, but as uneven as possible, and merely form stepping-stones from one ledge to another.

Where a stream comes over the face of the rock, its volume and course should be so controlled that even in time of flood it can do no damage to the plants growing beside it.

The two chief things to remember in the

preparation of natural rockwork are first to ensure thorough and efficient drainage of every pocket, and next to provide space sufficient to give that depth of soil all rock plants so urgently require.

Great care should also be taken, when putting soil into the pockets and crevices, to work it thoroughly into every corner, so that there is no possibility of leaving any air space, which so often proves fatal to plants. With regard to the soil required, full particulars will be found in Chapter VI.

CHAPTER IV

THE ARTIFICIAL ROCK GARDEN

EVEN more care and study are required to lay
out the artificial rock garden to the best
advantage than is the case with the natural
rock garden ; for whereas in the latter the
position chosen will to a great extent, if not
altogether, determine the type it has to be,
this is not so with the artificial garden, or at
least not to the same extent.   Take, for example,
a narrow field, sloping gradually from one end
to the other, which all will agree does not

appear the most promising material on which to work. Yet even this can be developed into three different types of garden.

By levelling a piece of ground across the face of the slope, and raising the upper part with the soil removed, we have the foundation for the bank type ; again, by sinking a path up the slope of the field a little valley is obtained ; and, lastly, by excavating into the slope the foundation for a garden is made, which will in a great measure correspond to the horseshoe type. It is therefore quite evident that it is necessary to devote considerable thought and exercise no little skill in laying out the ground, if it is to be done in the best possible, and at the same time most economical manner, and full advantage be taken of all its natural formations.

The fact that the same piece of ground can be laid out in several very different ways, all equally good, or nearly so, does not simplify the task.

It should also be realised that one cannot expect to get quite such bold effects in the artificial garden as are found in the natural, and

the reason of this is not far to seek, for in order
to obtain them large masses of rocks, weighing
at least several tons, would have to be put into
position, a Herculean task involving no little
cost, and a bigger undertaking than the majority
of people would care to attempt.   But let it
not be for a moment supposed that these large
boulders are an absolute necessity, for quite as
attractive gardens can be made by using comparatively small rocks, so long as these rocks are
skilfully placed.   On the placing of them the
ultimate result will in a great measure depend.

As it would be best perhaps to take the
several types by themselves, the little *valley*
shall be dealt with first.

Having selected a site of ground sloping, if
possible, for reasons already stated, the first thing
to be done is roughly to lay out its general lines.
Place a few stakes in the ground along the proposed lines and study the effect from various
points.   There are several things to be noted
when doing this.   Let the valley lie as nearly
east and west as possible, and especially let it lead
from one definite point to another, and not look
as if it had come there by chance and with no

THE BANK.
(Roughly formed before rocks are put into place.)

FIRST LINE OF ROCKS LAID.

object. Study the contour of the ground, and if, owing to the surroundings, it appears as though a path should come from one special place and lead to another, mark these two points and lay out the garden between them. The garden should neither begin nor end too abruptly; let it commence with a barely perceptible hollow, the height of the banks on either side of the path gradually increasing; while in a similar manner they should decrease in height at the further end, merging by degrees into the rising ground beyond. Nothing could look more unnatural than to come suddenly from comparatively level and probably rockless ground upon some bold rockwork which is there for apparently no reason, and which ceases equally abruptly and inconsequently. The same rule applies to all artificial rock gardens; avoid anything sudden in the way of rockwork, but lead up to it gradually, with odd rocks scattered here and there, increasing in number as you approach your garden proper. If this be done it will only be copying nature, which should always be your guide.

If the space available for working upon be

rather limited, and it is desired to obtain the utmost possible surface on which to plant, resist the temptation to make two small valleys in preference to one large one. This is most important and one of the most essential points to be noted, and I cannot impress it too strongly on the reader; for in laying out a rock garden, one of the chief objects is to obtain the boldest effects the site will permit of. This cannot be achieved if more is attempted than the space conveniently allows. If space is available and it is desired to have two parallel valleys, they should be at least 20 or 30 yards apart, in order to allow for planting on the top. The path should so wind about that it is impossible to see both ends simultaneously from any spot. The garden will be far more attractive and its size apparently very much increased if we see only a small portion of it at a time, and if round every corner some fresh attraction can be provided.

Having laid out the general lie of the main path, the next procedure is to mark out lines on either side about 20 feet from it, following its course throughout, which we will call lines

of section. Then from the ground, between
the lines of section, the sod must be removed,
skinning it off as thinly as practicable and
stacking in a heap in some spot convenient, but
well out of the way. The next operation is
to begin to dig out the valley. But should the
work be done after the method practised in
railway and other similar cuttings, the top,
and most valuable, soil would become buried

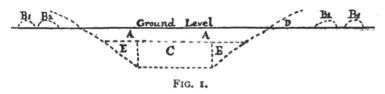

FIG. I.

beneath the almost useless subsoil. Therefore
some other method must be adopted. A
practical way of doing this is to divide the
ground between the lines of section into plots
about 10 yards long ; each of these will then
measure about 30 feet long by 40 feet wide.
From the first plot remove the top spit to
say a depth of 6 inches, putting it in heaps
($B_1 B_1$, fig. 1) on either side, and about 10
yards away. Next, dig out the soil down to
the subsoil, also putting it in heaps ($B_2 B_2$) on
either side, and about 5 yards from ground

marked out. Thus a cutting will be obtained
(A A) about 40 feet wide, and probably from
12 to 18 inches deep, with all soil of any
value in heaps (B_1 B_2) on either side. But the
banks must be quite 6 feet high, and at least
another 3 feet will have to be sunk in order to
achieve this. In the centre of the excavation
dig a trench (C) about 3 feet deep and 9 feet
wide, the bottom of which will be the path,
and throw the soil back on either side over
the ground (D) between the heaps (B_2 B_2) and
lines of section. Now cut out the portion
E E, and throw the soil over what has just been
removed from C. This will probably raise the
bank to from 4 to 5 feet above the bottom of
the path, with its sides sloping towards it. At
this stage it is well to work out the general
formation of the banks in the plot being dealt
with ; by this I mean that where it is ultimately
intended to have a long and gentle slope, keep
the subsoil further back and roughly make the
desired gradient, or if a bold and almost perpendicular bank is required, work accordingly.
For further particulars with regard to the
formation see page 47.

Having done this, the second plot is approached. Remove top spit as before, but the rest of the soil, down to the subsoil, instead of being put into a heap, should be thrown over the two sloping banks of plot 1. Then proceed to dig out the subsoil as before, again making the general formation of the banks as the work proceeds. Plot 3 is dealt with in a manner similar to plot 2, and so on till the last plot, when the soil removed from plot 1 and left in a heap (B_2) must be put over it.

The result of all this will be a cutting with sloping banks on either side about 5 to 6 feet high, with the good soil over the subsoil, and with heaps of the top and best soil available for use later on when the time comes to place the rocks in position.

This method undoubtedly entails considerable labour. The only alternative is to treat the whole in a way similar to that adopted for plot 1, and after having roughly formed the banks to throw back the soil removed. This, of course, has the advantage of saving the labour of carting the soil from the first to the last plot, and also it is easier to work out the general

formation of the banks when all excavations
are completed ; but, on the other hand, there is
more labour in throwing the good soil into
heaps and then putting it back again than in
placing it directly over that plot which has
iust been dug out.   It is, however, a matter of
individual taste which method to choose, and
though perhaps the latter alternative does entail
a little more work, it is the better of the two,
on account of its being easier to lay out the
general scheme when all digging is completed.

I have described these operations rather fully,
as I wish them to serve as a basis for the reader
to work on ; but he will, of course, have to
modify them according to the circumstances
of each individual case.

Where, however, there is a natural valley it
may only be necessary to make it a little deeper.
This can easily be done by sinking the centre
path and throwing the soil up on either side,
having first removed the sods, or whatever was
growing on it, for it is essential to have clean
ground to start with.   The chief point to look
to when excavating is that the subsoil shall be
in its proper place beneath the upper soil, and

also that the latter shall be of the greatest possible depth.

It has been already pointed out that the course of the valley should wind about considerably. The slopes forming the banks must also vary as much as possible, in order to avoid presenting a too artificial appearance. In some places let the bank recede in a gradual slope, whilst in others a more abrupt formation will lend a pleasing contrast. Here and there some flat patches may skirt the path and be almost on the same level with it; further on they may be raised considerably above the path level. These are a few suggestions whereby to break a stiff and formal outline and give the variety which should be aimed at. As I said before, it is far more satisfactory, and will probably in the end save considerable trouble, if the rough formation of the banks is made when cutting out the valley and before the rockwork proper is commenced. Nothing is more annoying than to find, when making a hollow in a certain spot, and when it is nearly completed, that the subsoil appears, for this entails removing the good soil for some distance round the spot and sinking the hollow deeper, with every chance of leaving it in a form that will retain water—the last thing to be desired. For these reasons let the rough scheme be worked out in the initial stages.

It may perhaps assist the reader and be the simplest way of showing what is meant by these variations in the slope of the banks, if I describe one artificial valley that I know.

This valley is made in a piece of ground about 85 yards long by 35 yards broad, with a fall of about 1 foot in 16. Owing to the circuitous course the valley takes, its actual length is about 105 yards, with a path varying from 7 feet to 12 feet wide, while the banks on either side vary from 5 feet to 9 feet in height.

Particulars of the formation of the right bank may now be given, beginning from the lower end of the valley.

For the first 15 yards or so the slopes are very gradual, but increasing in gradient until some bold rockwork at A (fig. 2) is reached. This is almost perpendicular, and is from 8 to 9 feet high. Round this the path turns sharply to the right, and then follows an almost semicircular course to the left for about 15 yards.

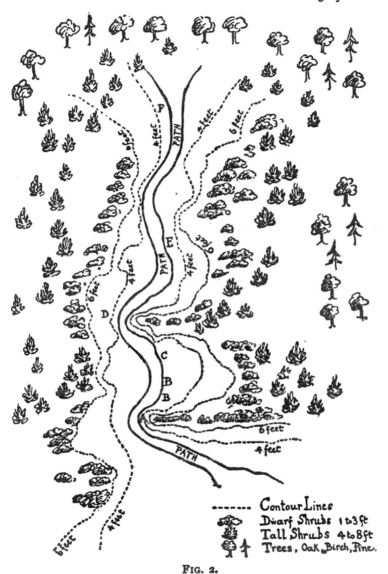

FIG. 2.

After passing the corner at A, the bank gradually takes a more gentle slope, receding from

4

the line of the path, thereby forming an almost level piece of ground at B between the base of the bank and the path. This continues to about the centre of the semicircle, when at C the bank again advances towards the edge of the path, at the same time increasing its gradient until, by the time the end of the semi-circle is reached at D, the slope again reaches the line of the path. Here it bears rather sharply to the right and continues to wind on gently for the next 17 yards, when it takes a decided bend to the left at E for about 20 yards, then once more curves gently to the right and gradually dies away towards the rising ground beyond.

Beyond the rather steep part at D, the bank by degrees assumes the form of two terraces, the lower one about 3 feet above the level of the path, and of a very gentle gradient, while the upper one is much steeper. This formation continues until about the point E, when the terraces once more merge into one bank, with a gentle gradient, which does not vary very much for some distance, when it again becomes steeper as it winds round the curve, after

SECOND LINE OF ROCKS IN POSITION.

ROCKWORK ADVANCING UP THE HILL.

which it gradually dies away into the rising ground beyond.

If the reader has been able to follow this description, he will see the necessity of working out the general scheme of the banks as he proceeds with his excavations.

There are a few things to be observed which may help him in deciding where the level or where the steeper places should be. It is generally found to be more effective if the sharper gradients are made on the convex curves, while on the concave are the level spots and more gentle slopes. The advantage of this is fairly obvious, for in the former case the steep rockwork will stand out boldly and naturally form a corner, while in the latter the banks form a hollow which lends itself to the formation of a level spot at their base.

If these ideas are carried out, there will be no danger of having the same formations opposite each other on either side of the path, for where the curve is concave on one side it follows that it must be convex on the other, and *vice versa*.

It will give a pleasing variety if in some

places the valley has the appearance of forming a gorge, while in others it may pass between two hills ; but even then the steep parts need not be exactly opposite, for the high ground can be cut diagonally.

It is only the general outline of the banks that is being dealt with at present. In the chapter dealing with the placing of rocks in position, it will be shown in more detail how they should be worked up to give that appearance of natural rockwork which is to be aimed at.

There is yet another point to be noted before leaving this type of garden, though, indeed, it applies generally to all gardens which have to be artificially dug out. It is this, when excavations have to be made, always be careful to get the top soil well away from where actual work is being done. You will thus ensure there being plenty of room, if, as may easily happen, it is found desirable to slope the top of the bank further back than had originally been intended. If the good soil be in the way, extra labour will be entailed clearing the required space.

The next type of garden is what may be called *the hollow*. If it is to be made on the face of a hill or rising ground, lay out the site in a manner similar to that adopted in the case of the valley; the outline should be as varied as possible, and be careful to avoid the appearance of its being marked out with a compass. Remove sods or whatever may be growing on it, then take off top soil to a depth of about 6 inches, putting it in heaps at a convenient distance from the ground marked out. After this has been done, dig out the remaining soil to the subsoil, also putting it aside. Then continue the excavations, throwing the subsoil removed on to the ground above until the required depth has been attained. The banks must not be made too steep; they should have a general slope of not more than 1 foot in 4 feet, because the steeper the formation the more numerous and the larger are the rocks required. In places, of course, the slope may be fairly perpendicular; but even there a gradient of 2 feet in 5 feet is quite enough, and effects as good, if not better, can be obtained than if a miniature cliff be constructed. After having dug out the garden in the rough, the good soil can be spread over the bank that has been made, keeping the first 6 inches for use when making the rockwork.

In this case also it is advisable to work out the formation of the banks in a general scheme before commencing to build in the rocks. Make it as varied as possible—a steep place here, there a little hollow looking like a tiny gorge which might at one time have been a watercourse. In another spot let the slope of the bank be very gentle, merging into a level stretch at its foot. Variety should always be aimed at, and the sequence of formations should not be repeated.

When deciding on the depth to which the hollow is to be sunk, always look to the drainage to see that there will be a good fall towards the entrance, in order that the water from the surrounding rocks may be carried off.

This type of garden should always face south, or as nearly towards that point as possible.

If there is a natural hollow to work on, then the labour of making the garden is considerably reduced. All that is required to be done is to first clear the ground and then to develop it as far as is deemed necessary, treating it in much the same way as in the more artificial type. For a natural hollow merely means that Nature has already done a certain amount of the work, and man will have to take it up where she left off.

Now to deal with the *bank* and *knoll* types. These, as may be expected, do not require the same amount of work in the earlier stages as those types already described, for, instead of the general formation having to be made, the outline is already there and only requires judicious development. If they are not sufficiently high, this can be rectified by sinking the ground at the base and raising that above with the soil dug out, having previously cleared the ground of whatever was growing on it. Very probably there will be occasional and solitary rocks just showing above the surface. Dig round these to ascertain their size and how they can eventually be worked into the general scheme of the rockwork. The banks in gardens of this type are usually higher than in the case of the valley gardens, and it will be expedient to make paths over them ; it will therefore be advisable that their general lie should be planned out, and the formation of the banks made in the rough.

The *rocky bed* requires comparatively little work in the preparatory stage. It usually is made on ground that is level or fairly so ; therefore make sure that it can be properly drained. When the site has been marked out, making its outline as varied as possible, dig out the soil to a depth of about $2\frac{1}{2}$ feet, and put in 6 to 9 inches of broken stones, coarse first and smaller above, which will facilitate drainage. At the same time take care that there is a proper outlet for the water to get away. The soil can, if necessary, be replaced, adding more then to bring it to the required height ; for the top should be quite 3 feet above the surrounding ground.

In dealing with the *large garden* it is difficult to give any very definite instructions for its treatment, as so much depends on the natural formation of the ground. One of the more important points is to lay out the garden in correct proportions : a most difficult thing to achieve. Try to avoid having a number of small and abrupt hills with wide valleys between, looking like a collection of ant-hills dotted over the ground. If the valleys are wide, let the hills be large, not necessarily high, but covering a good extent of ground. Three or four, or even two, are quite enough, rising gradually in long and gentle gradients. For example, we have two fairly large hills, each covering about half an acre or more, with a curving valley about 30 feet wide between them. As we advance up this valley another and rather larger hill appears in front, round the foot of which the valley winds towards the left, while on the right a miniature pass crosses the range. These three hills, with the valley and pass, are quite enough to cover a couple of acres of ground ; any more would look out of proportion and give a fussy effect, which should always be avoided. This is merely a description of the main scheme, for the hills will need to be broken up and varied in outline.

As the rockwork is on the higher ground,

the paths leading through it will probably
have to be on almost the same level as the
plants, or at least more nearly so than in the
types of gardens hitherto described. Therefore, in order to show the plants to advantage,
and to be in keeping with the surroundings,
the rocks should be considerably larger and
the whole scheme worked out on bolder and
broader lines. Where, for instance, in the
valley type, the level spots cover a couple of
square yards or so, three or four times that
extent would be scarcely sufficient here.
Again, when in the former case the bank
rises 6 feet in a distance of as many yards,
here it may take 15 or 20 yards, and the
eventual height from the bottom of the valleys
to the tops of the hills will be anything from
10 feet to 30 feet. The inclines should
always be more gradual than in any of the
gardens thus far noticed. In fact, to put the
whole matter concisely, in the former types
the idea was to copy some small portion of an
alpine scene, while in this it is to produce,
though on a very reduced scale, the scene in
its entirety.

NEARING COMPLETION.

THE COMPLETE ROCKWORK.
(Note general dip of stones from right to left.)

How difficult it is, only those who have tried can fully realise ; but if it is successful, a masterpiece of engineering and artistic skill will have been achieved.   There are few who, on account of expense, could attempt a garden of this description unless they had ground that lends itself naturally to it, when it would perhaps only be necessary to make the valley or valleys deeper and slightly raise and vary the heights and contours of the hills.   In this case one need clear only the ground that is intended to be rockwork, namely, the heights, unless indeed the valleys are overgrown with trees or scrub, when it should be thoroughly cleaned.

As the surface to be planted is so large, and as it is always necessary to reach all parts easily and without fear of walking on the plants, a number of paths will be required. Not paths in the generally accepted term— nice gravelled walks with stone edges—but almost imperceptible ways winding in and out amongst the boulders, starting from the main valley up a gentle slope for perhaps a few yards, then round some large rock and on, ever gradually rising, through some tiny gorge, then perhaps a rock-strewn valley, bending its way round some lesser peaks of the main hill, till at last the top is reached. Then let this summit, while bold and conspicuous, be no mere incongruous mass of piled-up rocks.

The object of a rock garden is to grow plants, and the rocks are merely an adjunct, though an important one, but still only the means to an end.

So unlimited is the scope for variety in a garden of this sort, that space will not admit of the enumeration of all its possibilities, so much must be left to the reader's discretion. Almost every type of garden thus far described can be worked into it more or less ; the object being to get the greatest variety of aspect and formation. To him who is in want of ideas there is no better teacher to go to than Nature. There is, however, no need to travel all the way to Switzerland. Let him but study the rocks and hills at home, and on his return try to reproduce the formation or scene on a smaller scale in his garden. More ideas can be obtained in a day's walk in a wild and rocky country than in a week's reading, and a few studies of natural rock made with a camera will prove of untold assistance. The chief difficulty is found when one comes to try to reproduce and adapt these pictures on the reduced scale : such at least has been my experience.

Those who, undeterred by expense, or the magnitude of the undertaking, wish to make such a garden, but have only sloping ground out of which to form it, will have to dig out the valleys and raise the hills. To such I should recommend working on lines somewhat similar to those laid down for the valley, only, of course, on a very much larger scale, the valleys wider in proportion to their depth and the hills with a more gradual incline. To get the soil in its proper place and to avoid burying what is wanted on the top and to distribute it evenly will be even more difficult than before. For while alpines require at least 12 inches of good soil as a general rule, the shrubs in the valleys require far more, and great ingenuity will have to be exercised to provide all this.

Keep the very best fibrous loam for the alpines, because shrubs, though requiring more depth, are not so particular as to quality. Even if the soil is mixed with a little subsoil, " weathering " will soon improve this and do no harm.

In all artificial rock gardens aim at variety of outline, but avoid too sudden transitions from one formation to another. Let the change be gradual, and always try to make it look as if there was a reason for it, for such is invariably the case in nature. Try to keep the lines of the garden in proper proportion. It is not an easy thing to do, for in ten yards you must reproduce what in nature covered ten times that distance ; but as proportion is the keynote to success, it is worth taking considerable trouble to achieve it.

Do not attempt more than the size of the ground will allow. One good wide valley looks far better than two narrow ones. There should always be the feeling of openness and expanse. Also remember that all-important point, drainage. Whenever making a hollow or forming a level plateau, see that there is no chance of water lodging : this is the stage

at which to do it, and not after the rockwork is finished. It is hardly necessary to say
that the real effect cannot be judged until after
your rocks have been placed in position ; but
please remember that the hills and banks are
not made to grow rocks, but that the rocks
are placed there to keep up the soil in which
the plants are to grow. Without the rocks
the soil on any steep gradient would soon be
washed down, although there is an angle, called
" the angle of repose," at which soils of every
description will remain stationary. But this
angle is generally of a far more gentle gradient
than is suitable for a rock garden, therefore it
will be necessary to adopt the other alternative
and build the slope up in the form of terraces,
each of which will, in all probability, have
a gradient considerably less acute than the
" angle of repose," and there will, therefore, be
less chance of the soil being washed down by
heavy rains.

CHAPTER V

THE ROCKWORK

Kind of rock to use and what to avoid — Principles of particular construction—Types of rockwork to avoid —The placing of individual rocks—Fissures and how to make them—Strata—Principles of general construction—Paths—Steps—The moraine.

HAVING made the garden in the rough, the next step will be to construct the rockwork, and the first thing one naturally wants to ascertain is the best description of rock for this purpose. On this point there is a diversity of opinions, but the majority consider that sandstone, which has special properties of retaining moisture, is the best all round, though others prefer mountain limestone. But almost any kind will do provided that it has a sufficient variety of forms, the greater the variety the better for our purpose. The stone from the nearest quarry will, generally, be found most desirable, if for

EXAMPLE OF ROCKWORK.

EXAMPLE OF ROCKWORK.

economical reasons only. Quarried stone will give more pleasing results, and is easier to build, the faces of the stones working in better together than is the case with those rounded by the action of the weather or water. Some people indeed object to the freshly hewn rock as looking too new, but the advantage of having rocks that will join closely together more than makes up for this, and a couple of years will give the desired weather-beaten appearance.

It is impossible to build rocks with rounded surfaces properly together, for, being invariably convex, it follows that on either side of the point where they touch there must be a gap, which has to be filled up somehow or other with small stones. This is seldom satisfactory, for frost and rain have a marvellous way of working soil through any opening, no matter how small.

The rock for building should consist of solid blocks, with as much variety of surface as possible, and must have a good base to rest upon. The area of the base should be about two-thirds of the surface exposed, and quite one-third of the rocks should be buried in the ground ; some people say even as much as half, but this is rather more than is necessary.

As I have already stated, almost any class of rock will do ; but avoid anything in the shape of thin slabs or round boulder stones—the former because they have an ugly and monotonous face and are difficult to make steady in the ground, the latter on account of the difficulties already mentioned in working them together satisfactorily ; though a few indeed may be half buried on the summit of a mound to give the idea of the point of a rock just appearing over the surface of the ground.

Above all things, avoid anything in the nature of artificial rock, clinkers, burrs, bricks, or the like. The bottom of a drain is the only place for such as these. Equally to be shunned are old tree stumps or wood in any form, for it so quickly rots away and promotes the growth of fungus, which is pretty certain to kill any plant growing near it. Nothing but good rough stones should be used. The size will in a great measure depend on the facilities for dealing with them, and also on the nature and size of the garden ; the larger the rocks, the bolder the effects obtained. All sizes can be used, weighing from a few pounds to a ton or more. A good building material is about 15 or 20 rocks to a ton.

Not only do I recommend quarried stone, but go so far as to say that it should all come, not only from the same quarry, but even from the same part of it ; for you will then get both a uniform colour and strata, which will to a great extent simplify the building and also give the ultimate rockwork a more natural appearance. It should never look like a collection of geological specimens.

The fundamental principle governing the construction of rockwork is to make the visible rock appear as if it is merely a part, and only a small part, of what is hidden by the soil. To carry out this idea, there must be uniformity in the arrangement of the strata. No rock should look isolated, but part and parcel of those adjoining. If this is carried out, a very different effect will be obtained from that found in those so-called rock gardens, now fortunately becoming less common, which consist of a mound of earth and a number of stones. Long, flat, spiky ones are generally chosen, and stuck up on end like so many solitary gravestones, without the least connection one with the other ; in another, though perhaps less objectionable, form, the stones are laid flat ; or, in yet another type, a number of large and ugly boulders are strewn over the ground, apparently for no special purpose, and certainly with no sense of cohesion. In none of these types are the stones of the least use, either for keeping the soil in position, or for showing off the alpines planted there. The general result is that the owners of these gardens, despairing of ever making them " a thing of beauty " or " a joy for ever," cover them as best they can with Ferns, Sedums, Nasturtiums, or anything that can be found to quickly hide their ugliness. Mr Reginald Farrar, in his book *My Rock Garden*, so aptly designates these forms as the " almond pudding," the " dog's grave," and the " devil's lapful."

But bad as the above types are, they are yet a great advance on that form, remains of which are still occasionally seen — hideous arches, grottos, or bridges, without a spot to hold more than a handful of soil. The constructors of such atrocities must have thought, if indeed they were guilty of thinking at all, that alpines lived on air and stones alone. For nothing else was provided. It is needless to say no self-respecting plant would grow under such conditions. The only remaining hope was that some friendly ivy would soon cover their nakedness.

These, then, are some of the most usual forms to be avoided ; but there are others more or less on the same lines, all hideous and unnatural. Why they were ever made will always remain a mystery. It may be presumed that the object in view was to grow alpines in a place somewhat akin to that from which they originally came. But how was this attempted ? A home was prepared for them as diametrically the opposite in every way as human ingenuity could contrive. The result was a foregone conclusion. It is only within comparatively recent years that the more natural and reasonable method has been adopted, with the result that success in place of failure has crowned the efforts of those copying Nature more faithfully.

Having now pointed out how the rocks should not be placed, there is no need to dwell further on the subject, and I will proceed to show how they may be used to the best advantage.

There are a few rules that should be observed in the construction of rockwork. In the first place, every rock, big or little, should be made quite firm in the ground; as this is often rather loose owing to the bank having so recently been made, the bed for each rock should be well trampled in order to get as solid a foundation as possible and minimise its chances of moving. The soil also should be rammed in well around it; for although the rocks will get firmer in time as they settle, it is better not to rely too much on this.

Each rock should be sunk for at least one-third of its height below the surface; it should be able to bear the weight of a man without moving, for it will often be necessary to stand on the rocks when working in the garden, and if they should move, considerable, if not fatal, damage might be done to the plants growing over and around them. Another advantage also gained by sinking the rocks is that most alpines like to get their roots amongst stones.

To all rock plants moisture is most essential, but at the same time it must be accompanied by sharp drainage to prevent any water lodging at the roots. For this reason the top surface of all rocks should slope down towards the bank behind, in order that the moisture may be directed towards the roots of the plants growing there.

The faces of the rocks should not as a rule overhang so as to prevent the rain reaching the ground at their foot, for this would prove fatal to many kinds of plants. There are indeed some, especially those species having woolly leaves, that require some shelter over- head, for damp lying on their leaves soon kills them ; but even these require that their roots be kept moist, which can be achieved by sink- ing flat stones in such a manner as to catch the rain from the rock above and direct it to the roots of the plant.

In the construction of rockwork, more

especially when negotiating the bolder masses,
it may often be found necessary to deal with
spaces, or, to use a more correct term, fissures,
between two rocks.   These are of three kinds,
oblique, vertical, and horizontal.

The oblique fissure looks externally very

FIG. 3.

much the same as the horizontal, the difference being that in the case of the former
it slopes down towards the back, while the
latter keeps to the same plane.   In both of
these it is very important to make sure that
the under rock projects beyond the upper,
otherwise rain falling on the sloping face
of the rock above will miss the fissure

altogether, and whatever is planted in it will in all probability soon die ; for if no moisture reaches the roots from the front, they will have to extend 12 inches or more to the back of the rock before they obtain any. This is more than most are capable of doing, certainly in the juvenile stage, in which they must be planted.

It is necessary to keep the rocks slightly apart in order to give room for a good layer of soil between them, and this should be done, while building the rockwork, by inserting some pieces of hard stone. The layer of soil should be filled in before the upper rock is put in position, so that no air space may be left, which it may be found very difficult to avoid later on.

Vertical fissures should, when feasible, be made wider at the top than the bottom, for then, as the soil settles, its tendency will be to compress itself against the sides of the rocks, instead of leaving them, as would occur were the shape reversed. Where the fissure is sufficiently large, wedge-shaped pieces of stone should be inserted, and care should be taken

to place them in such a way that their thin
ends are uppermost.

The object of placing the stones in this
manner is to separate up the fissure in such
a way that each of the divisions may form an
integral part of the whole and become com-

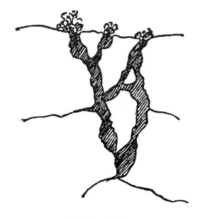 

Vertical Fissure.   Vertical Fissure.
Wrong Method of Building.   Right Method of Building.

FIG. 4.

pressed as the soil sinks under the action of
the rain and its own weight.

This indeed is the theory on which a
vertical fissure is built. It is, however, in
practice far from easy to carry out with any
degree of success, for it will generally be found
that, no matter how carefully it is made, nor
how tightly the stones are rammed into posi-

tion, a few winters' frosts and rains will work them loose and a quantity of the soil be washed out, to the great detriment of whatever is growing in it. This applies chiefly to the larger fissures, for in the smaller ones the soil is less likely to be dislodged.

A number of the rarer alpines, however, so dislike moisture lying about their crown that they can only be grown successfully in this type of fissure ; the chief difficulty is to get the plant well established ; but once it is established, the roots will help to keep the soil in position and the leaves protect it from being washed away by the action of the rain.

The oblique and horizontal fissures are, on the other hand, quite easy to make, and prove very satisfactory. Of the two the oblique is to be preferred, as it ensures utilising all available moisture.

On studying the face of a quarry, it will be seen that there is a certain uniform grain or strata running through it ; this may vary greatly in form, and is very much more marked in some kinds of rock than in others. In limestone it is very apparent, and in a less degree in granite or sandstone. Now this grain should, in a great measure, rule the construction of the rockwork. When in its natural position the strata runs in a certain uniformity ; therefore when building the rockwork each stone should be so placed that its grain coincides with that of those next it.

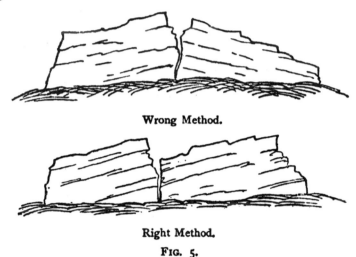

Wrong Method.

Right Method.

FIG. 5.

Examine carefully the formation of each rock, and, if its strata is vertical, the rock adjoining must be the same ; if oblique, it should be built into one having a similar formation. In this case it is necessary to note that its dip should continue in the same plane, as otherwise the lines of grain would meet in a V shape (fig. 5). If, as is sometimes the case, a certain amount of " live " rock exists and it is necessary to add to it, the rocks added must observe the same " dip " or formation as the " live " rock.

If these rules be carefully followed, little if any difficulty should be experienced in building the rocks into one another. Each will, however, have to be chosen with some care, in order that it may correspond both with its neighbour and also with the general formation that has been laid out ; that is to say, if it is required to form a corner, the stone chosen should have one of its faces to correspond with and be in the same line as the last previously placed stone, whilst another face will give the direction in which to continue the rockwork.

Having now dwelt at sufficient length on the way in which the individual rocks should be treated, the next thing is to show how to construct the rockwork in general.

As was pointed out in a previous chapter, the primary object of the rocks is to keep the soil in position and prevent it being washed down the sides of the garden by heavy rains.

The most usual and effective and also the

simplest method of accomplishing this is, with
the help of the rocks, to make the banks into
a series of terraces ; at the same time the rockwork should follow the same line or dip of the
strata throughout.

These terraces should vary in every con-
ceivable manner : height, width, outline, and
gradient.   This last is important, for if it is too
steep the moisture will run off too quickly and
not percolate the soil, and if it is too flat the
ground is apt to get sodden.   A fair gradient,
such as 6 inches in 2 feet, is about right.   It
will also be necessary during the construction
to make a number of pockets or compartments
in order to give a variety of aspects, the
advantage of which will be fully appreciated
when the time for planting comes.

In order to avoid getting the terraces in
regular planes, let them, in places, merge into
each other ; perhaps where they join a fresh
one may be started on yet another level.

In the long and gentle gradients the terraces
will naturally be wider and not so deep, very
different from the formation in the bolder and
steeper parts, where each rock almost touches

A WELL-COVERED ROCK BANK.

Saxifraga trifurcata and *Dianthus suavis* in foreground.

that below it. Keep the largest rocks for the boldest and most perpendicular formation. Where the banks slope back with a gentle gradient there should be no hard and defined line of rockwork along the top to give the impression of a ridge, but rather they should recede gradually, with the rocks becoming fewer and more scattered, until eventually the formation is lost in the shrubs beyond. On the other hand, in the bold and precipitous formation, the top of the rockwork may be abrupt and well defined, but even in this case the effect is more pleasing if the ground beyond rise gradually towards the shrubs forming the background.

Build up the main rockwork first, keeping in view the chief object, which is to maintain the soil in position. Afterwards, if there appear to be any large extent of ground without rocks, it will be easy to put in a few here and there to break the monotony, or form a position for some plant requiring a special aspect or treatment.

Do not fall into the rather popular error of imagining that a rock garden must be covered

with rocks : it is a mistake from every point of
view.   The cost will be greater, for more rocks
must be used, and the effect be less pleasing.
The rocks should monopolise the ground in
only a few places, as is the case in nature,
and, as a general rule, in the wider terraces
an odd one appearing here and there is quite
sufficient.

In the case of the large garden, where the
shrubs are in the valleys instead of being on the
heights, the rocks should increase in number
as you ascend.   They should also become
larger and the construction of the rockwork
bolder as the summit is approached, for this is
how it is in nature.

Once more, let me advise the would-be con-
structor of rockwork to go to that master-
builder, Nature, and study some natural rock
formation ; it will prove of great assistance in
carrying out the directions I have just given.

As a parting word of advice, have some
definite scheme and stick to it.   Do not let
the rockwork meander about in an aimless
sort of fashion, but endeavour all through to
carry out some well-defined geological forma-

tion ; if this is done, the extra trouble it entails
will be more than repaid.

Paths are an important and necessary factor
to be considered. The main paths, such as
those that go through the centre of the valley or
across the bank and knoll types, may be from
7 feet to 12 feet wide, and should be well
made. A good surface may be obtained by
laying a foundation of about 4 inches of stones,
broken fairly small, and covering it with
about 2 inches of the finest riddlings from a
stone-crusher. They should be rolled well
together to make them bind properly. The
path should have a decided fall from one
end to the other, in order to ensure efficient drainage of the banks on either side.
This is a point that should be carefully
noted.

It is also very advisable to lay flat stones
throughout the rockwork at convenient dis-
tances apart, in order to facilitate getting at
the plants and to avoid treading on them.

The main paths will require something in
the way of a rocky edging, if only to prevent
the soil from being washed over them from

6

the banks ; but anything the least formal must, of course, be most carefully avoided.

In order to prevent formality the line of rocks should be varied as much as possible. In some places, especially where the construction of the rockwork is abrupt, they may be as much as a couple of feet high, while in other places they need not be more than a couple of inches above the level of the path.

Steps are often a necessary adjunct, and, if well made, will prove a very attractive feature. Here again there must be no formality, nothing built up with cement. Large flat stones, the more varied in size and shape the better, may be just laid on the ground, after it has been made level and solid, to form the steps. The commoner Sedums, Saxifrages, Campanulas, and other dwarf-growing species should be planted between each of the steps, so that in a short time but little of them is visible.

In conclusion, when building the rockwork, make quite certain that the soil is well packed in behind and between each rock, and that there is not the least chance of an air space being left. Myriads of plants have been lost through

ROCKY STEPS.
Sedums and *Campanulas*.

neglecting this apparently unimportant detail. It must be done in the building stage, for later on it may be found very difficult, if not impossible, to do it properly.

Some of the higher-growing alpines would, if planted in anything like good soil, quickly succumb to over-feeding. Many of these plants are found growing in the moraines deposited by the action of the glaciers, the soil of which consists chiefly of grit and small stones, with just a trace of vegetable loam in it. There some of the rarest alpines will be found growing in a state of health never arrived at in this country. For them a special place will have to be prepared, to supply as nearly as possible the conditions to which they have been accustomed. Choose some bank the drainage of which is ensured, facing south, about 3 to 4 feet above the level of the path, and having a gentle gradient of not more than 1 foot in 16 feet. Remove the soil to a depth of about 18 inches or 2 feet, and put a layer of about 4 inches of coarse stones in the bottom; then about 2 inches of smaller stones. On top of this place a layer of fibrous loam or sods, then fill up with a mixture of stone chips, sand, loam, peat, and leaf soil, in the proportion of four parts of chips to one of the other constituents in equal proportions. For those plants requiring lime, chips of limestone should be added.

The alternative method is to build up instead of sinking. This can be done with large blocks of stone, filling up the intervening space with the required compost. Though somewhat more expensive to make, it will probably give better results. The one essential need of the moraine is drainage of the most perfect description; for this reason let it be fairly high and exposed, when it will also be less liable to suffer from ground damp.

Many people might imagine that in such a spot as this plants would suffer greatly from drought during a dry summer, but this is not the case, for so well does the stone retain moisture that even in a dry season the soil a few inches below the surface remains damp.

CHAPTER VI

THE SOIL

Importance of climate—Best type of soil—Supplying deficiencies in soil—Necessity of loosening ground—Drainage.

CLIMATE has more effect on rock plants than either soil, aspect, elevation, or any other natural factor. This may not sound encouraging, for, whatever else we may do, we cannot control the climate, so all that remains is to adapt ourselves to, and make the best of, existing conditions. Perhaps it is just as well that it is so, for the result would indeed be curious were we able to secure the amount of sunshine or rain that each desired. Uncertain as the climate of the British Isles now is, it would then be a hundred times more so.

Next to the climate, the soil, as might be expected, is of the chief importance. But

with regard to it we can assist or adapt the
natural soil to meet our needs.

Leaving for the present those plants which
require a special receipt for their nutriment,
as a general rule the majority of alpines
like a cool, deep, light, and gritty soil, rich
in humus, such as a good light fibrous loam.
Anything in the nature of a clay-soil is to be
avoided, for in winter it is liable to get sodden,
owing to its being very difficult to drain effectively, and in summer to bake and crack. It
would be difficult to get anything better than
the top 6 inches or so of an old pasture, if
the soil is of a loamy description.

Unless the soil is naturally very light and
gravelly, sand will have to be mixed with it :
good sharp river sand is the best. Small broken
stones, such as would pass through a $\frac{3}{4}$-inch
riddle, are beneficial. Alpines like, above all
things, to get their roots round and between
stones ; it keeps them cool and damp, as stones
retain moisture much longer than the soil
and are not so easily affected by change of
temperature.

If the garden is of large extent and the

soil is not of a gravelly nature, spread sand
and broken stones over it to the depth of
about 2 inches. This, when well dug in,
about 18 inches deep, ought to give a good
material to work on. Some plants will require an even lighter mixture, but it can
be prepared for them when they are being
planted.

It is a fallacy, and I fear rather a popular
one, to imagine that alpines do not require
good soil. This may have arisen from the
fact that they are often found, and in a thriving condition, in places where apparently
other herbage could not exist. To a great
extent this is due to the deep-rooting powers
of the alpines, which enable them to obtain
moisture and nourishment in places where
other species of a more shallow-rooted nature
would soon die.

But although these alpines require and
appreciate a good light soil, anything rich and
heavy is very detrimental, for, if they do not
damp off in wet weather, they will probably
run to leaf so much that the flowers will be
but sparse, and, in addition to this, the foliage

will lose that hard and compact form which
it should have, and which is the joy and pride
of those who are successful in the cultivation
of rock plants.

If the soil be deficient in humus it may be
supplied in the form of leaf-mould, but it
should be old and well decayed.

Many and various are the opinions about
lime-hating and lime-loving plants, but on one
point all are agreed, namely, that some plants,
such as the peat-lovers, will not live if there is
any lime in the soil ; this unfortunately cannot
be eradicated if there naturally, but it is easy
to supply artificially if required ; it is clear,
therefore, that a soil free from lime is to be
preferred.

Lime can be supplied either in the form of
old lime-rubbish or well-slaked lime ; but in
order to be sure that the latter is quite "dead,"
it should be dug into the ground some weeks
before planting. It is recommended by some
authorities, such as Mr Robinson, that separate
portions of the garden should be prepared for
those plants exclusively requiring lime, or
peat, or so forth, in preference supplying the

necessary ingredients to the individual plant. This method, while having much to recommend it, has, I think, the disadvantage of rather restricting one as to the position of certain plants, irrespective of the suitability of aspect or how they will work into the general scheme of planting. On the whole it seems a better plan to supply each plant, or group of plants, with whatever they need at the time they are being put in. This, however, is entirely a matter of individual taste, so long as each plant gets what it specially requires. But it will not do to just put the soil each plant likes round its roots; there must be sufficient for them to extend through.

It has been proved by experience that some plants, although found in nature growing in soils of a special character, will thrive quite satisfactorily in ordinary soil; as an example, most of the Ericas, Rhododendrons, or Azaleas, which are essentially peat-loving plants, will thrive quite satisfactorily in good fibrous loam, provided it has no trace of lime. In fact, the only exception I know of to the above rule is that those plants disliking lime will not, as already mentioned, live if there is any present in the soil.

There are some plants indeed, and amongst them some of the most difficult alpines to grow, that require the very poorest of soil, composed chiefly of grit and small stones, and to these anything in the nature of high feeding quickly proves fatal.

For these the moraine, as described in the previous chapter, is eminently adapted, ensuring as it does the quick and efficient drainage so essential to maintaining them in health.

Alpines, even those that are found most difficult to cultivate in this country, grow freely in their native habitat, and it is now becoming generally recognised that this condition of things is due, not so much to the soil as to the climate, the altitude, rainfall, temperature, length of growing season, duration of snow, humidity of the air, etc.

Although the winter in high altitudes is so much longer and far more severe than is ever experienced in this country, the alpines lie dormant during it, nursing their strength and vigour under a thick blanket of snow, which keeps them dry and warm and protects them from sudden changes of temperature or extremes of cold. When the spring comes again, melting the snow, they are found ready to shoot up and adorn those arid slopes with the glory of their bloom.

How very different are the conditions in this country, where the winters are made up of sudden changes, one day dry and warm, the next bitterly cold, and always the ever-present damp, which is more fatal than anything else !

Owing to the mild days the plants never become really dormant, and are, therefore, far more susceptible to cold than they would be if they had ceased growing.

As, however, the climate cannot be altered, all that can be done is to protect those plants which are most affected by the damp, such as the Androsaces and other of the woolly-leaved species. This protection can be obtained by placing sheets of glass over the plants during the winter months, say from November to April, which, though unattractive in appearance, will often save some treasure from extinction.

Many plants are not only affected by damp in winter, but also may suffer from drought in the summer, and generally it will be those kinds which are found fully exposed to the sun in their native homes. This may perhaps, to a certain extent, be accounted for by the difference of altitude, for there is a theory that the sun, owing to the air being so much more rarefied, does not have the same parching effect as at a lower level. The only remedy for this is watering, which in a large garden may prove rather an arduous task, but is preferable to losing the plants.

It is also advisable in dry weather to keep the surface of the ground loose. It is rather a popular error to imagine that stirring the soil conduces to evaporation; the result is quite the reverse, for by loosening the surface the capillary action of the soil is encouraged and moisture is drawn up from below.

A very useful tool for this purpose is the "Baby Bucco," a miniature form of that very excellent cultivator, "The Bucco," so widely advertised in all gardening papers.

If one comes to analyse it, it will be seen

how impossible it is to supply the climatic needs of a collection of plants gathered from all parts of the globe, such as is found in the modern rock garden, where such extremes as Mesembryanthemums and Androsaces grow side by side, the former almost a semi-tropical plant, while the latter comes from the snowline of the Alps. So it can scarcely be a matter of surprise if difficulty is experienced in growing them equally well. But be the climate what it may, there is one thing that must always be seen to, and that is drainage, to which I have so frequently referred, for damp is more fatal than anything else in this country.

If the subsoil is of a very open and porous nature, few drains will be required ; but if, on the other hand, it is heavy and retentive, the drainage will need to be most thorough.

In the artificial rock garden, where the subsoil during primary operations is exposed, it should be left in a slope, so that there may be no hollows for the water to lodge in. A few inches of broken stones over it will greatly assist the drainage. At the foot of the bank it is well to make a drain of loose stones which can run along at the back of the rocks bounding the pathway ; this will act as a main drain, and other short ones, if thought necessary, can be made to lead into it. This main drain should be made in the earlier stages and before the good soil is filled in.

Although drainage is so very important, it is a mistake to imagine that it cannot be overdone, for this is quite possible.

The object to be attained is to direct all moisture to the roots of the plants, and then to remove whatever the soil cannot readily absorb. If this is done the excess of moisture will not lodge in the ground and prove fatal to the plants.

CHAPTER VII

THE BOG GARDEN

Position—Natural bog garden—Artificial bog garden—
The stream.

A BOG garden, on any extensive scale at least,
should not be amongst the rockwork, but
should rather adjoin it in such a way that the
approach to the rock garden may lead through
it. But marshy patches of, say, from 5 to 10
square yards in area, here and there throughout the garden, will be found an additional
attraction, and give scope for a wider range
of plants.

These spots should have a variety of aspects,
some in shade and others in the sun, to suit
the requirements of the different plants ; they
should not have any formal or well-defined
outline, but should merge imperceptibly
from the rockwork. To those who are

fortunate enough to have a stream through
their garden the task will be easy, for then
all that is necessary to do is to remove the
soil to a depth of about 3 feet, where these
boggy spots are required, and fill the hollow
so made with about 6 inches of coarse stones, a
little charcoal, and a compost made up of about
equal parts of peat and fibrous loam, with a
little sand and broken stones added.   If there
is difficulty in procuring peat, leaf-mould will
do, but peat is to be preferred.   The course of
the stream should then be directed in such
a way that it flows through the spots so
prepared ; and in order that the water may
be evenly distributed, it is well to divide up
the stream into several smaller channels, thereby
ensuring the thorough percolation of the soil,
and the maintenance of constant moisture all
over these marshy spots.   Sink the bog garden
slightly below the level of the surrounding
ground, in order that it may catch all the
surface moisture from the rockwork adjoining.

As many of these spots as desired can be
made by directing the course of the stream
from one to the other.   It is, however, a

troublesome matter when the stream is so small that there is not sufficient volume of water to supply all the boggy patches with the required amount of moisture, or when it is liable to dry up in summer ; and still more difficult when there is no stream at all to work with. In either of these cases it will be necessary to prepare these marshy beds in such a way that the moisture will be retained.

To accomplish this it will be necessary to make the bottom of the bed fairly water-tight with either concrete or yellow clay. Of the two, concrete gives better and more permanent results.

The directions are fairly simple. Dig out a hollow about 2 feet 6 inches deep of the required size and shape.

Over the bottom of it put a layer 4 to 6 inches thick of concrete, about 6 parts of coarse sand to 1 of cement. At the lower end, about $\frac{1}{4}$-inch above the level of the bottom, put a pipe of 1-inch or 1$\frac{1}{2}$-inch bore ; this should lead into some drain or other means of carrying off the water, in case it at any time be thought expedient to run it off from the bog-bed. There will have to be a plug or tap at the lower end of the pipe, in such a position that it can be easily got at, and the end which is in the hollow should be covered with per-forated zinc to prevent it getting choked.

Having fixed this pipe, build a wall of concrete, or bricks if preferred, round the sides of the hollow, about 4 to 6 inches thick, and about 10 inches high, making sure that the top of this wall is approximately on the same level all round.

On the lower side, and about 8 inches from the bottom, fix a pipe of about $1\frac{1}{2}$-inch bore. This will act as an overflow, and also conduct the water to the next marshy spot and keep the water in the hollow at a constant level, and should have its end covered with per-forated zinc. This being in position, put a layer of about $\frac{1}{4}$-inch thick of pure cement all over the bottom and sides to ensure their being water-tight.

It is advisable to put on the cement before the concrete has set very hard, say on the following day, for it will be found to bind together better and not be liable to chip off.

BOG GARDEN IN AUTHOR'S ROCK GARDEN.

It should then be left for several days to thoroughly set, when it can be tested by filling up with water, which should rise to within about 2 inches of the top of the wall and give a depth of about 8 inches. If all is found satisfactory, empty by means of the bottom pipe. Now put in a layer about 6 inches deep of fairly large stones, brick-bats, or any coarse rubbish, to act as drainage ; over these place a layer of sods, with the grass sides next the stones. When doing this make sure that the end of the overflow pipe is quite clear and that the water can easily get to it. Having made all secure, now fill in with a compost of peat, leaf-mould, fibrous loam, sand, and broken stones in the same proportions that were given in the beginning of this chapter.

If these directions have been carried out, you will have a small (underground) pond with the water kept at a constant level just over the sods covering the drainage. The capillary attraction of the soil will draw the moisture up and keep it constantly damp. If the water to supply these marshy beds has to be brought in pipes, they should have a tap, so that the flow may be regulated. It is scarcely necessary to mention that every trace of cement and all pipes or taps should be hidden from view by either soil, stones, or plants. When circumstances will permit, it is advisable to have a constant flow of water through these beds; and although this be but a mere dribble, say 10 to 15 gallons per diem, it will be sufficient to keep the water from becoming sour or stagnant.

If the supply pipe is arranged so that it reaches the bottom of the bed, it will ensure the water being constantly changed.

If it is desired to make the bottom of the bed of yellow clay, the same directions will have to be followed, except that it will be necessary to puddle in about 6 inches of yellow clay instead of the concrete; but neither so water-tight nor lasting a result may be expected.

If it is wished to make a bog garden on a scale larger than that just described, and the water supply for it is limited, a concrete basin should be made, following the directions already given. Owing, however, to the expense and the difficulty of getting the levels correct, it is

not advisable to attempt a bog garden of this
description of over 150 or 200 square yards
in area.

But where there is a stream, provided the
volume of water is sufficient, there is nothing
to limit the size of the garden. It will be
necessary, of course, to spread the water from
the stream over the bog garden in such a way
that it can reach all parts; and as in all probability the proposed site is not level, the simplest
and most efficacious method is to cut small
channels running from the stream on either
side, in the way the farmer irrigates his fields.
This method has also the advantage that the
moisture can be regulated at will. Another
plan, if the channels are considered unsightly,
is to lay pipes with a number of holes bored
in them a couple of inches below the surface
of the ground and connected with the stream.
The great disadvantage of this method is that
the pipes are so liable to become choked with
mud or leaves.

The surface of the bog garden should not
be flat; undulating or, more correctly speaking,
uneven ground is much to be preferred. This

will give different degrees of moisture, which
will be found most useful, for all plants do not
need the same amount.   In the hollows can be
planted those kinds that require a wet soil,
while the higher-lying ground can be reserved
for those preferring a drier position.   If desired,
a pool here and there can be made, and a very
charming and attractive addition to the garden
these will be, if judiciously placed.   They can
be made of either concrete or yellow clay.   In
either case it will be necessary to edge these
patches of water with stones or plants, in order
to avoid the possibility of any formal outline,
and, needless to say, all concrete must be carefully
hidden from view.

Should the garden be of any considerable
size, it will not be feasible to fill it up with any
specially prepared compost, such as was recommended for the smaller bog beds ; nor indeed is
it necessary, for the majority of bog plants, and
certainly the coarser-growing ones, are quite
happy in any cool, rich, and moist soil ; but in
places the ground should be prepared for those
which are more delicate or fastidious in their
tastes.   These spots may be of peat or other

compost, according to the requirements of the future inhabitants.

As the soil of the bog garden in general needs to be richer and heavier and to contain more vegetable matter than does that of the rock garden proper, some old manure, leaf-mould, and peat can be dug into it with advantage, after the surface has been thoroughly cleaned. The reader should note most particularly the necessity of getting the ground perfectly clean, for nowhere do weeds grow so rampant or increase and multiply with the same extraordinary rapidity as they do in the bog garden. If the ground be not clean and free from weeds to start with, the rightful denizens will have but a poor chance in the struggle for existence, so let no trouble be spared nor time grudged in the preparation of the garden, for if properly done the extra trouble expended will be more than repaid.

A few stones half buried may be placed in the bog garden, more especially on the higher and drier spots, for many bog plants like to get their roots under and around them, just as do their neighbours in the rock garden.

Whatever paths are required should be made of flat stones in the form of stepping stones.

The bog garden should be made in such a position that part of it is exposed to the full sun, while part is in shade, to suit the requirements of the different plants. This can be done, either by planting the edge with bamboos or similar suitable and fairly tall-growing plants, or by making part of the garden in the shade of some higher-lying ground.

As has been mentioned earlier in this chapter, a bog garden of any size should not appear amongst the rockwork, but may adjoin it. A very suitable place is at the foot of the rockwork in the hollow or bank types. Or, in the case of the valley, the approach to the main walk may be through the bog garden.

These are merely suggestions, and individual taste and skill will need to be exercised as to where the bog garden would look most natural and work best into the general scheme of the rock garden.

Another point that must be taken into consideration before fixing on the site is the water

supply, which should be brought by the easiest
and most direct route possible, and care must
be taken that the overflow can be readily
disposed of.   Fortunate indeed are those people
who have a stream, no matter how small, running through their garden, or are able to
conduct one to it.   My advice is to have one,
if it is at all feasible, for it is the means of
adding enormously to the charm of the garden
and of considerably extending the range of
plants possible to cultivate.   If the rock garden
is of either the hollow or hill types, the stream
may be brought down the face of the rockwork in a series of little cascades into a pool
at the foot.   The ground on either side should
slope gently towards its course.

The banks of the stream, at least so much of
them as are affected by the water, should be
made of fairly large rocks to prevent its encroaching or washing them away.   These
rocks, it is scarcely necessary to say, should not
be placed in the form of a straight wall; the
stream should be made to wind about, for it
will then look so much better.   The bottom
of the stream should be paved with flat stones,

CHAPTER VIII

THE WILD AND WATER GARDENS

The wild garden—Treatment—List of plants suitable—The water garden—Treatment—List of plants suitable.

THE wild garden has frequently been referred to in previous chapters, so a few words upon how best to deal with it may be found useful. As may be supposed, there is no making in a garden of this description ; all that is needed is to plant with discretion and judgment. That the secret of obtaining effect is to plant in bold masses has already been pointed out ; and important as this is in the artificial garden, it is many times more so in the case of the wild garden. Whereas in the former type the available space is more or less limited, in the latter case the ground is not so curtailed ; therefore, in order to be in keeping with the surroundings, the planting should be done on very bold lines.

It is a great mistake to imagine that only so-called wild-flowers are suitable for the wild garden ; many of those species now found in the herbaceous border or enclosed garden would not only look better, but also grow more luxuriantly when introduced into wilder surroundings. Another advantage to be derived from a garden of this sort is that one is enabled to cultivate in it a number of lovely plants which, on account of either their undue vigour or encroaching habit, cannot be associated with choicer and more delicate species. For these the wild garden is the fitting home, in which the full value of their beauty can be obtained. In short, any species of plant can be used, so long as it is strong enough to take care of itself without the attention of the gardener.

Every spot should be planted. The ground under trees may be carpeted with the lovely Wood Anemones, Trilliums, Cypripediums, Cyclamens, Snowdrops, Dielytras, Ferns, and a host of others ; while by the margins of streams or in damp meadows the Caltha, Trollius, many species of Primula, Ranunculus, etc., should find a congenial home, and in any grassy spot may be planted Narcissus, Daffodils, Crocus, and other bulbous plants. The Genistas, Cistus, Helianthemums can be used to cover dry and stony banks. In short, whether it be under trees or in the open glade, on margins of a stream or on sunburnt slopes, there is no spot that should not be fully planted.

When the approach to the rock garden is through an open glade or fairly exposed bank, no more suitable plants can be found than those of the Heath family, which should be grown in bold masses, and will indeed make an ideal setting for a home of alpine treasures. The best kinds for this purpose are *Erica arborea, Codonoides mediterranea*, which grow from 3 to 8 feet high. The dwarfer kinds are *Erica carnea, carnea alba, ciliaris, cinerea, tetralix, vagans, vagans alba, vulgaris.*

The large rocks and trees may be covered with many kinds of Roses, the numerous hybrids of the *wichuriana* type, the Polyantha and Wild Roses, also Clematis, Vitis, Lonicera (Honeysuckle), and such-like. When rearranging the herbaceous border in the spring or autumn and dividing up the clumps of plants, instead of assigning the pieces taken off to the rubbish-heap, let them be planted in the adjacent woodland, which will shortly and with no expense be converted into a garden that will vie with, if not excel in beauty its more formal prototype.

The following is a selection of plants specially adapted for the wild garden :—

Achillea Eupatorium.
A. millefolium rosea.
A. Ptarmica.
Aconitums, in variety.
Anemone apennina.
A. blanda.
A. nemorosa.
A. japonica, in variety.
A. sylvestris.
Aquilegias (Columbines).
Asphodelus luteus.
Asters, in variety ; any of the taller-growing
    species are excellent.
Astilbe, in variety.
Caltha.
Campanula celtidifolia.

C. persiciflora Moorheimi.

Cardamine trifolia.

Crocus, Cypripedium spectabile and calceolus.

Delphiniums, Daffodils.

Dictamnus, in variety.

Dielytra spectabilis.

Digitalis (Foxglove).

Doronicum excelsium.

Dracocephalum virginicum.

Echinacea purpurea.

Echinops exaltatus and giganteus.

Epilobium angustifolium, and other varieties.

Epimedium, in variety.

Erodium Manescavi, and other varieties.

Eryngium giganteum, planum, and other varieties.

Euphorbia polychroma and Lathyrus.

Geranium, armenium, sanguineum.

Heleniums, in variety.

Helianthus : Miss Mellish, giganteus, multiflorus, and others.

Helleborus (Christmas Rose).

Iris, in variety.

Lobelia cardinalis, Queen Victoria, and others.

Mimulus.

Monarda.

Montbretia, in variety.

Myosotis (Forget-me-not) palustris, sylvatica.

Œnothera Lamarckiana, macrocarpa and
    speciosa.

Papaver orientale, in variety.

Pœonies, in variety ; these look very well planted
    in grass.

Polemonium, in variety.

Polygonatum (Solomon's Seal).

Primula cashmiriana, Japonica, in variety ;
    sikkimensis.

Ranunculus aconitifolius, speciosus.

Sanguinaria canadensis.

Saxifraga peltata and megasea.

Senecio, in variety.

Spiræas in variety are excellent subjects for
    shady or damp positions.

Symphytum caucasicum, Bohemicum.

Telekia speciosa.

Tradescantia.

Trillium grandiflorum.

Trollius, in variety.

Veratrum album and luteo-virides.

Verbascum olympicum (Mullein), and other
    varieties.

THE WATER GARDEN

Fortunate indeed are those people who
possess some pond or lake on the margins

of which they can carry out some water gardening.

These margins should be always left in their natural state, provided, of course, the pond has not been made artificially, in which case it may be necessary to break the outline, for anything formal should be carefully guarded against. It will be necessary to have access to the plants which are grown on the margins, and as these latter, in all probability, are soft and boggy for some distance from the water-line, some sort of path will have to be made. Where a firm bottom can be found, this may be done by laying down some rough ballast, ramming it well in and then placing flat stones over it. But where the ground is too soft, a good foundation can be obtained by laying brushwood tied in bundles or by driving piles into the ground.

It is scarcely necessary to emphasise the fact that these paths must be in no way formal ; they should meander through rushes, sedges, and other plants growing on the margins.

As before, plant in bold masses to get the

[*To face page* 114.

WATER GARDEN.

(Photo. by Mrs Delves Broughton.)

best effect. The following are a few of the best species for this purpose :—

Acorus calamus and gramineus variegatus.
Alisma natans, and plantago ; will grow in shallow water.
Aponogeton distachyon ; will grow in shallow water.
Brasenia peltata ; will grow in shallow water.
Calla palustris. These Arum Lilies can be grown in water 3 to 4 feet deep, but are not very hardy.
Caltha, in variety ; boggy, moist ground or shallow water.
Cyperus longus ; shallow water or boggy ground.
Gunnera manicata ; grows very large, moist ground.
Gunnera scabra ; moist ground.
Heracleum giganteum and mantegazzianeum ; for wet margins.
Hottonia palustris (Water Violet) ; for shallow water.
Hydrocharis Morsus-ranæ.
Iris Pseudacorus, sibirica ; lævigata.
Menyanthes trifoliata (Bog Bean).
Nymphia (Water Lilies).

Polygonum amphibium and Sieboldi ; sacha-
linense.

Pontederia cordata.

Sagittaria japonica, fl. pl., sagittifolia variabilis.

Thalictrum flavum.

Bamboos, in variety.

Zizania latifolia.

CHAPTER IX

THE WALL GARDEN

Position and Types—Building—Beautifying the old wall.

WHERE shall I make my wall garden? This may appear a difficult problem at first, but perhaps the answer may be easy. Make it just where it is most needed. Wherever there has been levelling for lawn or garden, banks will be found of, perhaps, some height. These may not have been laid in grass, owing to the trouble and expense of keeping them constantly mown, and they may be easily clothed in a way more attractive than the usual carpeting of ivy or periwinkle. This is just the place for a wall garden, and if it be made here a double purpose will be achieved, for the wall will give a support to the bank, and in a short time, when covered with masses of rock plants, will prove a very attractive addition to the landscape.

But it is not only as a support, or retaining wall, as it might more correctly be called, that a wall garden can be made ; for by building what is known as a dry wall (which is in fact a wall without mortar), a very effective division can be made in a garden or elsewhere, which can soon be turned into a home for rock and alpine plants. Nor is it only in walls built specially for the purpose of growing this type of plant that they can be cultivated. Many old walls—the older the better—which are now but an eyesore, can with very little care and trouble be converted into a veritable garden that for many months of the year will be a blaze of colour. Unlike most other gardens, these, when once properly established, will practically look after themselves and require but little further attention.

It will surprise many people that not only will they be able to grow a great variety of plants in the wall garden, but they will be able to cultivate there, with comparative ease, some kinds acknowledged to be amongst the most difficult to keep in the rock garden proper. Nor is the reason difficult to find, for in the wall there is the perfect drainage, and there is not the same risk of loss from excessive damp, which more often than anything else proves fatal to alpines in this country. The chief and only difficulty connected with wall gardening is that of establishing the plants. If planted after the wall is finished, they can only be very small and therefore young ; for they will have to be inserted in the narrow crevices between the stones, often no easy task to accomplish, and, having to be so young, they are more liable to be affected by the vicissitudes of temperature than would the older and better-matured plants. For these reasons it will be found advisable, when at all practicable, to plant as the building proceeds. Larger and stronger plants can then be used, and their roots can be properly spread out and encouraged to penetrate into the cooler mass of soil behind the stones forming the wall. This will render them far less liable to suffer from drought.

Although this method of building the retain-

ing wall is very similar to that used in the
construction of the division wall, I think it
would be better to deal with each separately,
and afterwards I will show what can be done
to metamorphose the old wall.

The main principle underlying the construction of retaining walls made for the purpose
of growing rock plants is to place the stones
in such a way that all available moisture be
directed back towards their roots. For this
reason, and also because additional strength
will be obtained, the walls should not be built
perpendicular, but should rather slope back
from the foot at say an angle of 60 degrees.
Fairly flat stones may be used, and it will
simplify the building if they be of much the
same thickness, for then the " courses " will
work in evenly. These stones should be firmly
fixed and should all slope down towards the
back. The lower stone should slightly
protrude beyond that immediately above it, in
order to catch the rain falling from it. No
mortar should be used, but soil only, and not
very much of that—just a sprinkling between
each course of from $\frac{1}{2}$ to $\frac{1}{4}$ inch thick ; if

PART OF WALL GARDEN, MOUNT USHER.

(Photo. by Mrs Delves Broughton.)

more soil were used it would be liable to be washed out by heavy rain. Pieces of slate may be inserted between the stones, and provide a little room to plant in, and also to take off undue pressure on the plants. As has been said earlier in this chapter, it is advisable, when possible, to insert the plants as the building proceeds, for larger plants can thereby be used and their roots properly spread out, and also the chances of leaving vacant spaces behind them, which is so often the cause of plants unaccountably dying, will be reduced to a minimum.

The advantages of planting at this stage can only be fully realised by those who have spent many and weary hours, both trying to the temper and not unfrequently most painful and damaging to the skin of the knuckles, endeavouring to insert the delicate and obstinate roots of alpines into chinks where they did not wish to go.

So, having laid a course of stones, put a sprinkling of soil over them ; then the plants, spreading the roots out well ; then a little more soil, making sure that all the crevices are well

filled, and on top another course of stones, and
so on till the desired height is reached.

Where a dry wall, which is also to act as
a dividing wall, is required, it must be built
hollow in the centre, to allow for the soil
which is needed for the plants.

FIG. 6.

Both sides of the wall should slope back
from the foot at an angle of 80 degrees, and
there should be at least a foot of soil in the
centre. A wall of say 6 feet high and 2 feet
thick at the top would require a base of 4 feet
6 inches wide, allowing for the stones being
about 12 inches long (fig. 6). This wall

should be built in exactly the same way as described for the retaining wall, and the stones must slope back so as to catch the rain.

It will be found a good plan if about 6 inches of stones are laid in the bottom of the wall to act as a drain, and this will also reduce the chances of heavy rain affecting its stability.

In this case also it is advisable, when circumstances permit, that the planting be done simultaneously with the building. The soil in the centre should be filled in as the stone-work progresses, and should be well rammed home and made solid.

We now come to the old wall which requires beautifying; and the older it is the better, so long as there is no danger of its collapsing and thereby burying our treasures or ourselves in its ruins.

The first thing to do is to open up as many holes in its face as is consistent with its stability. In the bottom of these holes it is a good plan to place pieces of slate or flat stones, tipped up in front and slightly protruding, say about $\frac{1}{2}$ to $\frac{1}{4}$ inch, in order to catch the rain;

these may be, if necessary, made secure by a little cement or mortar, which, however, should not be visible. Into the holes thus prepared a compost made up of finely sifted loam, leaf-mould, and a little sand should be packed, every care being taken that all nooks and crannies are well filled and that no empty spaces are left.

The top of the wall will most probably be covered with grass and weeds. This should all be carefully removed, and then as many pockets as possible made, using, as described above, pieces of slate or stone to keep the soil in position. It is well, when making the pockets in the face of the wall, to vary their position as much as possible. By this I mean avoid having the protruding stones immediately one above the other, for the rain will be prevented from reaching the lower one, a state of things that should be carefully avoided. One of the chief difficulties to contend with in wall gardening is the liability of the plants to suffer from drought when young and tender and before their roots have had time to work back into the cooler regions behind. As the space available for planting is generally so small and cramped that it is necessary to use very tiny plants, which will often be found difficult to establish, it is advisable to use seed. There is then a better chance of the seedlings establishing themselves, for they will not at any time suffer from disturbance. One method which will be found particularly useful when dealing with some very tiny crevice is to mix the seed and soil into a sort of paste, which can be worked into the required spot.

As the aspect of the wall must unavoidably be governed by the circumstances of the case, all that can be done is to adapt the plants to suit the situation ; if in shade, plant with those preferring a shady home, and *vice versa*.

A list will be found in Part II. giving the names of plants best suited either for sun or shade.

CHAPTER X

PROPAGATION

Propagation by seed—By division and cuttings—Methods
of raising from seed — Methods of propagation by
division—By cuttings—By layers.

MANY alpines when in cultivation enjoy at
the most but a short life ; in some cases not
more than five to eight years. Whether it is
the same in nature is for obvious reasons
difficult to say, but the fact remains that plants
will have to be frequently renewed. It is
therefore advisable to keep a stock at hand to
meet the deficiencies.

There are four ways of propagating
alpines, namely, by seed, division, cuttings,
and layers.

Reproduction from seed is in some ways the
best. It ensures healthy and vigorous plants,
which, being more acclimatised, are therefore

more likely to thrive than would be the case if propagated by any of the other methods. Seed also provides the only means of raising a new variety and of improving a freshly imported strain. But, on the other hand, unless artificially fertilised, the results from seeds are often disappointing, for, in place of being an improvement, they frequently turn out to be only very inferior copies of the parent plant. This is due to cross-fertilisation, especially noticeable in the case of Aubrietias, Aquilegias, and many of the Saxifraga family. Nevertheless, many species do come quite true, a great deal, of course, depending on whether there are varieties of the same species grown sufficiently close for bees to carry their pollen from one to the other. Another disadvantage in raising plants from seed is that they often take two or even three years before they flower; indeed, the seeds of some kinds take as long as eighteen months, or even more, to germinate at all. During this time the seed-pans need to be carefully looked after and kept free from weeds and that arch-enemy, Marchantia; to say nothing of the trouble and difficulty of judicious watering, neither letting soil get too dry nor keeping it too moist.

Propagation by division or cuttings, when possible, is on the whole preferable, for the plants are then sure to be true and reach maturity much sooner. As this method, however, can only apply when one either possesses or has access to a plant from which to take the pieces or cuttings, and when it is possible to pot them up soon after being removed from the parent plant, it would not be feasible when collecting abroad, in which case try to get seeds and raise plants from them. There are some kinds, indeed, though not many, which will neither admit of division nor grow readily from cuttings : for example, many . of the Aquilegias family ; these can therefore only be raised from seed. In growing alpines from seed, the secret of success lies in procuring fresh seed that will germinate readily, and also yield a much larger percentage of plants. In order to ensure its being fresh, when possible save the seed yourself. Therefore look out carefully for seed, especially in the case of the rarer kinds. Often the first intimation that is given of fertile seed having ripened is the finding of small seedlings round the parent plant. It is a great mistake to be in a hurry to remove the flower-heads as soon as they are withered, and, more-over, the seed-pods are in many cases nearly as ornamental as the flowers themselves. At the same time it is well to exercise discretion, for the seedlings from some plants may prove as troublesome as any weed.

Having gathered the ripe seed, sow at once. Nature sows her seed as soon as it is ripe ; why should we imagine we know better and lay it aside for several months ?

Seeds may be sown in the open or in pots, but many species of plants do not ripen their seeds till late in the autumn, and these should be sown in pots and wintered in a frame or cold-house. In any case I should recommend this treatment for any of the rarer species. The best time to sow in the open is in April, but seeds may be put in any time from April to August. So, should seeds come to hand during the summer months, it is better to sow at once rather than to keep them over for the following spring, for then a whole season's growth is gained. Even if sown as late as the beginning of August, the seedling ought to be strong enough to take care of itself during the winter. Yet it is not advisable to sow in the open so late in the season except in the case of seed from plants of a hardy nature, which germinates quickly.

The seed-bed, which should not be more than 4 feet wide, will require to be carefully prepared, in some warm but sheltered position. Dig the soil well to a depth of 8 inches, making it as friable as possible ; clean the ground well, removing all weeds and large stones, and, if not naturally light, add plenty of sand and leaf-mould. Over this put a layer about 4 inches thick of a good light compost made up of loam, leaf-mould, sand, and refuse from the potting bench. This mixture should be all put through a $\frac{1}{4}$-inch riddle. Now level the surface of the bed, which will be ready for the seeds. Choose a day for sowing in calm, mild, and open weather, when the ground is rather dry and in good friable condition. Make little drills across the bed about 6 inches apart. These should not be made with a hoe or similar tool, but get a piece of straight stick about $1\frac{1}{2}$ inch wide, and, laying it on the ground, press it gently down till it leaves an even and smooth hollow about an inch deep. This will give a good firm bed for the seeds. Therein sow the seeds as evenly and thinly as possible, and cover sparingly with some good light soil put through a $\frac{1}{16}$-inch riddle. In many cases the merest sprinkling will suffice, for seeds should only be covered to a depth about equal to their diameter.

Nothing more need be done except to keep down weeds and see that the beds do not get too dry; but watering will have to be done very carefully and with a very fine rose, otherwise the ground will become baked and hard. Watering should be limited as much as possible, and, in order to prevent undue evaporation, the beds should be protected from hot sun. It is a good plan to put a little cocoanut fibre between the drills, which will help to keep the ground damp and lessen the chances of its getting baked. The seedlings may be left where sown until they are fit to transplant to their final habitat. In the stronger-growing kinds, if they come up too quickly, a little thinning can be done with advantage ; but care should be taken not to disturb the roots of those that are to remain.

In this way many of the best rock plants may be raised. They have this advantage over those sown in pots, that they are less liable to suffer from the vicissitudes of temperature, nor do they receive any check when being pricked out. But do not imagine that your bed of seedlings is free from all dangers, for sooner or later hungry slugs will find them out during their midnight forays, and then woe betide them, for untold havoc will be wrought before you visit in the morning what was the night before the pride and joy of your heart. There is one thing, however, no slug or snail will cross, and that is zinc. So get a sheet of zinc and cut it into strips about 3 inches wide, and after the seeds are sown put this all round the bed, thereby making a rampart which, from the slug's point of view at least, is impregnable.

I never sow, nor would I recommend other people to risk sowing, the rarest or finest seeds in the open air when they come to hand at a time unsuitable for sowing out of doors, such as the late autumn. But as they should be sown at once, it is advisable to use pots which can be put in a frame or cold-house.

In this treatment there are two great difficulties to contend with, namely, the growth of Marchantia, and keeping the pots at an even degree of moisture.

With regard to the first, there are several ways of preventing its growth. The best and surest means is to bake the soil thoroughly and use nothing but boiled water. This is an absolute preventative, but entails rather more trouble than most people would care for.

Another way is, to prepare the pots for sowing, and then to water them thoroughly with boiling water—but it *must* be *boiling*

—and then leave them for a day or more before using. This will destroy most of the seeds and spores of weeds and kill all worms and insects, which is no little advantage. For subsequent waterings use nothing but boiled water. If neither of these plans is adopted, the only course left is to pick off every particle of the Marchantia as soon as it appears, which is by no means easy to do without disturbing the seed or young plants, and will entail considerable labour if there are a large number of pots to look after.

It is most essential to keep the soil at the proper degree of moisture, which is not at all easy to accomplish, and will require constant attention. Nothing proves more fatal to seeds than to allow the soil to become dust-dry ; while, on the other hand, if it is kept too moist, the seeds are very liable to rot away. Above all, avoid alternate conditions of wet and dry. For, germination having once commenced, if the soil is subsequently allowed to dry up, the seeds will be irrevocably destroyed.

Watering overhead is all right in the case of seeds that germinate fairly quickly, say in a month or two ; but not when, as is the case with some, it will take twelve or even eighteen months before any signs of life are visible. Under such circumstances it is very difficult to prevent the surface getting hard and baked, when the pots will not " take the water." So, for all seeds which are slow in germinating, I should advise not watering from overhead, but supplying the moisture from below. This may be done by placing the pots in a saucer of water, when the capillary attraction of the soil will draw it up, and if there is plenty of drainage in the pots, as there should always be, there is no danger of the soil becoming water-logged. Personally, I am trying another method, which so far seems quite satisfactory, and will, I hope, still further reduce the attention required. As perhaps my readers may care to try it for themselves, I will explain my system. Into one of my small two-light frames, 6 feet by 4 feet, I put a wooden partition down the centre from back to front. In one of these divisions I fixed a lead trough or tray, completely filling the bottom. This tray, which is filled with water, is therefore 4 feet by 3 feet, and about 4 inches deep. An inch pipe connected with the tray goes through a hole cut in the back of the frame, and protrudes about $2\frac{1}{2}$ inches beyond the woodwork. By means of this pipe it can be seen at a glance what amount of water is in the trough, and, through it, more can be added if necessary.

When I had ascertained that the trough was quite level, which can easily be done by filling with water, I placed perforated zinc all over it, about 2 inches from the bottom. The zinc I kept in position by resting it on some flat tiles about 2 inches thick. Over this I put small stones to a depth of about half an inch, and then about 8 inches of granulated peat. If this description has been carefully followed, it will be seen that about 1 inch of the peat is in water. By this means moisture will be drawn up through the whole mass, which will be kept constantly damp, and all that will be necessary to maintain this condition is occasionally to look at the pipe which protrudes outside the back of the frame, and, when required, to add water to keep it up to the desired level.

Pots containing seeds should be plunged up to the brim in the peat, which will keep them sufficiently damp, and also tend to preserve them at an even temperature. By this device the danger of the pots becoming too dry is reduced to a minimum, and as the moisture is merely absorbed from the outside, there is no chance of their becoming water-logged. A few minutes two or three times a week is all the attention they will require.

Much time may be gained, especially in the case of the slower germinating seeds, by making, in a pit or frame, a very gentle hot-bed, and either sinking in the bed the pots in which the seeds are sown, or else covering it with about 4 inches of fine soil and sowing the seeds on that. Personally, I think the chief objection to this method is that the seedlings will require to be very carefully treated until they are sufficiently hardened off. There is also the danger of the hotbed cooling down before the seedlings are strong enough to look after themselves. I therefore much prefer the cold frame, for although its action is slower, better and stronger seedlings are thereby obtained. Some people also recommend soaking the seeds for a short time in warm water before sowing. This treatment rather tends to hasten germination, as it softens the outer covering of the seed, which with some is so very hard that it would take, in the ordinary course, a long time before it becomes affected by the moisture of the soil.

There is a right and a wrong way of doing most things, and, although it may be thought difficult to make a mistake in sowing seed, it is by no means as simple a process as many people imagine.

With the seeds at hand, choose out the requisite number of pots of 5 or 6 inches, according to the amount to be sown, a separate pot for each kind. Into these put the drainage of broken crocks, filling to about a quarter the depth of the pot, and over this put a layer of moss to prevent the soil getting into and choking up the drainage.

Next prepare the compost, which will of course vary according to what is to be sown, but for general purposes it may be made up of good light fibrous loam, mixed with a fair amount of sharp sand and leaf-mould in the proportion of about three to one. Put this through a $\frac{1}{16}$-inch riddle, keeping a sharp look-out for worms, which should be promptly removed. Put the coarse part remaining in the sieve over the drainage in the pots, filling them half full. Then fill up the remainder with the fine soil. Now press all down firmly, either with a piece of wood or the bottom of a pot, which will answer just as well, until the surface is about half an inch below the edge of the pot and fairly smooth. This will leave things ready for sowing.

Take the seed packet and open carefully, either over the pot or a sheet of paper, if the seeds are very small, and then sow as evenly and thinly as possible. To cover, hold the riddle in one hand at an elevation of about 6 inches over the pot, and on it scatter the soil, keeping the riddle gently moving all the time. By this method the soil will be spread evenly over the surface of the pot. The depth of covering is generally supposed to be equal to the diameter of the seeds ; but these are often so very small, that a better way is just to cover till no seeds are visible on the surface. In some cases the merest dusting will suffice. Over this I find a thin layer of fine silver sand very beneficial in keeping the surface clean and free from moss, which, even if it does grow, can easily be removed without disturbing the seeds.

Special mixtures of soil will be required for some seeds. For those that like lime, the Saxifrage family, for example, and especially the encrusted section, it can be added in the form of lime rubbish, and less loam and leaf-mould used ; whilst for those that like peat, such as the Ramondias, Rhododendron, etc., the compost should consist of fibrous loam, peat, and leaf-mould, with a little sharp sand. In the case of the Androsaces, sandstone broken up quite small will be found of service. In short, whatever soil the mature plant does best in should be used for its seeds. The soil for either potting or sowing seeds should not be so dry that it will not take water readily, nor yet so wet that it is liable to cake or stick to the riddle ;

it should just be sufficiently damp to work easily.

Having sown the seeds, label carefully, and then cover the pot with a piece of glass to prevent undue evaporation. This should not be removed till the seedlings are well up. Now place in a cold frame, close to the glass, and see that each pot is as level as possible. The frames should be kept shaded from the direct rays of the sun, whilst admitting as much light as possible. Try to keep the temperature as even as can be. Before the seedlings appear, the frame may be kept closed ; but when they are up more air will be required, or they will be liable to damp off.

As some seeds take such a very long time to germinate, do not be in a hurry to throw them away, even should they not appear within twelve months. Presuming the seeds are sown in March and nothing appears up to the autumn, they should be surfaced with a light dusting of soil and kept over the winter, being watered sparingly during the winter months. Except in the case of seeds that are known to germinate quickly, I should not despair of their coming up, even had they been sown eighteen months; but after that they may be thrown away, for the chances of success are by then almost nil.

If there is no frame available, the seeds should be sown rather later, say about the beginning of April, and the pots plunged in sand or cinders in a warm and sheltered corner, protected from the hot sun and heavy rains. But I strongly recommend a frame whenever possible, for the temperature and moisture can then be so much more easily regulated and kept even.

After the seedlings are up and strong enough to handle easily, they may be pricked off into 4-inch pots, or, still better, into shallow boxes about 5 inches deep. After pricking out, the pots or boxes should be kept protected from the sun for a few days until the seedlings have recovered from the move. As frost has great effect on pots and is very liable to loosen the roots of plants in them, some protection will be required during the winter months, although this may be obviated to a certain extent by plunging into a bed of sand or fine cinders.

The seedlings may remain in these boxes or pots till the following spring, by which time they should have made good roots and may be transferred to their final home, or, if required for stock, be potted up into $2\frac{1}{2}$-inch thumb-pots, which should be plunged in the sand or cinder bed. Another method which may be adopted in the case of stronger-growing plants is to prick out direct from the seed-pot into a bed specially prepared with fine soil. Plants so treated will also require protection for a few days from hot sun.

If the instructions just given are carefully followed there is every reason to expect that the result will be a success. But, to give it every chance, it is absolutely essential to obtain fresh and fertile seed, to provide ample drainage in seed-pots, keep them clean and free from all weeds and moss, and, above all, to keep the moisture even, for nothing proves more fatal to germination than alternate conditions of moisture and drought.

Most alpine and rock plants lend themselves very readily to propagation by division, especially that large and typically alpine family the Saxifrages, as do also the Androsaces, Primulas, and a host of others too numerous to mention.

As an example of the method to be adopted, let it be assumed it is wished to increase the stock of *Saxifraga apiculatum*. Remove from the parent plant some of the shoots next the ground, breaking them off as close to the main stem as possible. A careful examination will disclose tiny rootlets attached to every piece so removed, each of which, when potted up in suitable soil, will grow readily. In a similar way any number of rooted pieces may be obtained from the mossy Saxifrages, without in the least spoiling the appearance of the plant from which they are taken. In dealing with the rarer kinds of Saxifrages, especially those of the encrusted section, such as *diapensioides, Burseriana, Boydii*, etc., more care will have to be exercised, and it is advisable, before removing a portion of the plant, to see if it is rooted. With some Saxifrages, such as *trifurcata, Whitlavii*, roots will be found springing from joints along the creeping stem, much in the same way as with strawberry runners. In the case of *S. Cotyledon* and its varieties, hybrids of *S. longifolia*, *S. Griesbachii*, and others of a like habit, the rosette from which the flower-spike springs dies after flowering, but round it will appear a number of offshoots, each of which will have developed roots by the autumn. They can easily be separated from the main stem, and will have formed sturdy plants by the following year.

The Androsaces also are easily increased by division. Take a plant of *Androsace Chumbyi*: after flowering, a number of small woolly rosettes will appear attached to the parent plant by thin wire-like stems. Each of these in a month or more will develop roots and form a complete plant which can easily be separated. *Androsace lanuginosa*, and its variety *Leichtlini*, will, on careful examination, be found to have made roots on some of their trailing stems, and these will readily grow when separated from the parent plant and potted.

Few families lend themselves better to division than do the Primulas; in fact, it is essential to their successful cultivation that

10

they should be taken up and divided annually, owing to the way they have of growing out of the ground. This is especially applicable to the alpine Auriculas. When the plant is lifted, break off each crown or shoot, and roots will be found attached to each of the pieces, which will soon form a good-sized plant.

Most of the dwarf Campanulas, such as *pulla*, *pulloides*, *Stansfieldii*, *G. F. Wilson*, etc., spread by means of a creeping rootstock, from which pieces can easily be detached, each of which will readily grow.

The various Phloxes, and some of the Dianthus family, especially *suavis* and *cæsius*, will, if closely examined, be found to have made roots in places. These rooted bits should be separated from the parent plant, and then carefully raised with a ball of earth if possible. There are, in fact, very few alpine or rock plants from which rooted bits cannot be obtained, which, when divided and carefully potted, appear usually to gain increased vigour and strength, instead of suffering from the effects of the division.

The best time to propagate in this manner

is immediately after flowering, when the fresh growth is commencing and the sap is most active. Having taken off the rooted pieces in the ways just described, make up a compost, similar to that in which the parent plant is growing, and put each piece in a 2½-inch thumb-pot. It is advisable to put a pinch of sharp silver sand round the roots, for it encourages growth and lessens the chances of their damping off. After planting, keep the pots fairly close in a frame, plunged up to the rim in sand or fine cinders, and keep moderately, but not too moist. They should remain in the frame till they are thoroughly established, and are forming roots, which will be shown by their making growth, and then they may be moved to the open and plunged in a sand or cinder bed.

It may be taken as a universal rule, to which there is no exception, that all pots containing plants should, when in the open, be sunk up to the rim in either earth, sand, or cinders. The latter two are much to be preferred, for in earth the pots are liable to become water-logged. The object of sinking the pots is to keep the temperature as even as possible, for, treated in this manner, they have but the top surface exposed to either the frost of winter or the hot rays of the sun in summer, and the plants in them are therefore much less likely to suffer from cold or heat than would be the case if the whole surface of the pot were exposed.

It will be found a good plan in many cases to put small pieces of sandstone round the neck of the plant ; they will keep it secure and prevent undue evaporation.

Propagation by cuttings is an easy method, and especially applicable to shrubs and any of the hard-wooded plants. The best time to take cuttings is between August and November. They should be made from well-ripened wood of the year's growth, choosing vigorous shoots. These should be shortened to about 3 inches and the lower leaves trimmed off ; then take a sharp knife and cut through immediately below a joint from which the roots will eventually spring. The cutting is now ready for insertion in pot or bed. Another method is to break off the cutting

with what is known as a " heel." This is, in
fact, a portion of the main stem. This heel
should be cut across immediately below where
it joined the stem. Of the two methods the
former, namely, without a " heel," is that most
generally preferred.

Having prepared the cuttings in either of
the above ways, the next procedure is to insert
them in pots or in an open bed. For any of
the choicer or less hardy kinds, pots are to be
recommended. Take a 4-inch pot, put in
drainage to about a quarter of its depth ;
then fill up as full as possible with a compost made up of about equal parts of good
fibrous loam and sharp sand. Round the
edge of the pot, and about 2 inches apart,
make with a pointed stick small holes about
$1\frac{1}{4}$ inch deep, into each of which drop a
pinch of silver sand. Now put a prepared
cutting into each of these holes, making sure
that they reach the bottom. Then place the
thumb of each hand on either side of the
cutting and press the soil firmly down: this
should be done to each cutting in turn.

The great secret of putting in cuttings is to

make the soil round each quite firm. It is nearly impossible to make it too firm ; while, on the other hand, it is very easy to have it too loose.

Place the pots containing the cuttings in a frame or cover with a hand-light, and keep close, well shaded from the direct sun, until the cuttings begin to grow. Watering should be done sparingly ; for while the pots should on no account be allowed to get too dry, on the other hand, excessive moisture might cause the cuttings to damp off. Of the two extremes it is better to err on the dry side.

For the hardier plants or shrubs, such as the Helianthemums, Cistus, Philadelphus, etc., it is preferable to strike them in the open in a specially prepared bed, which should be situated under a wall in some shady and sheltered corner. Some people, indeed, recommend having it under a wall facing south and exposed to the full sun, but personally I prefer a western aspect. Having decided on the site, remove about 2 inches of the soil, and make the hollow so formed as firm and solid as possible. On this prepared surface put about

6 inches of soil, composed of fibrous loam and sand in equal parts, which should be put through a ¼-inch riddle. Consolidate this also as much as possible.

The bed is now ready for the cuttings, which should have been prepared as already described, and which may be inserted by making a hole and dropping in a pinch of silver sand, much in the same manner as was done in the pots, except that in this case, instead of being 2 inches apart, they should be placed quite close to one another. As before, make quite sure that the end of the cutting reaches the bottom of the hole, and above all see that the soil is pressed firmly round its stem. After the cuttings are inserted give a good watering to settle the ground. Little further attention will be needed, except to shelter, if necessary, from strong sun or to protect from severe frost or snow. By the spring it will be found that a large percentage of the cuttings have rooted.

Aubrietias are frequently found rather difficult to strike, owing to their liability to damp off. The following treatment should, however, be found to yield a good result. Take the cuttings in early summer, choosing the young growth, and cut to joint, as already described ; then insert in the prepared bed, and cover with a hand-light, keeping quite close for a couple of weeks ; after that let a little air in at night, closing again in the daytime.   In all probability a very large proportion of the cuttings will be found to have rooted by the autumn.

Some of the hard-wooded shrubs are often very slow in striking. If at the end of the year the bark remains fresh and firm, but still there are no signs of growth, remove it from the pot. On examination it may in all probability be found that although there are no roots, a covering will have formed over the end of the cutting, which is known as a " callus," and from which the roots will eventually spring. If this is found to be the case, pot it up again with fresh soil, using plenty of sharp sand. Very likely in a few months' time growth will appear, showing that it has made roots. In fact, as long as the cutting continues fresh and the bark un-shrivelled, there is always the chance of its striking. I have had cuttings as long as two years before they made any roots, but in the end I was successful by adopting this treatment.

Layering is found a useful way of increasing some plants which do not, in this country at least, produce seed, or are difficult to strike from cuttings; the Rhododendron, Azalea, and Daphne species, for example. By layering, stronger plants can often be obtained than from cuttings. The process of layering is quite simple. Choosing a convenient branch or shoot near the ground, cut it half through near a joint, and then peg firmly to the ground, which should at the point of contact consist of fine loam and sand in equal parts; then cover about 2 inches deep with the same compost. If, as is sometimes the case, it is found impossible to make the branch touch the ground, it may be inserted in a box, raised to the required height. The great thing to remember is to make the piece that is to be layered quite firm, so that it cannot be shaken about in the soil. In the following spring, if roots have been made (which may be ascertained by trying if the layered portion is firm in the ground), cut this piece from the parent plant, but do not take up for another month, when it will be quite safe to move it. Many shrubs and plants layer themselves quite freely : all that need be done is to place a little fine soil over the stem, and on it place a stone to keep it firm.

CHAPTER XI

CULTIVATION

Climatic difficulties—Contrasting natural and artificial conditions—Tendency to loss of characteristic growth—
Methods of overcoming climatic difficulties—Importance of proper planting—Time to plant—Importance
of top-dressing in spring—Weeding—Garden pests
and how to deal with them.

BEFORE discussing the cultivation of rock and
alpine plants in general, let us for a moment
study them growing in their native homes.
We shall then be able to realise and be in a
better position to cope with the difficulties to
be contended with when cultivating them in
the rock garden in this country.

Long, cold, dry winters followed by hot, dry
summers of short duration are the conditions
in which they thrive. From the time of the
first snows in late autumn until these are melted
by the summer sun, the plants are covered

with a thick mantle of snow, which keeps them dry and protects them from the severe frosts.   Then, during their flowering and growing season, their roots are kept constantly moist by the melting snows, which gives them a vigour of constitution which is unaffected by the scorching sun of late summer.

How very different are the conditions at home, where, during the winter, there is no friendly covering of snow to keep them dry and warm.   Instead, there is constant damp, varied by occasional frosts, which, though not nearly so severe as they would experience in their mountain homes, have a much more harmful effect, owing to their never having become properly dormant.   Then the flowering and growing season in March, April, and May is, in this country, so often accompanied by parching east winds.   And this lack of moisture at the period when it is so essential for them to have abundance of it, to swell the flower-buds and to promote growth, has the not unnatural result that when the summer comes, though they are not subject to anything like the heat of their native place, they have neither the vigour nor constitution to withstand it, and will surely pine away, unless kept constantly watered.

From this we learn that the failure to keep such choice alpines as *Eritrichium nanum*, *Gentiana bavarica*, *Androsace glacialis*, and many others, or to flower with any success such plants as *Soldanella alpina*, *Androsace obtusifolia*, is due not to the severity of our winters, nor yet to the heat of our summers, but to the fact that, owing to the conditions of our climate, the plants never become dormant, and their constitution is thereby so weakened that they are unable to withstand the comparatively temperate heat of our summers. And, in addition, though alpines at certain seasons must have abundant moisture at their roots, they dislike above all things the continual humid atmosphere which is one of the characteristics of the British Isles. From this one may infer that the secret of success and the chief thing to aim at is to encourage strong and vigorous growth in the spring by careful watering until the plants are sufficiently established to enable them to withstand a great deal of drought during the latter part of the year.

In parts of the Alps, and especially in the higher valleys, the ground, with scarcely a rock upon it, will be found carpeted with alpine flowers, just as daisies and buttercups carpet an English meadow. There will be found growing side by side *Anemone sulphurea*, *Myosotis alpestris*, *Gentiana acaulis* and *verna*, *Silene alpestris*, *Primula farinosa*, *Androsace Sarmentosa* and *obtusifolia*, *Aquilegia alpina*, *Pinguiculas*, *Ranunculus*, and a host of others, covering the bare and rockless ground. Should we, however, with this scene in our minds, be tempted to try and reproduce the dazzling picture at home, we shall only court disaster, for it cannot be done, or at least it has never been achieved up to the present. With us it is found to be impossible to grow *Silene acaulis* and *Primula farinosa* in the same spot, nor will the *Pinguiculas* flourish with the *Androsaces*. And why is this? The reason is not difficult to discover; it is that the Swiss valleys suit all these plants equally well. Moreover, there is no need of rock to protect them during the winter from moisture or from drought in the summer.

But since, in this country, similar conditions cannot be reproduced, it is neither possible to have a spot free from drought in summer and excess of moisture in winter, nor to persuade the plants themselves to retire to rest for at least half the year : all that remains is to try to learn the peculiar weakness of each and to provide to the best of our ability what may suit their several needs.

Yet another lesson is to be learnt from the study of alpines in their own land, where they are found growing so close together as to form a regular turf, and carpeting the ground so thickly that they leave no bare spaces. It is that the rock garden at home should show nothing but plants, and rocks half hidden by them, and, if this is done, the plants will not be so liable to suffer from drought. As one might expect, there will be some difficulty in accomplishing this, especially in the beginning, when plants must have room to grow, and when they are also most liable to suffer from bare spaces and the attendant danger of drought. To a certain extent this may be guarded against by covering the bare spaces with chips of stones, but plants are more beautiful than stones, therefore endeavour to clothe the ground completely. But while it is right to aim at the ideal, it will require considerable skill to combine the plants in such a way that one will not crowd out the other; we must seek to eliminate, as far as possible, that struggle for existence which is the predominant feature in nature.

Another point to remember, and one which does not help us in the choice of subjects to plant together, is that alpines, when brought into cultivation, in a great measure lose their characteristic growth, and not unfrequently the brilliance of their bloom. It will be necessary, therefore, to know the habit of the plants when growing in an English garden, to enable one to combine them together successfully. Therefore it should not be taken for granted that those which live together harmoniously on the Alpine slopes will do the same with us.

One reason, and probably the correct one, why some alpines, when brought into cultiva-

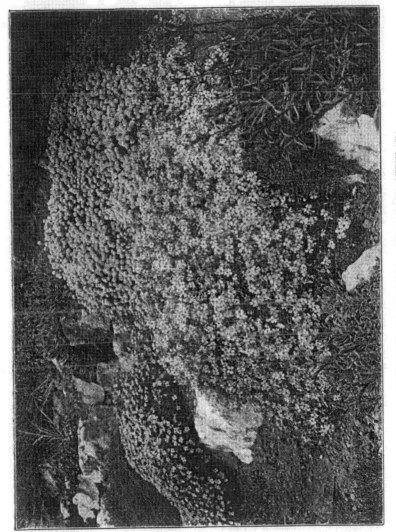

ÆTHIONEMA GRANDIFLORA AND PHLOX SUBULATA.

tion, lose the characteristic dwarf and stunted habit they display in their native homes, is that there they have not time to make much growth, for within the space of perhaps three or four months at the outside they have to perform the whole cycle of growth — leaf, stem, flower, and fruit—while at the same time they are exposed to every wind.

Nature provides for this by making the typical alpine close growing, with short-stemmed flowers. But when the growing season is extended and plants protected from exposure to wind, the flower-stems are apt to become taller and the foliage more straggling and rank.

We should aim at combining and massing the same species together in our rock gardens as far as space will admit, for in nature we see them growing in large masses or forming a carpet of different kinds interwoven together ; and it is unnecessary to have many rocks, only a few here and there for the plants to get their roots under and around.

So much for the different conditions in which the alpines find themselves when gleaned from their mountain homes and brought to an English garden. It is, unfortunately from the alpines' point of view, impossible to create a climate similar to what they have been accustomed to ; we must therefore see how best we can make up for the deficiencies by artificial means.

A study of the chief characteristics of the Alpine climate will show that, when compared with that of the British Isles, the chief difference is in the certainty of the former and the uncertainty of the latter.

In the Alps, once the frost and snow come in the autumn, they hold all nature in their grip until the summer sun dispels them for a few short months.

What a contrast to this country, with its wet and cold summers, its parching springs, uncertain autumns and winters ! One day we are frost- and snow-bound, on the next revelling in misplaced summer weather, which induces the tortoise-shell butterfly to disport itself over the few withered remains of the past summer's flowers.

Since it is out of the question for us to

attempt to reproduce the conditions necessary
to induce alpines to become dormant during
the winter, as they are in their native homes,
all that can be done is to protect them from
undue moisture, and, as far as possible, from
sudden variations of temperature. This is
best achieved by covering them from about
November to April with sheets of glass. We
shall be amply repaid for the temporary dis-
figurement during these months by the healthy
appearance of the plants when the glass is
removed in April. This treatment is especially
necessary in the case of the Androsaces and
other woolly-leaved species, which, if left fully
exposed to the winter's damp, will be very
liable to disappear. It is, however, often very
difficult, owing to the adjacent rockwork, to
fix these panes of glass so as to prevent their
slipping or being knocked down by wind or
the midnight cat. If fitted in a regular frame
with legs, these will be sure to come in
contact with some rock, when it is a case
of either removing one of the legs or the
offending obstacle, neither of which is
desirable.

To overcome this difficulty the following
contrivance will be found quite simple and
easy to make :—From a length of round bar
iron ¼-inch diameter, cut pieces 6 to 9 inches
long. Hammer out the top inch of each
quite flat, and bore two holes in it ; then
screw on, at a slight angle, a piece of fairly
hard wood 2 inches long by 1½ inch, pro-
jecting over the top of the flange about ¼-inch.
On the top of this block nail a strip of sheet
lead about 1½ inch wide and 2 inches long,
which will fold in two to hold the glass,
much as is done in Simplex lead glazing, an
illustration of which can be found in almost
any garden paper.

To fix the covering, select a piece of strong
21 oz. glass large enough to completely cover
the plant. Put the supports into the ground
wherever possible on one side ; slip the glass
into the lead clips and place the supports
on the other side of the glass wherever
required, and by gently closing the lead clips
together make all secure. If the glass is too
high above the plant, the whole can be easily
pressed down. The glass should always be

slightly inclined, to throw off the rain. By using these supports and employing a little ingenuity, the glass can be fixed in any spot and at any angle without danger of damaging the plant.

So much for the protection of the plants from the winter's rain. We shall now see how we can best supply the moisture necessary during the growing season, which too often in this country is the driest and most trying time of the year. For this there is but one remedy, and that is constant watering. This can, to a certain extent, be assisted, or rather the moisture may be retained, by placing round the plant pieces of stone, which will prevent undue evaporation. The spring is the crucial time; for if strong, healthy growth is then produced, there will be little need to trouble about the drought of the summer. Strong plants will be well able to withstand any that is likely to be experienced in this country.

The beginner must not, however, imagine that all alpines or rock plants require this amount of attention, or are so exacting, for it is only these difficult and tantalising higher alpines, such as the Androsaces, Gentians, some of the Campanulas, and a few others, that demand so much care. But there is, and always will be, a certain fascination in trying to grow those kinds that others have failed with, and with every new treatment tried there is always the hope that the secret of success has been found. Moreover, so many of these perverse plants are so typically Alpine that no rock garden worthy to be called by that name is complete without them.

But the numbers of other plants are countless, and amongst them are some of the most attractive, which will need little attention, but will increase and multiply as freely as weeds, provided there is good light soil and plenty of it, sufficient and ample drainage, as well as plenty of light and pure air.

Some plants, such as varieties of the Androsaces, *Campanula lanata*, and others, so dislike much damp lying on their leaves and about their crowns that they should at all seasons of the year be protected from moisture from overhead. Therefore plant them under an overhanging ledge ; but since in this position they will be liable to suffer from drought, thin pieces of stone and slate should be inserted in the ground round the plant in such a way that they will catch the moisture falling from the rock above and direct it towards their roots. Others, again, are found to do best when planted in the perpendicular face of the rockwork—such, for example, as *Saxifraga longifolia*, the Ramondias, the Edrianthus ; whilst some, such as *Gentiana verna*, prefer a slight hollow. In short, there is no spot in the properly made rock garden for which an inhabitant cannot be found, whether it be in sun or shade, or partial sun or partial shade, whether in a hollow or on the level, whether on the perpendicular face or gentle slope.

In Part II. will be found, after the description of each plant, the position and aspect that suit it best and the soil it specially prefers.

Many plants die owing to their not having been properly planted. How often are people seen planting in somewhat the following fashion :—Scooping out a slight hollow, sometimes even using their hands ; then, placing the plant in it anyhow, with its roots all bunched up, and covering it with soil, they press the earth down closely round the neck of the plant. If the plant is too high out of the ground, they try to rectify the error by pressing down still harder, and with what result ? The tender and delicate roots get broken and bruised, and, even if they survive such treatment, take a long time to establish themselves and become reconciled to " pastures new." The proper way is, to make the hole rather larger and deeper than the plant will require, then to draw the soil up into the shape of a mound in the centre ; then, very gently disentangling the tender roots, place the plant on the top of the mound, spreading its roots out all round and over its sides, and cover them with soil; press it gently but firmly down on the outside, but not close to the neck of the plant, or at least only as much as is required to keep it firm and unaffected by the wind. If the specimen you wish to plant is growing in a pot, remove it from it by placing the left hand over the surface of the pot, if necessary allowing the stem of the plant to come up between the fingers ; then, taking the pot in the right hand, turn it upside down, and strike the rim sharply two or three times against some solid object, such as the side of a barrow, or corner of a rock ; if this fails to dislodge the plant, push a piece of stick through the drainage hole at the bottom, and press it firmly up. On removing the plant from the pot, its roots will often be found to have formed a solid mass, completely filling all the available space. In this case it would be a hopeless task to try to unravel them, and would, in fact, do more harm than good ; so all that need be done is to pick out the pieces of drainage which will be found encased in the roots at the bottom ; then squeeze the mass gently, and, having shaken out the roots a little at the bottom, plant as already described.

If the plant should be tall-growing or likely to catch the wind, stake at once, for before the roots have established themselves the plant is much more liable to be affected by the wind.

Never, under any consideration, plant when the ground is sodden or in such a wet state that the clay sticks to the trowel or fork used ;

it is far better to leave the plants "heeled in" for a week, or even more, than to plant when the ground is unsuitable.

Nor should you plant during hard frost. The ideal time is in mild, open weather, but not too hot, when the ground is fairly dry and in good friable condition. If it is found necessary to plant in very dry weather, after putting in the plant, and before completely filling the hole, give it a good soaking with water. The hole can be made up to the required level as soon as this has drained away.

With regard to watering in general, there is one golden rule which should never be broken. *Never* water unless it can be done to the extent of thoroughly soaking the ground to a depth of at least 3 inches. This is applicable equally to either the newly planted or the old established plants. The effect of a light sprinkling is merely to encourage the roots of the plants to come to the surface, which is exactly what should be avoided, for they will then be far more likely to suffer in hot weather. So if the watering cannot be done thoroughly, it is much better not to water at all. Watering, once commenced, should be continued; but if the garden is properly made and the slopes not too steep, little will be required when once the plants are established, unless in an exceptionally dry summer.

It is a good practice to put stones, pressing them in firmly, close to and round the neck of alpine plants. These help to keep the roots moist and cool, and prevent the leaves lying on the damp ground.

Top-dress the rock garden in spring to counteract the effect of the winter's rain and frost. It is a very important and necessary operation, and one which is too often neglected. Nature herself does it by bringing down with the melting snow, soil and grit, which are deposited over and around the plants.

The best compost that we can use for this purpose is the refuse from the potting bench, mixed with sharp sand and grit, or, failing this, fibrous loam, leaf-mould, and sand in about equal parts will do well; the addition of a little powdered granite will be found beneficial and suit many plants.

This mixture should be fine and be put through a $\frac{1}{8}$-inch riddle.

Every spring we should carefully examine our plants, especially such kinds as *Androsace villosa*, *Chamæjasme*, and *Laggeri*, many of the Potentillas, Saxifrages, Erigerons, Asters, Campanulas, *Daphne cneorum* and *Blagayana*, Silenes, Dianthus, Anemones, Primulas, Gentians, etc., and wherever it is found that the soil has been washed away from the plants, expose their roots and stems, gently open the tufts out, and carefully work in the soil and grit through them. Small chips of stone can with advantage be used to keep straggling shoots in position and encourage them to layer. It may, and probably will, be a troublesome operation, but the result will more than repay the time expended, for plants so treated will shortly appear to take a new lease of life and display that vigour of healthy growth that is the pride and joy of all gardeners.

The surface of the whole garden should be gone over, and wherever roots or off-shoots of plants are exposed they should be covered. Frost also tends to loosen plants, which, when so found, should be firmly pressed home again. In places where rain has formed a miniature channel, it should be filled up and a stone or two put in to keep the soil in position.

The frost, snow, and rain of winter, besides removing the soil from the plants, has often the effect of dislodging or loosening the very rocks themselves, no matter how carefully they have been originally built in. Therefore in the spring examine the rockwork carefully, and whenever a crack appears in the soil behind some rock it is a sure sign that it has moved. It should immediately be made firm, either by packing the soil around it or driving in a wedge-shaped stone at its base to get it back into position. When this is accomplished, make quite certain that no air space is left at the back of the rock, even if it should entail removing some of the soil to ascertain it. During the summer, and more especially in very hot, dry weather, the exposed surface of the ground should be kept loose and well pulverised, and, when doing this, care should be taken not to disturb the roots of the plants.

Weeds must, at all costs, be kept down. The secret of success is never to let them seed. The only safe and sure way to remove the weeds is by the hand. The hoe is a dangerous instrument, even in the hands of the skilled, and fatal in the hands of others. Besides, alpines should be encouraged to sow themselves, and the young seedlings would most certainly come to a speedy and untimely end. When feasible, do the weeding yourself, unless you are lucky enough to command the services of a man, or boy, who can distinguish the difference between weeds and plants—by no means an easy thing to do when they are in the seedling stage—and who possesses that rare and divine gift of walking over a rock garden without treading on the tufts of one's most precious plants. Personally, I have not yet met this gifted creature, for my experience is that a month's weeds do less harm than an hour of the labours of the garden boy ; but others, perchance, may be more fortunate.

How very true is that trite old saying, " One year's seeding gives five years' weeding " ! and especially so of the rock garden ; not, indeed, that weeds seed more freely there than they do in the ordinary border, but that the weeds, once established, are so much more difficult to dislodge, owing to the way they have of getting their roots around and behind the rocks, choosing generally the largest and hardest to get at. Sometimes, indeed, the only way to exterminate them is to remove the rock itself. This should, however, be the last resource.

Garden pests ! I cannot say whether it is more in sorrow or in anger I write these words ; a good deal of both perhaps. In sorrow at the picture it recalls to my mind of tender and choice plants mutilated almost beyond recognition by some bird, or in one short night by the attention of one voracious slug. In wrath certainly at the spoiler of these treasures. Gardening is, alas ! one long fight against the elements and against nature in the shape of birds, beasts, and insects. Fishes, so far, have not yet attacked me.

Perhaps, however, if gardening were all plain sailing it would not have the same fascination.

In hard weather, when snails and slugs are not abroad, birds tear to pieces our choicest tufts of Saxifrages and Campanulas, seeking for insects. It was only yesterday that, going round my own garden after a week's frost and snow, I found my best plant of *Saxifraga Apiculata* strewn in small pieces over the path, and a patch of *Arenaria Balearica* looking as though an army of men had been at it with rakes.

In mild weather the birds very kindly leave us more or less alone, except when, in a playful mood, they amuse themselves by cutting off and scattering on the ground the open flower-buds of our alpines, choosing with an almost uncanny certainty those of the shyest-blooming varieties. But in case we should be congratulating ourselves on the waning interest in our garden displayed by the birds in mild weather, the slugs and snails will sally forth in quest of pastures new and rare! Is it towards such strong-growing plants as the Aubrietias, Arabis, or mossy Saxifrages that

DIANTHUS ALPINUS.

ROMAZOFFIA SITCHENSIS.

they wend their slimy way? Not at all. But
yonder is a plant of *Phyteuma comosum* just
showing its purple leaves. What more
could heart (if it has one, which I doubt) of
slug desire for a luscious supper? Or perchance it is a struggling plant of *Campanula
Zoyzii*, or *Erigeron*, or *Symphydra pendula*, or ! ! !
A volume could be filled with all the or's!
How can we cope with such difficulties? For
if the birds be destroyed, then there promptly
will be a plague of insects, and the last state
will be far worse than the first. So it were
better to destroy all the insects. But can this
be done? The answer is short. Quite impossible. So let the birds live, or some of
them at least, to keep the balance of nature.

Dire indeed would be the result if this
were lost. The one example of the rabbits
of Australia too easily proves the truth of
this.

Many mixtures are advertised for destroy-
ing these pests, but personally I have not found
any of them very efficacious. Perhaps I did
not use them properly ; but, be that as it may,
the result was that neither slugs nor snails

12

were destroyed or kept at bay for more than a few days at most. The only thing I have found really efficacious in warding off their attack is a ring of zinc round the plant. It is not ornamental, but can be removed as soon as the plant has made its growth, when the slugs can do but comparatively little damage, the crucial time being when growth is just commencing.

These zinc rings are simple to make. Get a sheet of zinc and cut into strips about $1\frac{1}{4}$ inch wide, and long enough to go round the plant, and fasten the ends together with copper wire. The theory is that as zinc and copper in contact create a certain amount of electricity, the marauding slug gets a shock on touching this barrier. Whether this is the case or not I cannot say, but the fact remains that they will not cross the zinc. When putting this ring round a plant, make sure there are neither slugs nor snails in the plant or ground around it. If any are within the magic circle, there they will remain and concentrate all their energies on the one unhappy plant, with dire results.

Powdered alum, which is quite harmless to plant life, is also a good preventative for slugs, and snails most strongly object to any astringent, though I doubt if it would kill them unless applied in considerable quantities. As an experiment I have tried sprinkling slugs with a mixture advertised for killing them, and the only result I could get was that, though they apparently very much disliked the stuff and at first seemed to be dead, after a short time they were able to throw off what appeared to be a skin of slime and then crawled away none the worse. There is, in my opinion, but one way to get rid of these pests, and that is by hand-picking. The earlier in the year this is done the better, before they commence to breed. The practice I adopt is to go out as soon as it is dark with a lantern (those " ever-ready " electric lanterns I find very light and handy), and armed with long pointed scissors, such as are used for thinning grapes ; and every slug or snail, be he large or small, I—well, the guillotine was supposed to be an instantaneous and painless death, and I can assure my readers that, judging from appearances, the scissors are equally speedy in dealing with slug or snail.

By persevering with this treatment, these pests, though not completely banished, can be kept within reasonable bounds. Wire-worms, of which there are several varieties, are the larvæ of various kinds of beetles, known by the popular name of the click, or skip-jack. These wire-worms, especially in new ground, are a great scourge. They are about half an inch long, and somewhat thicker than an ordinary knitting-needle, and of an orange colour. They obtain their name from the toughness of their skin. They can be hammered into the ground, which treatment, unless it be peculiarly hard, appears to have but little effect on them. They are most destructive, especially to any of the Dianthus family, and dearly love the tuberous-rooted plants. "Vaporite" is very successful in warding off their attacks, and will in fact kill them, while it is perfectly harmless to even the most delicate plants. It can be obtained from almost any seedsman or chemist, and full instructions are given with each tin.

A very good and simple way of catching wire-worms is to bury a carrot or potato in the ground, marking the spot, and after a day or so dig it up again. By that time all the wire-worms for some distance round will have found it out and burrowed into it.

Earwigs are especially harmful to the blooms of carnations, cutting the petals off at the base. They can be easily trapped. Being night-feeders, they rest during the day, choosing for preference such a spot as a hollow stalk; so by placing pieces of bean-stalk about 6 inches long, or any other hollow stalk, amongst the flowers of the plant attacked and blowing the contents into a tin of boiling water every morning, many of these troublesome pests may be destroyed. For caterpillars, aphis, and the like, hand-picking and spraying with some of the many mixtures advertised for that purpose are the only remedies.

The wood-louse has got a bad name, but has done me little or no harm in my garden.

To catch him, cut a potato in half and hollow out each portion, then place on the ground, hollowed side down. Examine each day, and destroy the wood-lice that will be found hiding in these traps by shaking them into boiling water.

CHAPTER XII

PLANTING THE ROCK GARDEN

Points for consideration—Difference between alpines and rock plants—Grouping—Examples of same—Planting bulbs — Ferns — Caution against rampant-growing plants—Importance of proportion—Planting shrubs.

IF the reader has been able to derive sufficient help and information from the earlier chapters, he will naturally be anxious to know how to plant his garden, and the best varieties of plants to use, and as the ultimate result will largely depend on the selection made and whether the plants are judiciously grouped, their choice and arrangement should most carefully be considered. Otherwise the result will be but chaotic and inartistic, no matter how skilfully the garden has been engineered.

How to group plants so as best to show off the beauty of the individual, while at the

same time producing the most telling effect in
the general scheme, is in my opinion one of,
if not quite the most difficult branch of rock
gardening, while it is also the most important.

It is at times almost impossible to know
how best to produce the desired effect ; there
are so many points to be considered before the
final home for any plant is selected. First
arises the question of aspect, whether that
chosen will suit it ; then how it will combine
in colour, habit, and time of flowering with
its next-door neighbour.   One is sometimes
almost in despair, for no place seems to answer
all requirements, and one is almost induced to
follow the slovenly and lazy gardener's motto
of " Oh, put it in anywhere."   But anywhere
is nowhere, and there must be some spot that
will suit it best, and that spot should be found,
even if it entails a considerable amount of
trouble.

I do not profess to be an artist, nor will I
attempt to venture into those mystic schemes
of colour of which one hears so much, but
sees so little, except in the catalogues of
nurserymen.

SAXIFRAGA APICULATA.

SAXIFRAGA OPPOSITIFOLIA.

In rock gardening, and in fact in all kinds of gardening, the best results are frequently obtained by the simplest means. The chief thing to avoid is a confused mixture of many brilliant colours, giving crude contrasts ; at its best it has but a patchy appearance, and does not give that harmony of colour which it should be one's object to obtain. And the beauty of the individual plant will suffer no loss from a judicious blending for general effect; rather the contrary, for by a good combination the individual also will be shown at its best.

Before proceeding to discuss further the planting of alpine and rock plants, it would perhaps be as well to explain what is meant by alpine and what by rock plants, lest some confusion should arise, owing to the two names being often used synonymously. Alpines derive their name from their original home—the Alps. Rock plants, which include alpines, are those collected from all parts of the temperate world, be it mountain or valley, which, so long as they are suitable in habit and height, are used in the rock garden.

Henceforth it may be understood for the sake of brevity that in " rock plants," alpines and all suitable varieties are included.

Rock plants, looking at them with a view to grouping in the garden, may be divided into two classes : (1) those which, on account of their freer growth and more generous bloom, can be effectively used for massing ; and (2) those which are grown chiefly on account of their intrinsic beauty, but which, owing to their slower and more diminutive growth, will not, in this country at least, give the same bold dashes of colour.

In the former class may be included such families as the Aubrietias, Rock Roses, Arabis, Cerastium, Campanulas, etc.—in fact, most of the commoner plants grown in the rock garden. In the latter class one has such lovely things as *Soldanella alpina*, the rarer Saxifrages, such as *S. diapensioides, cæsia, Burseriana, Faldonside* etc., *Campanula Zoyzii, Rainera, Edrianthus serpyllifolius, Phyteuma comosum*, and many others too numerous to mention here, all and each lovely in themselves, but whose beauty would be lost if planted beside, say, a yard-square avalanche of Aubrietia. So it is advisable that these more diminutive treasures be grown in a part of the garden reserved for them alone, and not mixed with the coarser kinds. It is all very well for people to talk about carpeting the ground with *Androsace glacialis*, *Eritrichium nanum*, or *Campanula Rainera*; it is so in Switzerland, but it cannot be achieved in the British Isles.

Keep all the choicer Saxifrages together, choosing a well-drained spot fully exposed to the sun, with soil containing a good proportion of lime-rubbish, sand, and broken stones. I have grown together, and bloomed well, *S. diapensioides*, *Faldonside*, *cæsia*, *Ferdinandi*, *Coburgi*, *Boydii*, *Burseriana*, and others of the choicest kinds, which would have been lost and passed unnoticed if scattered throughout other parts of the garden. There are numbers of other Saxifrages strong-growing and beautiful, such as *apiculata*, *sancta*, *Wallacei*, *Rhei*, *Guilford*, and *Cotyledon*, which will make as much growth in one season as the previous mentioned kinds will in ten. So use these latter in large bold masses for covering your rocks and level spaces.

The following general scheme of planting might well be adopted :—To fall over the rocks bordering the paths, mass Aubrietias of all kinds, *Arabis*, *Hypericum reptans*, *Androsace lanuginosa* and its variety *Leichtlini*, *Dianthus suavis*, Thymes, etc.; while in places where the rocks are but little over the level of the path, tufts of mossy *Saxifrages*, *Campanulas*, etc., may be allowed to spread on to the path. Behind this, which may be called the edging, plant over the rocks the lower-growing kinds and creeping varieties, while on the level spots place such plants as *Silene alpestris*, *Campanula pulla*, and *Gentians*, *Dianthus*, etc., interspersed here and there with plants of a taller - growing habit, so as to avoid a too flat appearance. Behind these again the bolder-growing plants and smaller shrubs or shrubby plants, merging gradually into the shrubs which form the background.

Always endeavour to plant in bold masses. Avoid single specimens dotted here and there. If the garden is large, one or even two square yards is not too much space to devote to one variety ; but this is not always easy to accomplish. It takes so many plants of one kind to cover the space desired, especially considering how small they usually are when received from nurserymen, and the expense of a large number is often prohibitive. But if only two or three plants can be obtained in the beginning, instead of the dozen or more required, I would still advise assigning the larger space, and in the autumn propagating from one of your own plants. It cannot be expected that the garden will be properly clothed much under four years, unless a very large number of plants are purchased to begin with. And even when this cannot be done, it is still better to adopt the system of massing, for massing is the secret of effect. Though often the individual flowers of rock plants do not possess much intrinsic beauty in themselves, when grown in large quantities they are most effective.

When massing plants, endeavour to vary the shape and outline of each group as much as possible, for otherwise a formal effect will be produced, which is very objectionable. The formation of the ground will help in this, to a certain extent at least.

As an example of what can be obtained by this method, imagine a drift of Campanulas stretching half way up the face of the bank, with a tuft of mossy Saxifrages covering the rocks which bound the path, while in another place a cascade of *Androsace lanuginosa* falls on to a strip of *Silene alpestris* growing at its foot ; while again a dazzling patch of *Gentiana acaulis* is seen extending right up to rocks covered with a snow-white torrent of *Thymus Serpyllum alba*. Many such pictures as these could be suggested did space permit.

Annuals may give a great show of bloom for some months during the summer, and are usually very easy to grow; but they have the great objection that once their bloom is past they die away, leaving an ugly blank in the garden. With the majority of perennial rock plants it is different. They are beautiful even when not in bloom, on account of their foliage and habit of forming compact tufts, which increase year by year, and give that idea

[*To face page* 190.

ANDROSACE LANUGINOSA, IN THE AUTHOR'S GARDEN.

of permanence so lacking in annuals. For these reasons I never use annuals of any kind, if I can avoid it, except that dainty little yellow Saxifrage, *Cymbalaria*, which appeared in my garden of its own accord, and goes on sowing itself from year to year, but never encroaching.

Many varieties of bulbs can be used with delightful effect on the slopes of the rock garden. They have, however, one objection, that they only make a show during the flowering season, which, alas! is all too short. Once that is over, little else but withered leaves remains. To remedy this defect, put your bulbs under dwarf- and close-growing plants, such as the Thymes, Sedums, mossy Saxifrages, etc. In the spring they will push up through these carpets, have their flowers, and disappear until the following year.

Ferns can also be used with good effect in the shadier and damper parts of the garden. Their lovely green foliage will show off and accentuate the livelier colouring of the flowers.

My reiterated emphatic advice with regard to the scheme of planting is to mass. Mass boldly, covering the rocks and all the surface of the ground. The fully matured rock garden should have no untenanted spot, nor in summer show any bare spaces. Therefore, mass ; but it must be left to individual taste and circumstances to decide how to obtain the best effects from the material at hand.

With regard to what are the best species to plant together, colour and time of flowering will have especially to be considered, provided always that the aspect suits both species equally well.

It is not advisable to devote too large a space to plants of the same flowering season, for though the result during that period may be pleasing, it will be apt to make rather a blot on the general effect when their bloom is over. So I prefer to mix the plants in such a way that from April to September there will be no part of the garden quite devoid of bloom, though, as might be expected, the garden will be much gayer at some times of the year than at others.

Another point to look to, and one often rather liable to be forgotten, is that no very strong and rapid-growing plant should ever be put beside one that is of slow growth and delicate habit, or the former will sooner or later smother the latter.

Never plant rubbish. Do not be persuaded by your friends "just to fill up your garden with anything to make a show the first year." This is the greatest mistake, for you may afterwards have difficulty in getting rid of what you planted merely as a "stop-gap."

A word of warning may not be out of place with regard to very strong and rampant-growing plants, especially those that have a creeping rootstock, for great discretion will have to be exercised in planting them owing to the difficulty of removing them when once established behind some large rock. Nothing in the shape of a rampant grower should be planted in the part of the garden reserved for the choicer kinds. The wild garden is the place for such dangerous characters, for their encroaching habits will not so much matter there.

I speak from experience. In a weak moment, and I must confess in ignorance of its

13

habit, I planted in one of the choicer parts of my garden a plant of *Convolvulus althæoides*, a very attractive plant in itself. In two months it had made wonderful growth, clothing the adjacent rocks with its creeping stems. My suspicions having been aroused, I examined the ground around, and about 4 feet from the parent plant I found a sucker of it just appearing in the middle of my best plant of *Daphne Blagayana*. To get there it had to work its way behind a rock weighing about a quarter of a ton. Further investigations showed that it was spreading in all directions, and had reached as far as 5 feet from the original plant, which was hastily banished to the· wild garden. All the rockwork had to be taken down in order to thoroughly clean the ground. So that two days' hard work was the result of a thoughtless moment. Let this experience of mine be a warning to the reader on no account to plant anything, except in the wilder parts, that will be likely to take possession of his garden.

Leaving the rock plants, we will now deal with the shrubs, the dwarf-growing kinds, which can be mixed with the plants, or form a connecting link with those of stronger growth which are to make the background of the garden.

Too much care and attention cannot be devoted to the planting of the shrubs, both large and small. On their judicious and skilful arrangement the success of the garden from an artistic point of view will greatly depend.

The modern rock garden is usually a copy, or more often an attempt to copy, some mountain scene on a very reduced scale, and that it is on a very reduced scale is evident from the fact that where in nature we find rocky crags or cliffs 30 feet or 40 feet high, we, in our puny imitations, have to be content with rocks measuring as many inches. In order, therefore, to carry out this idea correctly, we should use trees and shrubs proportionate in size to our rocks. Amongst the rocks should be planted dwarf shrubs, such as *Ledum buxifolia*, *Azalea amæna*, or *Cistus florentinus*, and such miniature trees as the dainty little *Pinus sylvestris Beuvronensis*, or some *Retinospera obtusa pygmæa*, pigmy reproductions of those gnarled and aged giants found on the scene we wish to copy.

The secret of a faithful reproduction is proportion. For example, by planting one of these dwarf trees at the foot of some rock, or inserting it in some fissure, such an added value of dignity and height will be imparted that the rock will appear to be transformed into a rugged cliff. So again, by planting on some height a group of *Juniper Sabina*, the idea is conveyed of a wind-swept mountain crag. Time will indeed be well spent in working out pictures like this and trying where such as these will look best and most effective. Place a group here or a single specimen there, and study the effect from different points before finally planting. The results that can be obtained are wonderful so long as the sense of proportion is preserved. So also with the dwarf shrubs, though in a somewhat lesser degree, for they are not such faithful copies of their larger prototypes. But with the grouping and arrangement of these dwarf trees and shrubs, the faithful picture ends, for I must confess

SEMPERVIVUM ARACHNOIDEUM.

I find it difficult to assimilate a pigmy Scotch fir of say 8 or 10 inches high with a 4 feet specimen bush of *Cistus ladaniferus* or *Olearia Hastii*, though it is undeniable that such shrubs are a necessary and attractive adjunct to the rock garden. The only way I can find out of the difficulty of combining dwarf shrubs and trees with those of larger growth, is by planting the latter so far away from the pigmy specimens that they form merely a background.

As it is imperative that this background should be permanent, evergreen shrubs should chiefly be used. But do not for a moment think it is desirable to ignore the deciduous section, containing, as it does, many of the most beautiful of flowering shrubs. These should be so placed that the full value of their beauty when in flower is obtained, while not at other times affecting the permanent scheme.

This may appear to be somewhat contradictory advice, but by judiciously mixing the evergreen with the deciduous, such an effect can be achieved. The advice as regards the massing of the plants applies also, in a certain degree, to shrubs, for when several of the same species are planted together, the effect is far more striking than when they are grown singly.

Of shrubs suitable for covering the heights and the intermediate space between the rock plants and the larger shrubs, I should advise a selection from the following :—The family of Rhododendron is of chief importance, and varieties suitable for our purpose will be found in such dwarf-habited kinds as *ciliatum, hirsutum, ferrugineum, Racemosum, myrtifolium* ; also *Azalea amœna* and its varieties ; the Menziesias, *polifolia, polifolia alba,* and *Bicolor* ; and of the Ledums, *Palustris* and *latifolium* ; while amongst the numerous Cistus family such varieties as *florentinus, formosus, lusitanicus,* and *Rosmarinifolius* will be found most useful. Of the Genistas and Cytisus one cannot go far wrong in selecting the following : *Cytisus Ardoini, Kewensis, purpureus,* and *Purpureus albus, Genista prostrata, saggitalis,* and *tinctora, fl. pl.*

Some of these, such as *Cytisus Ardoini*

and *Kewensis*, and *Genista prostrata*, which grow only a few inches high, will creep over a rock, covering it with a compact green cushion, which in summer will be transformed into a sheet of cream or gold.

It is not, however, a good plan to line all the heights with these dwarf shrubs, for that would tend to give a monotonous appearance. Therefore, vary the effect by planting here and there, almost up to the rock plants, a group of the stronger-growing brooms, such as *Cytisus Præcox* and *Præcox alba*, *Carlieri*, *scoparius*, etc.

Shrubs, deciduous and otherwise, suitable for massing in the background, are legion, and every year new varieties are being introduced — some hardy, and others only half hardy.

Therefore, to a certain extent, the selection made will depend on the climate. For instance, in my garden in County Wicklow, I can grow without the least protection during the winter such shrubs as *Metrosideros floribunda*, *Carpenteria Californica*, *Cistus formosus*, *Myrtus apiculata*, *Grevillea rosmarini-*

folia, and many others which are considered only half hardy ; but all people are not so fortunate.

Unfortunately, Rhododendrons will not grow everywhere, for they belong to that group of shrubs which includes so many lovely and rare species, namely, the peat-lovers, or, as they should more accurately be called, the lime-haters. I have a little lime in the soil of my garden, and Rhododendrons, though they live, will not thrive as I should wish them to ; otherwise I would grow them as freely as I would advise all others to do, whose soil is more suitable.

In Part II. will be found a list of the choicer shrubs, both dwarf and free-growing.

CHAPTER XIII

COST

Points affecting the cost — Labour — Clearing scrub —
Drainage—Estimated cost of rocks, sand, etc.—Cost
of making artificial bog garden—Cost of plants.

WHEN undertaking any work, whether it be
the laying out of a pleasure-ground, the building of a house, or the making of a rock garden,
the question that first arises is the probable
cost; and very rightly so too, for to commence
an operation of this kind without having any
idea of the expense incurred, is, to put it
plainly, the act of a fool.

With regard to buildings, the estimate
is, comparatively speaking, simple, for it
merely resolves itself into a mathematical calculation, with a well-recognised basis, such as
the cost of a cubic yard of masonry or a square
of roofing. These are known and acknowledged

factors, and, except in very exceptional cases, not liable to much variation.

But very different is the case in landscape gardening, for difficulties may arise, such as finding unexpected rocks or a very hard stratum of subsoil, etc., which could not have been foreseen or guarded against when the work was commenced. So any estimate made must be more or less approximate, and it is wise to leave a good margin.

In the case of a rock garden much will depend on whether it is natural or artificial; if the former, on whether much clearing has to be done to expose the rock, and on what facilities there are for making and draining the necessary pockets. The texture of the rock, whether hard or soft, will also affect the estimate. In the artificial garden there are even more points to consider: if the ground has to be cleared from scrub, when it will cost less than if there are also trees to be removed; if it is necessary to excavate for the site, and, if so, to what extent; also, what the facilities are for getting rocks, sand, water, and many other things.

But in order to form an estimate some data will be needed as to labour, quantities of rocks required, etc. I therefore propose to give some figures which may be found useful, based partly on my own experience and partly on engineering tables.

I shall take labour first. But as wages vary so much in different parts of the country, I think the most practical way of dealing with it is, instead of giving cost, to give particulars of the amount of work an ordinary labourer might reasonably be expected to accomplish in a day, and then, with a little calculation of quantity and knowledge of the local rate of wages, a very fair estimate of the probable cost can be made.

One man in a day of eight hours should dig out and throw up on either side of a cutting ten cubic yards of light friable soil.

If the soil is stiff clay, which entails much pick-work, he probably would not be able to remove more than half that quantity. If there are large boulder stones mixed with the earth, it may take even longer. About three cubic yards of soft rock, or about half a cubic yard of hard rock should be removed in the day's work.

Should the soil have to be removed in a wheelbarrow to a distance, say, of fifteen to thirty yards, two men and two barrows should be able to remove ten cubic yards of friable loose soil ; if of stiff clay, about five cubic yards.

This is presuming the run to be fairly level. If up a steep incline they will only be able to remove about two-thirds of the above amounts. The method of work is for one man to dig and fill the barrows, while the other wheels. If the soil should be hard or difficult to dig, three men will be required altogether ; two to dig and fill, and one to wheel, for otherwise the barrow-man would be idle, waiting till the load was dug out and filled.

When the earth has to be removed some distance or the gradient is too steep for barrow-work, carting will be necessary. Assuming the distance the soil has to be drawn is a quarter of a mile, four men with two horses and carts should remove about twenty cubic yards of loose earth in the day. An extra man would be required if the soil is hard.

Sometimes, while yet too steep for barrow-work, it is not possible to work a horse and cart, as was the case when I was making my garden. The means I adopted of overcoming this difficulty was as follows :—I made a small tilting truck, holding about a ton, similar to that used in quarries, etc., which I ran on some light rails, about nine pounds to the yard; these were quite portable and could easily be moved about in sections. The motive power I used was an old ship's winch, and with about thirty yards of a three-inch cable I had a most useful little railway, by means of which I drew and deposited where I wished many hundred tons of soil, up a gradient of nearly one in five. The winch being geared very low, a small boy could work it easily, even with a full load on the truck. In place of the winch, horse power could be used, but this was not in my case feasible. However, even had I the choice, I would prefer the mechanical power.

Some few suggestions as how best to utilise labour may be found to be a help.

Two men will get through more work in

one day than one man in two days. It is, nevertheless, a mistake to have too many men working at the same spot, for they are apt to get in one another's way. If possible, try to arrange your workmen so that one has to keep steadily working in order to keep another supplied with work ; for example, with two men and two barrows, one should be digging and filling while the other is wheeling ; the first should have the barrow filled by the time the second one has returned from depositing his load. If the distance is considerable a third man and a barrow may be worked into the cycle of operations. So also with carting : arrange your men and carts so that an empty cart is never kept waiting at the scene of operations while another one is being filled ; but time it so that the empty cart arrives at the spot as the full one leaves. It is wonderful, the amount of time, and consequently money, that can be saved by a little arrangement of this sort.

It is difficult to make anything of an accurate estimate of the cost of clearing land from scrub, so much depends on its nature and age. But—and I think it may be taken as a maximum—one man ought to clear and stub one square perch of thick scrub in the day. This does not include the removal of tree-stumps, which may easily entail a good deal of labour and expense.

Piped drains sunk about three feet deep will, in ordinary soil, cost about two-and-sixpence per chain of twenty-two yards.

The cost of materials, such as rocks, broken stones, sand, peat, etc., varies so much in different localities and depends so much on the distance they have to be drawn, that it is difficult to give more than a very rough estimate.

Rocks of all sizes and broken stones, which have to be carted about two miles, I get for three-and-sixpence a load of one ton. Sand costs about four shillings per load. Peat, which has to be drawn five miles from a mountain, costs me five-and-sixpence a load of about twelve cwt. The quantity of rock required for making a garden largely depends on the gradients of the banks in it, and is difficult to estimate with any degree of accuracy. Judging from personal experience, I would say roughly, but it must of necessity be a very rough estimate, that, taking one part with another, banks varying in gradient from four in ten to two in ten would take about one ton of rocks to every ten square yards. The steeper the formation the more and larger the rocks required. Parts with a gradient of one in two would demand from two to three tons for the same extent of ground. The rocks I here refer to are not large masses weighing fifteen or sixteen cwt. each, but good serviceable stones weighing from one to five cwt. apiece, say about ten to fifteen rocks to a load of one ton. These figures are based on what I used in my own garden. In it the actual rockwork, including parts with rocks scattered only here and there, covers about twelve hundred square yards, and took about one hundred and thirty tons of rocks. The gradients vary from five and a half in eight, in the steepest parts, to two in ten, on the gentlest slopes. A good, useful, and effective gradient is about three and a half in ten.

The description of rock used will also, in a certain measure, affect the calculations, as some kinds of stone weigh so much heavier than others in comparison to their bulk. A solid block of sandstone (quartzite), weighing one ton, would contain fourteen and a half cubic feet, while the same weight of whinstone (basalt) would only contain twelve and a half cubic feet. So it is apparent that the bulk is very considerably affected by the nature of the rock.

For building a dry wall, estimating the stonework at two feet thick, it would require about three-quarters of a ton of stones for every square yard. I have not touched on the question of cost as regards the actual building of the rockwork, as this calls for considerable artistic skill, and is altogether outside the sphere of ordinary labour. There are many landscape gardeners nowadays whose services can be obtained, if desired, at fees varying from one guinea to four guineas per day, according to skill and reputation.

When it is necessary to dig sand or small

14

stones into the soil, it will be useful to have an idea of the quantities required.

One ton of dry sand contains twenty-four and a half cubic feet in bulk. So by spreading a ton one inch thick it will cover thirty-two square yards, and a ton of broken stones about twenty-five square yards. If either is very wet, the bulk will naturally be reduced as compared with the weight, and correspondingly cover less area.

Those who wish to make an artificial bog-bed with concrete, as described in Chapter VII., may find the following calculations of service. For the foundation, one ton of broken stones, laid six inches thick, will cover three square yards. For the concrete, use it at a strength of six to one. Take one bag of Portland cement (weighing two hundred and eleven pounds), and mix with eleven cwt. of gravel; this should give about thirteen cwt. of concrete, equal in bulk to about twelve cubic feet. By spreading this three inches thick it should cover about five and a half square yards. In order to make the basin of the bog-bed watertight, a coating of pure cement will have to be applied. This should be about half an inch thick. One bag of cement at this thickness will cover ten square yards.

The number of plants needed will vary considerably, according to their nature and habit, some requiring to be planted not more than six inches apart, while others may be left as much as eighteen inches or two feet ; but taking one with another, roughly, about twelve plants to the square yard would be a fair number to allow.

The cost of plants varies also not a little ; but, excluding the rarer kinds, I should say about five shillings a dozen is a fair price to pay. This, though only for the commoner kinds, would mount up to a large figure for even a garden of moderate dimensions, and when the cost of rarities is added, the total will often frighten one.

But nobody expects to fully plant their garden the first year, so I should recommend, if economy is an element to be considered, not buying more than half a dozen of one sort of the commoner plants, and of the rarer kinds only one or perhaps three. As most rock plants can easily be increased by propagation, the full complement can be made up in the course of a couple of years or so, at a considerable saving to one's pocket, and with greatly added interest and knowledge of the habits of the plants.

PART II

ALPHABETICAL LIST OF PLANTS SUITABLE FOR THE ROCK GARDEN

GIVING FULL PARTICULARS OF THEIR HABIT, TIME OF FLOWERING, CULTIVATION, ETC.

ABRONIA (NYCTAGINACEAE)

A SMALL genus of plants of trailing habit, bearing clusters of verbena-like flowers. Only the following species are suitable :—

A. arenaria.—Fully exposed position in light sandy soil. Flowers lemon-yellow, borne in dense clusters in July. Fragrant. Not very hardy. Increased by seed, the outer skin of which should be peeled off before sowing, or by cuttings taken in spring.

A. Crux Maltae.—Open position in sandy soil. Flowers purplish, pink, with a green throat, in shape resembling a Maltese cross. Blooms in August. Increased by seed and cuttings same as above.

A. fragrans.—Same soil and position. Flowers white and fragrant, borne in terminal clusters. Blooms during May, flowers expanding during the *evening*. Increased by seed and cuttings. Grows 12 to 18 inches high, and of a more erect habit.

A. mellifera.—Exposed position in sandy soil. Stem decumbent, only rising some 4 to 6 inches high. Flowers orange-coloured, borne in loose clusters in July. Seed and division.

ACAENA (ROSACEAE)

Dwarf creeping plants, of which there are about twenty varieties in cultivation, but mostly of only secondary value for the rock garden, where effect is desired. They are all evergreen and quite hardy.

A. adscendens.—Any aspect. Sandy loam. Creeping habit. Rapid grower. Silvery leaves. Purplish-coloured burrs. Easily propagated by division.

A. Buchanani.—Any aspect. Any light sandy soil. Close creeping habit. Rapid grower, but at the same time does not appear to have the encroaching habit of some of the other varieties. Finely divided foliage of bright pea-green colour. Round, reddish burrs freely produced, flowering July to August. Division. This is one of the best of the family, and on account of its lovely foliage and less rampant growth may be used for the choicer parts of the rock garden.

A. inermis.—Any aspect and soil. Creeping habit and rapid grower. Bronzy-green foliage. Reddish, rather insignificant burrs. Propagated by division. Useful for carpeting the less choicer parts.

A. microphylla (syn. *Novae Zealandiae*). — Any aspect. Will thrive in almost any soil, but prefers that of a light and sandy nature. Creeping habit, forming a dense carpet about ½ inch high. It is slow-growing as compared with others of the family. The inconspicuous small round heads or burrs which are freely produced are furnished with bright crimson spines from July to December. Pretty finely cut, small, bronzy-green foliage. Easily propagated by division. This is quite the best variety of the family, being neat of habit, and during the autumn and even into December the crimson burrs make quite a feature. It is altogether an indispensable plant for some level spot beneath the eye.

A. ovalifolia.—Indifferent to either aspect or soil. Grows about 9 inches high; of vigorous habit. Purplish-coloured burrs, produced from July to September. Bright green fern-like foliage. Propagation by division. Too rampant a grower to plant in the choicer parts of the garden, but in the wilder will be found useful as a carpet under trees.

A. pulchella.—Any aspect and soil. Creeping habit and very vigorous growth. Bronzy-green foliage. Propagation by division. Is a useful plant for covering large stones or bare spaces, but owing to its growth should be reserved for the wilder parts of the garden.

A. Dryentea, A. glabra, A. myriophylla, A. Sanguisorbae.—Are all useful for carpeting, but should not be associated with the choicer rock plants.

A. laevigata.—Is a somewhat shrubby species, with glaucous green leaves.

ACANTHOLIMON (PLUMBAGINACEAE), Prickly Thrift

A delightful and attractive genus of dwarf mountain plants which should be grown in every rock garden. The flowers resemble those of the Thrift, to which genus they are allied. The plants form branching, cushion-like mats of rigid spiny leaves, from which they get the name of Prickly Thrift. They all require a sunny and well-drained position, and are slow of growth and not easy to propagate. The best method is by working plenty of sand and cocoa fibre well into the tufts in early autumn, having previously carefully torn some of the branches, at a junction, so as to half sever them. After this treatment water well to settle the soil. By spring many of the growths so treated will be found to have rooted. Cuttings are uncertain. The best time to take them is in August and September. Tearing them off with a *heel*, insert without further preparation in very sandy loam.

The following are the only varieties in cultivation, but none, with the exception of *A. glumaceum*, are at all common.

A. acerosum.—Sunny, sheltered corner. Light, well-drained soil. Close-tufted habit, forming a cushion of spiny, grey, glaucous leaves. Very slow-growing. Rosy-pink flowers on stems 6 inches high in July. Propagate as already described. Hardy. A rare and attractive species ; the grey, glaucous, spiny leaves rather remind one of the foliage of *Dianthus caesius*, but, on touching, they will be found to be armed with sharp spikes.

A. androsaceum.—Soil and aspect same as last. A dense tufted species. Leaves, grey, glaucous, spiny. Bright pink flowers with a shade of purple in them, on sprays 4 inches high. Flowers in July. Propagate as described. Hardy. A very good and choice rock plant of easy culture ; will spread over the ledge of a rock. Owing to the pliant nature of the leaves, the rosettes appear to be less spiny than in the case of *A. venustum*, which it resembles.

A. armenum.—Hot, sunny aspect and well-drained soil. Spiny foliage and pink flowers on sprays nearly 6 inches high.

A. glumaceum.—Sunny aspect and light, well-drained soil. Forms spiny cushions of narrow dark-green leaves 6 inches high. This is the most vigorous grower of the family. Bright rose-coloured flowers, six to eight in a spikelet, with bracts rather like a Thrift. Flowers June to August. Propagated by cuttings or layers as described. Quite hardy. The best known of the family, and should be in every rock garden, where, in any suitable position, it will thrive well.

A. cephalotes.—Well-drained soil in a sunny position. Rosettes less compact than most species, and composed of narrow spiny leaves. Globose heads of rosy-pink flowers. A rare species, but well worth cultivating.

A. Kotschyi.—Requires same soil and aspect as other kinds. Rather broader spiny leaves than most of the others, and about 4 inches high. White flowers freely produced.

A. libanoticum.—Dry, well-drained, sunny position. Dense in growth and very woody. Pink flowers.

A. venustum (syn. *A. laxiflorum*).—A sheltered, sunny aspect.

Deep, well-drained soil, composed of sandy loam, leaf-mould, and brick rubbish. Dark green spiny leaves with an overlying slightly grey or glaucous shade. Forms close tufts 6 to 8 inches high. It is a slow-growing plant, freely producing bright rose-coloured flowers on arching, one-sided spikes during July. The flowers are rather longer than those of *A. glumaceum*. Propagation by layers and cuttings. This is one of the most attractive and choicest of rock plants. It requires firm planting.

ACANTHUS (ACANTHACEAE)

There is only one variety of this genus suitable for the rock garden, namely, *A. Perringi* (syn. *Roseus Caroli* and *Alexandri*). Ordinary soil in a sheltered position. Leaves long and lanceolate, low-growing habit. Flower-spikes about 12 to 18 inches high, each producing twenty-four to thirty blooms of deep pink flowers. Quite hardy and vigorous. A useful and attractive new introduction, though it has not the brilliancy of some alpines.

ACHILLAE (COMPOSITAE), Yarrow

A numerous, though not particularly interesting family of Compositae, some of which, owing to their rampant growth, are suitable only for the herbaceous border; but the dwarfer-growing kinds come in useful for grouping in the rock garden, and are easily grown and increased. Some of the higher alpine kinds are liable to become "leggy" in our open winters and will occasionally require division and replanting. Most of the Achilleas are good subjects for the wall garden. All like a hot, dry position.

A. ageratifolia (syn. *Anthemis Aizoon*).—Sunny aspect. Light sandy soil. A neat and spreading plant about 5 inches high, of moderately rapid growth. The crinkled leaves, which are narrow and tongue-shaped, are covered with a white down. White, daisy-like flowers are freely produced in June. It is easily cultivated and readily increased by division or cuttings, and quite hardy. A useful plant on account of its silvery foliage.

A. aegyptiaca (syn. *taygetea*).—Requires a well-drained, sunny position. Rather a tall-growing, shrubby plant of 12 to 18 inches high. Not a very rapid grower. Stems and finely cut fern-like leaves of a silvery colour. Handsome heads of pale yellow flowers during August. Easily increased by cuttings. This Achillea is not very hardy, except in well-drained, sunny, and sheltered spots. A useful and attractive, half-shrubby plant for the higher parts of the rock garden.

A. alpina.—Indifferent to either soil or position. Grows 6 to

12 inches high, with pretty serrated leaves and white flowers in September. Propagated by root division, cuttings, or seed. Quite hardy. Not of much value for rock garden.

A. aurea.—Any position. Loamy soil. Grows about 12 inches high, with finely cut leaves, tufted habit. Showy, bright yellow flowers freely produced during July. Propagated by root division, cuttings, or seed. Is a good rock plant, and one of the showiest of the family.

A. Clavennae.—Prefers a sunny position in light loamy soil. A somewhat shrubby plant of compact habit, growing 6 to 9 inches high. Silvery-white leaves, which colour is due to the short silky down with which they are covered. Pure white flowers freely produced in May and June. Is propagated by root division and seed, and is quite hardy. One of the best of the family for the rock garden, if only for the foliage, but the flowers also are a good white, which many of the other kinds are not.

A. Griesbachii.—Sunny position and loamy soil. Grows about 4 inches high, with glaucous foliage and white flowers.

A. Huteri (*Huter's Yarrow*).—Sunny position in any soil. Grows about 6 inches high, of spreading habit, with bright green foliage. Good, pure white flowers during June and July. Propagated by division. Is quite hardy. This species should be divided and replanted every two years.

A. Jaborneggii.—Not particular as to soil or situation. Grows about 6 inches high, of spreading habit and moderate growth. Distinct silvery foliage. Pure white flowers during the summer. Quite hardy, and easily propagated by root division or seeds.

This Achillea is a hybrid between *A. Clavennae* and *A. moschata*. It is one of the most worthy of being cultivated, and is really beautiful.

A. Herba-rota.—Any aspect and soil. Grows about 6 inches high, with white flowers during May and June. Foliage aromatic smell.

A. tomentosa.—Sunny position in ordinary light soil. Of spreading, tufted habit, growing about 6 to 9 inches high, of moderately rapid growth. Woolly, fern-like, evergreen foliage, with flat corymbs of golden-yellow flowers, freely produced from July to October. It is quite hardy, and easily propagated by division. A good and attractive dwarf plant.

A. rupestris.—Warm sunny bank, in poor soil. Of compact, prostrate habit, only growing 4 inches high, producing white flowers from June to September. A free bloomer. Easily cultivated and quite hardy. Increased by division. A useful and attractive rock plant from Italy.

A. Vielleresi.—Loamy soil. Any aspect. Grows about 6 inches high. Silvery foliage. Pure white flowers during June and July. Hardy and easily propagated by root division and seed. A good rock plant.

A. nana, A. moschata, A. umbellata, etc.—Have silvery foliage and white flowers, and are all of dwarf habit, easily cultivated and increased. They mostly bloom during the summer months, and are useful for carpeting, but call for no special attention.

ACIS (AMARYLLIDACEAE), syn. LEUCOJUM

A small genus of bulbous plants, all hardy, and related to the "Snowflake."

A. autumnale. — Sheltered position. Fine, very sandy soil. Grows about 3 inches high. Narrow green leaves, which disappear during the summer. Flowers, which appear in September before the leaves, resemble delicate pink snowdrops. This is a very uncommon plant, and is a gem for the rock garden, and looks its best springing from a mat of delicate-rooted Sedum, such as *dasyphyllum.*

The following are all worthy of a choice spot, and should be cultivated in sandy soil :—

A. grandiflora.—Grows 6 inches high, with large, white, bell-shaped flowers in August.

A. roseus. — Grows 3 inches high, with bright rose-coloured flowers in August.

A. trichophyllum.—Grows 6 inches high. Rather hairy leaves. White flowers in January.

ACTAEA (RANUNCULACEAE), Baneberry

Hardy perennials, chiefly suitable for the wilder garden. Increased by seed and division.

A. alba.—Partial shade and deep sandy soil. Grows about 18 inches high. Long, white, feathery flower-spikes, rather like a Spiraea, followed by white berries. Flowers in June.

A. spicata.—Similar, with black poisonous berries.

A. spicata, var. *rubra.*—Same as above, only with scarlet berries.

ACTINELLA (COMPOSITAE)

A small genus of hardy plants. Increased by division of root in spring.

A. grandiflora.—Deep sandy soil, in a sunny position. Dwarf, tufted habit, about 9 inches high. Yellow flowers about 3 inches across, borne on many-branched stems, in August.

A. scaposa.—Similar, but with silvery leaves and yellow flowers on long scapes, in July.

ADONIS (RANUNCULACEAE)

Handsome plants of easy cultivation, belonging to the Buttercup order. They all dislike disturbance and are slow to increase. Planting should be done in autumn. Strong seedlings are preferable to pieces from old plants. Most varieties produce seed freely, which will easily germinate if sown in a moist, shady spot and lightly covered. The following are the best perennial varieties :—

A. amurensis.—Sunny position, sheltered from cold winds, in moist, rather heavy loam. Increases very slowly, and grows about 9 inches high. Beautiful fern-like foliage, which dies down towards the end of the summer. The flowers, which are yellow, and about 2 inches across, are borne on stout leafy stems, and appear as early as January. It is quite hardy, and can be increased by seed or division. An attractive and valuable plant, as it blooms when there is little else in flower. The foliage and colour tint of flower are rather variable.

A. amurensis, fl. pl.—A double form of the above, and a very handsome plant. Large, quite double, golden-yellow flowers, with a curious green circle formed of green segments, which rather enhances than otherwise the beauty of the flower.

A. Viekinsaki.—Has feathery leaves and small yellow flowers, which bloom in January and February. It requires same treatment as above.

A. pyrenaica.—Sunny position in stony, well-drained, though moist, sandy loam. Grows about 1 foot to 18 inches high. Pale green leaves, rather like curled parsley, at the base of the much-branched stems. These decrease in size, till round the flower they are mere mossy tufts. Rich yellow flowers, 2 to 3 inches across, which appear in June. Hardy and increased by seed. If drainage is deficient, the crown of the plant is liable to decay.

A. vernalis.—Sunny position in rather moist, heavy loam. Increases slowly and dislikes disturbance. Grows about 9 inches to a foot in height. Finely cut leaves. Each stem, which does not branch freely, bears a single flower of rich, glistening, golden-yellow, about 2 inches across, in March. Quite hardy, propagated by seed. A well-known border plant, but one that should be in every rock garden.

A. volgensis.—Requires same soil and treatment as *A. vernalis*, which it very much resembles as regards its flower. Its foliage is quite distinct, being of a bright green, stems much flatter and thinner and more branched.

A. pyrenaica.—It bears rich yellow flowers on all the branches of its slender stems in April.

A. walziana.—This is a hybrid : *A. vernalis* and *A. volgensis.* It requires same treatment and position as the last named. It bears narrow-petalled, yellow flowers in April that expand very fully. The stems, which are stiffly erect, and about 12 inches high, are clothed with finely cut pale green foliage.

ÆTHIONEMA (CRUCIFERAE)

A charming family of dwarf-growing rock plants, forming rather untidy little bushes, with leaves mostly of a glaucous blue colour. The flowers are borne in crowded terminal racemes. All the species can be cultivated on the warmer slopes of the rock garden, and increased by seed or cuttings in the summer. They are all deep-rooted, and dislike disturbance or damp soil.

Æ. armenum.—Warm, sunny position, requiring a deep root-run of a light, dry, stony nature. It does well in limestone. It is of dwarf habit, growing only 3 or 4 inches high, with dense spikes of small, purplish-rose-coloured flowers. Dislikes damp, and is liable to perish in a wet winter.

Æ. capitatum.—Same position and soil as the last. Numerous thick stems, growing only a few inches high, with somewhat acute linear leaves rather scattered. Small and inconspicuous flowers. It is chiefly remarkable for its dense heads of boat-shaped seed-vessels with entire wings.

Æ. cepeaefolium (syn. *Hutchinsia rotundifolia*). — Requires a deep, dry root-run in a sunny position. Densely tufted stems, rising 3 to 6 inches, with glaucous, green, fleshy leaves $\frac{3}{4}$ to 1 inch long, those from the root obovate, those on the stem sessile. Flowers pale lilac, with a yellow eye, half an inch across, in cylindrical, crowded, erect racemes. A pretty and attractive plant.

Æ. cordatum.—Sunny position ; deep root-run. A shrubby little plant, growing 9 inches high, with rather large sulphur-yellow flowers in dense heads in August. Propagated by cuttings or seed. A good rock plant for a dry bank.

Æ. cordifolium. — Sunny position and dry, deep root-run required. A compact, shrubby little plant, growing only about 6 inches high. Short, crowded leaves, and rather large, rosy-pink flowers in clusters. Blooms in June and July. Hardy in dry situation, and propagated by seed or cuttings. A handsome species.

Æ. grandiflorum.—Demands same position and soil. Forms quite a little bush about 12 inches high, with rather long slender branches and leaves oblong, linear. Spikes of rosy-purple flowers of a good size freely produced in June. Quite hardy, and easily propagated by seed or cuttings. One of the best of the genus, and should be grown in every garden.

Æ. iberideum.—Requires a deep, dry soil on a warm bank. A dwarf-growing species with white flowers. A good plant, and a new addition to this already large genus.

Æ. persicum.—Deep soil; dry, warm position. A prostrate and free-growing plant, with rosy-purple flowers in the summer; a good plant.

Æ. rubescens.—Same soil and position. A showy species with large rose-coloured flowers and elliptical seed-vessels.

Æ. speciosum.—Same soil and position. A densely tufted species, growing 3 to 4 inches high, with ovate, oblong leaves, and freely producing rather large rose-pink flowers during the summer. Seed-vessels toothed and tinged with purple. One of the best and showiest of the genus.

A great deal of confusion exists amongst the Æthionemas, and it is difficult to get them true to name. Those already described are about the best of the genus. The following are, however, in cultivation, and all require similar treatment, namely, a deep, dry root-run and a sunny position.

Æ. bourgei.—Flowers rose-coloured and of good size.

Æ. chloraefolium.—Leaves slightly papillose and scabrid at the edges. Rather large rose-coloured flowers.

Æ. cordiophyllum.—Stiff, densely leaved stems; leaves sessile, deltoid, cordate, lobes embracing the stems, lower ones opposite. Medium-sized rose-coloured flowers. Plant grows 6 to 12 inches high.

Æ. diastrophis, Æ. pulchellum.—Both of these are very nearly akin; the difference lies in the former having longer fruiting racemes and seed-vessels. Both bear dense heads of small rosy-lilac coloured flowers.

Æ. graecum.—Short, numerous stems; small, rosy-purple flowers.

Æ. Jucundum.—Dense, shrubby little plant. Glaucous leaves and pink flowers in July. Grows about 12 inches high.

Æ. Moricandianum.—Short stems and leafy, not of dense growth. Leaves opposite, sessile, obtuse, ovate. Large yellow flowers.

Æ. membranaceum.—Grows about 6 inches high, with erect stems. Small, oblong, linear leaves.

Æ. rotundifolium.—This is very like *Æ. oppositifolia*, and should not be confused with *Æ. cepeaefolium*, from which it is quite distinct.

Æ. sagittatum.—Stiff, many nerved, oblong leaves ; rather large white flowers.

Æ. thesiifolium.—Grows about 18 inches high, with slender twiggy stems and long narrow leaves. Large pink flowers marked with purple.

Æ. tenue, heterophyllum, and *cæspitosum.*—Are all densely tufted, dwarf-growing species, with pink or white flowers.

Æ. thomasianum.—Dwarf-growing ; glaucous leaves, and rosy-pink flowers.

Æ. trinervium.—Dwarf-growing ; leaves hard and three-nerved; large white flowers.

Æ. saxatile.—Twiggy branches with rosy-purple flowers, and freely produced.

AJUGA (LABIATAE)

A dwarf, free-growing genus of plants of procumbent habit. Though not of first value for the rock garden, they are useful for carpeting. Are all of the easiest culture in ordinary soil, and are indifferent to position.

A. genevensis (syn. *A. alpina* and *A. Rugose*).—Creeping habit ; bright, shiny green leaves. Flowers vary in colour from blue to rose and white, in spikes about 4 to 5 inches long. This plant should not be associated with the choicer alpines, which it would quickly overrun. There is a variety of this plant known as *A. genevensis Brockbankii* which is of dwarfer habit.

A. genevensis crispa (syn. *A. metallica crispa*).—The leaves of this variety are curly and have a metallic sheen. Spikes of deep blue flowers.

A. reptans.—A native plant useful for carpeting in the wilder parts on account of its vigorous growth and dark green purplish leaves and blue flowers. There are three varieties :—

A. reptans alba.—A white form.

A. reptans atropurpurea.—Dark bronze-purple leaves.

A. reptans variegata.—Variegated silvery leaves.

ALCHEMILLA (ROSACEAE), Ladies' Mantle

A genus of but little value except for their foliage. Light sandy soil and open situation suits them all. Easily increased by division of roots, and seed.

A. alpina.—Has evergreen silvery leaves, and grows about 6 inches high. Small greenish flowers in July. Other varieties are :

A. maxima.—Large leaves, downy underneath ; 12 inches high.

A. pentaphylla.—Grows 6 inches high ; silvery-white leaves.

ALLIUM (LILIACEAE)

A genus of bulbous plants with compact heads of flower, and not particularly suitable for the rock garden. They all like rich loam in any position. They are of easy culture and readily increased by offsets. The following are the most suitable :—

A. acuminatum.—Deep rose. Grows about 9 inches high, and flowers in July.

A. acutangulum (syn. *A. angulosum*).—Heads of rosy-purple flowers in July. About 9 inches high.

A. caeruleum.—Pale blue flowers in May. Grows about 6 to 9 inches high.

A. cyaneum.—Blue flowers ; dwarf habit.

A. glaucum.—Purplish blue flowers ; glaucous foliage. Grows about 9 inches high.

A. grandiflorum.—Pendant clusters of reddish-purplish flowers. About 9 inches high.

A. Holparowskearium.—Heads of light rose-coloured flowers of a good size.

A. narcissiflorum (syn. *A. pedemontanum*).—Pink flowers rather like a chinodoxa in shape. Grows about 6 inches high.

A. triquetrum.—Pretty heads of drooping white flowers.

ALYSSUM (CRUCIFERAE), Madwort

A numerous genus, of which, however, only the best are worthy of cultivation in the rock garden. They are all of the easiest culture in almost any light soil in a sunny position. Readily increased by cuttings of the young shoots.

A. alpestre.—Sunny position in rather poor soil. Forms compact tufts of hoary leaves. Only about 3 inches high, the whole plant being covered with minute, shining, star-like hairs. Golden-yellow flowers very freely produced from May to July. A pretty plant. There is a double variety of this which is rather better in colour.

A. gemonense.—A dwarf-growing variety about 6 inches high. Flowers good, pure pale yellow colour, in corymbs.

A. Idaeum.—A sandy soil in sun. A tiny, prostrate species. The small roundish leaves, which grow in pairs down the stem, are of a true silvery colour. Yellow flowers in summer. Fairly hardy, and can be increased by cuttings or division. One of the gems of the genus, and worthy of a choice place in the garden.

A. moellendorfianum.—Sun and sandy soil. Forms a compact plant 6 inches high, with silvery-grey leaves and yellow flowers

15

freely produced in June and July. Propagation by division and cuttings. After flowering, cut back to prevent the plant getting bare and "leggy."

A. maritimum.—Hot, dry, sandy soil. It is an annual with sweet-scented white flowers. It sows itself freely about, and is useful for tops of walls, etc. It is a native.

A. montanum.—Sunny position in sandy soil. Spreads into compact tufts about 3 inches high. Glaucous green foliage covered with stellate hairs plainly visible. Fragrant yellow flowers, like alpine wallflowers, in early summer. Quite hardy, and readily increased by cuttings or division. It is a very attractive feature when grown into a large mass partially falling over some rock.

A. podolicum.—Sun, and light dry soil. A dainty little species, only growing some 3 inches high, with small white flowers freely produced. Is quite hardy, but not of any special value.

A. pyrenaicum.—Sun, and sandy soil. A diminutive species growing only 3 to 4 inches high, with grey downy leaves and white fragrant flowers. Quite worthy of a place.

A. saxatile.—Sun, in any light soil. Spreading habit and fairly rapid growth. About 9 to 12 inches high. Covered from March to May with a profusion of golden-yellow flowers. Rather dislikes heavy, moist, rich soils, where it is liable to perish in the winter, otherwise of easiest culture. Readily increased by cuttings. An old favourite, and should have a place in every garden.

A. saxatile, fl. pl.—A double variety of above. Blooms quite as profusely, and is altogether rather an improvement.

A. saxatile citrinum.—A variety with pale, sulphur-coloured flowers, which are very pretty. Another indispensable plant.

Old plants of the last three-named varieties should be cut back after flowering to prevent their getting bare and leggy.

A. saxatile, "Tom Thumb."—A very pretty, diminutive form of *saxatile*, forming compact little cushions some 3 inches high. Also a plant for a choice spot.

A. serpyllifolium.—Fully exposed position in sandy soil. Forms small bushy plants about 3 to 4 inches high, which become as compact as moss. Grey-green leaves, and yellow flowers freely produced. A dainty and attractive little plant.

A. spinosum (syn. *Koniga spinosa*).—Light soil and exposed position. Plants form a pretty little silvery bush. Leaves covered with minute stellate hairs. Flowers insignificant and not pretty. This plant merits a place in some not over-choice part on account of its distinctive appearance. Easily increased from cuttings. There is also a very pretty form, *A. s. rosem*, with small rosy blossoms. A more attractive plant.

AMPHICOME (BIGNONIACEAE)

Very pretty evergreen Himalayan plants, rather like a Pentstemon. They unfortunately are only half hardy, but are well worth trying in favoured localities, giving them a position sheltered from cold winds and where they can be protected from severe frosts. Increased by cuttings struck in gentle heat.

A. arguta.—Requires sheltered position in sandy loam and leaf-soil. Dwarf-growing, shrubby plant about 12 to 18 inches high. Neat pinnate foliage. Drooping, rosy-purple flowers at the axils, and also in terminal racemes. Blooms in August.

A. Emodi.—Dwarfer-growing than the last, being only from 9 to 12 inches high. Rose and orange-coloured bell-shaped flowers borne in axillary racemes in August. A very handsome plant

ANAGALLIS (PRIMULACEAE), Pimpernel

Pretty dwarf plants, mostly annual, but so dainty that they may be used where bare spots occur in bog or rock garden.

A. Monelli (syn. *A. Linifolia*).—An Italian species with large deep blue flowers shaded rose.

A. tenella.—Our native bog Pimpernel. Creeping habit. Small round leaves on slender stems, among which appear the tiny pink flowers. A pretty and dainty little annual for the bog garden.

ANDROMEDA (ERICACEAE)

A genus of dwarf shrubs nearly allied to the Heath family. There is only one true species of Andromeda known ; the others generally known as Andromedas really belong to the families of Cassandra, Cassiope, and Pieris.

They are interesting plants, but not easy to grow, doing best in moist sandy peat in cool, but not shady spots, and should be associated with the dwarfer-growing plants.

A. angustifolia (syn. *Cassandra angustifolia*).—A pretty, small evergreen shrub growing about 2 feet high, producing sprays of white flowers in terminal racemes in April. Propagated by layers.

A. calyculata (syn. *Cassandra calyculata*).—Snow-white flowers in April. Very similar to the last.

A. Fastigiata (syn. *Cassiope Fastigiata*).—Cool position, fully exposed to sun and air in deep, moist, peaty soil well-drained. A beautiful heath-like shrub growing about 12 inches high. The leaves, which overlap along the stems, have a thin, silvery, chaffy margin, and a deep and broad keel by which it may be distinguished from *A. tetragona*, which it otherwise much resembles. White, waxy, bell-shaped flowers borne at the end of each branch. A beautiful little shrub, and worthy of some care, though difficult to cultivate. It should have stones placed round the neck of the plant and should be pegged down when first planted.

A. floribunda (syn. *Pieris floribunda*).—Requires the same position and soil as the last. A beautiful, compact evergreen shrub growing about 3 feet high, and producing white, waxy, bell-shaped flowers very freely. It is of easy culture.

A. hypnoides (syn. *Cassiope hypnoides*).—Requires a position, fully exposed to the sun and air, in moist, very gritty, sandy, well-drained, peaty soil. A tiny, spreading, moss-like shrub, only growing 1 to 4 inches high, with small wiry branches densely clothed with minute bright green leaves. Small, white, waxy, drooping flowers borne on reddish stems in June. It is one of the most beautiful and most difficult to grow of alpine plants, and is seldom seen in a robust state. The chief difficulty is procuring healthy plants to start with. It is advisable to carefully peg down the main branches, and place stones round neck of plant to prevent evaporation. Drought is fatal to its successful cultivation.

A. japonica (syn. *Pieris japonica*). — Open, though sheltered position, in good, moist, peaty soil. A graceful evergreen shrub growing some 3 feet high. It is of slow growth. Flowers white, borne in long pendulous clusters in May. Quite hardy. A choice shrub for the rock garden.

A. polifolium (Wild Rosemary).—The only true species of Andromeda, and a native of Great Britain. It requires an open position in moist, peaty soil, in which it forms a compact little shrub about 12 inches high, with beautiful, very dark glossy green leaves, glaucous beneath. Drooping, bell-shaped flowers of a lovely delicate pale pink shade, produced in May. Easy of culture and quite hardy, and can be propagated by layers or seed. One of the choicest shrubs for the garden. There are several varieties, which differ principally in colour of flowers.

A. tetragona (syn. *Cassiope tetragona*).—Half-shady position in very moist, well-drained sandy peat. Of compact habit, seldom more than 8 inches high. Deep green foliage. The whole plant has the appearance of a miniature Cypress. Beautiful drooping, white, waxy, bell-shaped flowers rather like Lily-of-the-valley, produced singly. Blooms in April. Quite hardy, and one of the most delightful and choicest of peat-loving shrubs. Easily increased by division. It may be distinguished from *A. Fastigiata*, which it much resembles, by the absence of the chaffy margin of leaf.

ANDROSACE (PRIMULACEAE)

The choicest and most typical plants of the highest mountain ranges. All are beautiful and gems for the rock garden. Whilst some are of easy cultivation, others are amongst the most difficult of alpines to grow. They all require a deep root-run in well-drained, gritty soil. Some varieties will grow on the level, while others need to be planted in vertical fissures of the rock, where they cannot suffer from damp lying about them, which quickly proves fatal, though at the same time they require moisture at their roots.

It is advisable to cover those kinds that have hairy leaves with a sheet of glass during the winter to protect the foliage from excessive moisture. A clear pure air, free from dust, is essential ; they are almost sure to perish in a smoky atmosphere.

A. alpina.—Vertical fissure shaded from the sun and protected from damp overhead, though it requires moisture at its roots, which must also have free escape. Requires gritty, fibrous loam mixed with pieces of sandstone, and at least 15 inches deep. Forms dense cushions about 3 inches high, with pink flowers in June. A lovely plant, but difficult to grow.

A. arachnoidea.—Can be grown on the level in fine, sandy, gritty loam. Grows about 3 inches high, forming little rosettes which in the early part of the year are not covered with the white silky hairs that appear later. Flowers white, with a distinct red eye, towards the end of May. Fairly easily cultivated.

A. brigantiaca.—Requires sloping ground, half-shady position, and sandy soil. Dwarf-growing, with deep green foliage, free from' the characteristic fine down. White flowers. This species does not require so much protection from the rain as do some of the others.

A. carnea.—Can be planted on a level, exposed spot in a mixture of peat and sandy loam at least a foot deep. A distinctive plant, growing about 3 inches high. The small pointed leaves, instead of forming rosettes, as most of the other kinds do, make a dense spiny cushion rather like *Saxifraga Juniperifolia.* The flowers rose-coloured, with a yellow eye, are freely produced in May. It is not difficult to cultivate, and can be raised from seed. It is one of the best of this attractive genus. *A. eximia* is a larger form.

A. Chamaejasme (syn. *A. villosa Chamaejasme*).—Plant in a position fully exposed to the sun, in light sandy loam mixed with pieces of sandstone. The surface of the ground should also be covered with pieces of stone. The foliage forms rather large rosettes of fringed leaves a few inches high. Flowers white at first, with a yellow eye, changing to crimson. Blooms in June, and fairly freely.

Not difficult to grow. A lovely little plant which no rock garden is complete without.

A. Charpentieri.—Forms a dense cushion with bright red flowers. Will do on a level in deep, gritty loam.

A. ciliata.—Requires sunny fissure in deep, gritty, sandy loam. Densely packed leaves, glabrous on the surface and downy on the margins. Carmine-red flowers in June.

A. cylindrica.—Requires a sunny fissure and deep root-run in gritty loam. Stems rise about half an inch, with leaves which form columns on the stems. Tufted habit. It has pure white solitary flowers in April and May. This is, by some, thought to be a variety of *A. ciliata.*

A. foliosa.—Requires an open situation on the level in full sun. Does best in good, deep, heavy limestone soil, with pieces of stone added. Grows about 6 to 8 inches high, with rather large, coarse, hairy leaves. It is free-growing, and will form a plant a foot across in one year. Rather large umbels of rosy-lilac flowers. A good plant, though much coarser than the type.

A. glacialis.—Requires fully exposed, open, sunny position in wet, very gritty soil, composed almost entirely of granite chips. Forms spreading tufts, the leaves of which are completely hidden in summer by the mass of the most lovely, pure, soft, rose-pink flowers. A gem amongst gems, and as difficult to grow as it is lovely, being one of those plants that have so far baffled nearly all attempts to cultivate. It comes from the high moraines, and is found growing there in wet debris.

A. helvetica.—Requires partial exposure to the sun in a well-drained spot tightly wedged between stones, which will guard it from excessive moisture, whilst allowing the roots to work into the gritty soil behind. It forms dense little masses of tiny ciliated leaves in diminutive rosettes and grows fairly quickly. The white flower, with a yellowish eye, is almost twice as large as the rosette from which it rises. Blooms in July, and very freely. Hardy, but requires careful cultivation, and is but short-lived. It is essentially a limestone plant. A lovely little gem. Propagated by seeds.

A. imbricata (syn. *A. argentea*).—Sunny situation in light, well-drained loam ; requires granite. Forms dense tufts of white, silvery rosettes. The flowers are stemless and rest so thickly on the rosettes as to overlap each other. Propagated by seeds and division.

A. lactea.—Should have an eastern or western aspect, in gritty loam. Vigorous habit. Numerous white flowers, with a yellow throat, borne in umbels in June. Forms compact rosettes. Of easy culture.

A. Laggeri.—Light, gritty soil in partially shaded situation. Tiny rosettes of sharp pointed leaves. Bright pink flowers, with a lighter eye, freely produced in April. Of fairly easy culture, and increased by seed or division.

A. lanuginosa. — Half-shady position in good loam. Forms trailing, many branched stems, with leaves nearly an inch long, and covered with white silky hairs. Of fairly rapid growth in a position it likes. Delicate, rose-coloured flowers, with a yellow eye, borne in umbels, and freely produced from May to October. Hardy and easily propagated by seeds or layers. It is advisable, when possible, to protect from rain during the winter. A most attractive plant, which should be so placed that its trailing stems can fall down over some rock.

A. l. Leichtlini (syn. *A. Oculata*).—Plant to fall over the edge of a rock in a half-shady position. Prefers a light, limestone soil. Foliage not so downy, and flowers larger and of a paler colour than the last, of which it is a variety. Quite hardy, and of easy culture in light soils.

A. primuloides.—Likes a sheltered, half-shady situation, protected from moisture overhead, in gritty soil. Forms rosettes of bright green leaves and produces rosy-lilac flowers. A rare species, but no better than many of those better known.

A. pubescens. — Sunny crevice in deep, sandy, gritty peat. Densely packed, rather hoary leaves, with large, solitary white flowers scarcely rising above the plant. Flowering freely in July, it is of easy culture, and is a very attractive little plant.

A. pyrenaica.—Requires fissures in rocks in deep, sandy, and peaty loam. It can also be grown on the level in similar soil and protected from drought by half-buried stones. Forms a compact mass of tiny grey, downy rosettes. The flowers are white, with a yellow eye, and rise about $\frac{1}{2}$ to $\frac{1}{4}$ of an inch over the plant. It is closely allied to *A. helvetica* and *A. imbricata*, and is not of particularly easy cultivation.

A. sarmentosa.—Prefers an open, sunny situation in deep, well-drained, sandy loam mixed with limestone. Forms dense rosettes of silvery foliage, from which spring runners bearing rosettes at their extremities, which, if pegged down and covered with sandy soil, will root quickly. Flowers, which are freely produced, are rose-coloured, with a white eye, and borne in trusses, rather resembling the Verbena. Blooms in May. Of easy culture. It is very advisable to protect during the winter with a sheet of glass. The surface of the ground under the rosettes should be covered with finely broken sandstone to keep them dry.

A. s. Chumbyi.—It requires the same treatment as *A. sarmentosa*, which it much resembles, except that it is a stronger-growing plant and the flower is deeper in colour and borne on shorter stems. It is quite one of the best species of this attractive genus, and should be grown in every rock garden. It also is the better of protection during the winter. It is a hybrid, *A. sarmentosa* × *villosa*.

A. spinulifera.—Tufts of spatulate leaves from which spring upright stems 3 to 8 inches high, bearing heads of rose-coloured flowers with yellow centres. A new introduction from China requiring treatment similar to *A. sarmentosa.*

A. villosa.—Plant in fine, sandy loam on level, in sunny position. Dwarf-growing; leaves covered with silky hairs, mostly on the underside. Pale rose-coloured flowers, yellowish eye, in umbels about 3 inches high, freely produced. Easily cultivated; a dainty little plant.

A. vitaliana (syn. *Douglasia vitaliana*).—Partially shaded situation in moderately damp, light, sandy, calcareous soil. Has little narrow leaves about an inch high. Yellow flowers of a good size and colour. Forms a good tuft in right position, but is a shy bloomer.

A. wulfeniana.—Should be planted on the level in light, sandy soil. Very compact foliage and deep rose-coloured flowers barely rising above the leaves. A good plant, and not very difficult to grow. Other varieties are—

A. coronopifolia (syn. *A. lactiflora*).—Biennial ; white flowers.

A. Hausmanni.—Like *A. ciliata*, with red flowers.

A. obtusifolia.—White, with yellow eye. Pretty.

A. sempervivoides.—Small rosettes and umbels of rosy-purple flowers in May.

Anemone (Ranunculaceae), Wind Flower

These, though more strictly meadow rather than rock plants, are of such beauty and variety that they should, the best of them at least, be grown in every rock garden. They are all of the easiest culture in any good, deep, warm, rather rich loam in some open, though partially shaded spot. To ensure success, in preference to old plants, get seedlings or good young plants to start with ; or, failing these, seed, which should be sown as soon as procured, for they make great woody rootstocks, which are nearly impossible to move without damaging them. All the following are deciduous, and are a selection of the best and most suitable kinds for the rock garden.

A. alpina (syn. *Pulsatilla alpina*).—Good loam. Open, rather damp position. Fern-like foliage, sometimes clothed with long silky hairs, growing from 6 inches to a foot in height. Of fairly vigorous habit. Big, starry flowers, white inside and pale blue outside, in May. Increased by seed or division. A dainty and lovely plant.

A. al. sulphurea.—A yellow form of the above, rather larger, and also very lovely, and requiring similar treatment.

A. angulosa (syn. *A. Hepatica*).—In any open spot in good loam.

A large form of the common *Hepatica*, with sky-blue flowers about 2½ inches across, blooming in February. It is of free growth, and is more suitable for margins of walks through woods than the rock garden. Varieties of the above are—

A. an. alba.—A white form.

A. an. lilacina, gd. fl.—Large lilac flowers.

A. an. major.—A large variety of *A. angulosa.*

A. an. rosea.—A pink form, rather scarce.

A. baldensis.—A rocky crevice in peaty loam in partial shade. Grows about 6 inches high. Flowers white inside and pale pink outside. A dainty little plant, and one of the best of the family. Easy of cultivation, and readily grown from seed.

A. blanda.—Good loam in sunny spot. Grows about 6 inches high. Spreads slowly. Deep sapphire-blue flowers. Is quite hardy, of the easiest culture, and quite one of the best of the alpine Anemones. There are two varieties :—

A. b. alba.—A pretty white form.

A. b. scythinica.—Large white flowers, pale blue on the outside.

A. fulgens.—Partially shaded position in good, rather moist, rich loam ; likes burnt earth. Hard, deeply lobed leaves, about 6 to 8 inches high. Flowers of a most vivid scarlet, in April. Hardy and easily grown from seed. Words can scarcely describe the appearance of a large mass of these plants when in bloom and the sun shining on them : the effect produced is quite dazzling. With me, at least, I find they are rather uncertain. Good young plants are essential to success. There are many varieties of shade, and some double, but the type is the best.

A. Halleri.—Sunny position in deep, well-drained, rich soil. Deep lilac-coloured flowers of good size, produced singly on erect, slender stems about 9 inches high, in April. This is the finest and perhaps the rarest of the Pasque-flowers.

A. Hepatica.—Half-shady position in good loam and leaf-mould. The well-known *Hepatica* of gardens, growing about 6 inches high, and making neat little plants. Pale blue flowers, rising just over the leaf, in February. Of the easiest culture, but dislikes disturbance, and is beloved of slugs. There are many varieties.

A. H. alba.—White form ; less robust.

A. H. alba, fl. pl.—Double.

A. H. coerulea.—Pale blue.

A. H. coerulea, fl. pl.—Double ; rather darker shade.

A. H. "Royal Blue."—Deep shade.

A. H. rubra.—Bright red. Poor grower.

A. H. rubra, fl. pl.—Double ; rather darker shade.

A. narcissiflora.—Any position in good, deep loam. Soft, velvety leaves, much lobed. White flowers tinged with pink on the outside, and borne in umbels on stems about 18 inches high in June. Propagated by seed. A very beautiful and rather neglected Anemone of the easiest culture. It should be found in every garden.

A. nemorosa.—Half-shady position in leaf-soil. Grows about 6 inches high. Flowers generally white. The well-known native Wood Anemone, of which there are several good varieties.

A. n. coerulea.—Very nearly, if not identical with *A. n. robinsoniana.*

A. n. robinsoniana.—Any position in loam ; leaf-mould with a little sand added. Soft, pale blue flowers about 6 inches high. Quite hardy, and easily grown, and increased by division. A most lovely and dainty form of the Wood Anemone, and should be freely used everywhere. There are several varieties, giving different shades of blue, purple, and rose, and are equally attractive.

A. palmata.—Level, sunny position, in deep, cool peat or peaty loam. It has leathery lobed leaves rather like a Cyclamen. Erect stems, bearing glossy, golden-yellow flowers in May and June. Of fairly vigorous growth, and quite easily cultivated. A handsome plant, readily increased by seed or division. There are two varieties, *albida* and *alba.*

A. patens.—Another Pasque-flower very like *A. Pulsatilla*, only a little larger, but not of as good a colour.

A. pratensis.—Sunny position in loam. Leaves finely cut, and pendulous flowers of a deep purple. Differs from the following in having rather smaller flowers.

A. Pulsatilla (Pasque-flower).—Plant in various aspects to secure a longer bloom. Does best in a light, dry loam. In heavy soil it is rather inclined to run too much to foliage. Likes chalk. Pretty finely cut foliage and violet-blue flowers, hairy on the outside. Golden-yellow stamens. Blooms April and May. Quite hardy, and of easiest culture. A lovely and quite indispensable plant, and one of the best of the Anemones. There are four varieties.

A. P. alba.—A rather dirty white form.

A. P. lilacina.—Pale lilac.

A. P. rubra.—Rosy-brown form. Golden stamens. Much smaller than the type.

A. P. Mrs Van-der-Elst.—Shell pink and very beautiful.

A. rivularis.—A wet, cool spot in the bog garden suits this Anemone best. Grows about 2 feet high. Leaves villous. Rather small white flowers, with deep purple anthers. Very easily cultivated. Is a most choice and lovely plant for the bog garden. Is readily grown from seed.

A. vernalis.—Deep, cool, rather moist peaty loam in a half-shady position. The dwarfest-growing of the Pasque-flowers, forming compact tufts, from which rise on shaggy stems large goblet-shaped flowers, pure white within, and covered with golden-brown hairs without. Is not of particularly easy culture; seedlings are best to start with. These, unfortunately, vary a good deal, as some of the flowers are of rather a greenish-white; but if the true white form be obtained, no more exquisite plant can be grown in the rock garden.

The above are the best of the Anemones for the rock garden. Others, though also very lovely, are better suited for naturalising in the woods. The following are the best for this purpose :—

A. apennina.—Clear, pale blue flowers.

A. coronaria.—Various shades of colours.

A. nemorosa, and its varieties.

A sylvestris.—Pretty white flowers.

ANOMATHECA (*see* LAPEYROUSIA)

ANTENNARIA (COMPOSITAE), Cat's-ear

Are of only very secondary value for the rock garden. They are all dwarf and neat-growing plants with silvery leaves, and are of the easiest culture, indifferent either to soil or aspect. Their chief merit lies in the colour of their foliage, and are useful for carpeting bare spots.

A. alpina (syn. *Gnaphalium alpina*).—White, downy foliage.

A. dioica (syn. *Gnaphalium dioicum*).—Silvery leaves and pink flowers.

A. tomentosa.—Only grows about 1 inch high. Silvery foliage.

ANTHEMIS (COMPOSITAE), Chamomile

Of those in cultivation few are worthy of a place in the rock garden. All of easy culture in any position or soil. Propagated by division.

A. Aizoon (see *Achillea ageratifolia*).

A. Biebersteiniana.—The pinnately divided leaves are covered with a white, silky down. Large, yellow, composite flowers, about 12 inches high. Rather a showy species.

A. macedonica.—Spreading tufts of silvery-grey leaves about 6 inches high, and large, solitary white flowers in July. A pretty plant.

A. montana.—Silvery-grey tufts of finely cut leaves and white flowers, freely produced from May to August. Only grows 6 inches high.

These represent about the best of the genus.

ANTHERICUM (LILIACEAE)

These, though scarcely suitable for a rock garden, should, on account of their beauty, be given a place amongst the more vigorous plants or shrubs. They all do well in rich, moist, sandy loam and partial shade.

A. Hookeri (syn. *Bulbinella Hookeri*).—Peaty bog suits this variety best. Bright yellow flowers growing 18 to 24 inches tall. Blooms in June. A showy plant.

A. Liliago (St. Bernard's Lily).—Pure white flowers in spikes, in August. Grows about 12 to 18 inches high. Free-flowering.

A. Liliastrum (syn. *Paradisia Liliastrum*, St Bruno's Lily).— Cool soil and half shade. Spikes of white, lily-like flowers in early summer. About 2 feet high. A very pretty plant, and one that slugs appreciate.

There are varieties of this, *A. L. major* and *A. L. giganteum* ; both showy plants.

ANTHYLLIS (LEGUMINOSAE), Kidney Vetch

Dwarf-growing plants of the Pea-flower order. Pretty and attractive rock plants.

A. montana.—Dry, sunny aspect in loam. Compact-growing, with white, downy, pinnate leaves about 6 inches high. Rose-coloured or purplish flowers in dense heads in July. Quite hardy, and propagated by division or seeds. One of the best little rock plants.

A. m. atrorubens.—Is a variety of the above, with deep, red-coloured flowers.

A. Vulneraria.—Dwarf-growing, with yellow flowers, useful for dry banks. There are red and white varieties.

ANTIRRHINUM (SCROPHULARIACEAE), Snapdragon

There are a few of this genus of Snapdragon which are suitable for the rock garden. They all require a warm, dry spot.

A. Asarina.—Hot, dry position in light, poor soil. Creeping habit and of rapid growth. Clammy, woolly, rounded leaves. Creamy-white flowers June to September. A free bloomer. A useful and pretty plant for old walls, or growing over a rock. It dislikes excessive moisture, and, being rather brittle, should be sheltered from the wind.

A. glutinosum.—Also requires a hot, dry position. Of trailing habit, with downy leaves and quantities of pale, primrose-coloured flowers all the summer. A charming plant for a dry spot, and also rather brittle.

A. sempervirens.—Of more bushy habit. It has whitish flowers and requires same treatment as *Asarina.*

APHYLLANTHES (LILIACEAE)

A. monspeliensis.—Requires a sunny position in almost pure sand. Rush-like leaves about 9 inches high, and clear blue flowers. A pretty plant.

AQUILEGIA (RANUNCULACEAE), Columbine

The genus of Columbines includes some of the fairest and daintiest flowers that can be grown in the rock garden, some of which, unfortunately, are not particularly easy to cultivate. They all like deep, moist, rich loam, thoroughly drained, in a sunny position. They come readily from seed, but interbreed so freely that it is difficult to obtain them true.

A. alpina.—Requires a sheltered but not shady spot in deep loam and leaf-mould soil with quick drainage. Bears lovely, big, soft clear blue flowers on dainty stems about 18 inches high. Is of easy culture. One of the most beautiful plants for the rock garden. This, as with most others of the family, is not easy to get " true." Propagation by seeds. There is also a white variety.

A. canadensis.—Looks its best planted amongst rocks in loamy soil. Sharply notched leaves and bright scarlet and yellow flowers, with long spurs, borne on stems about 12 inches high. Blooms in June. Easily raised from seed. *Nana* is a dwarf form, and also very lovely.

A. coerulea.—Sheltered spot in cool, deep loam well drained. Its exquisite, long-spurred, pale blue flowers, with creamy-white centres, are borne on slender stems 9 to 12 inches high, and is in flower from May to September. The plant is, unfortunately, little more than a biennial, and should be treated as such, for even if it lives over the second year, it rarely does well. It comes freely from seeds, which should be sown as soon as ripe. It is impossible to bestow too much praise on this glorious little plant, which is about the loveliest of a lovely genus.

A. flabellata.—Cool, ordinary soil. Pale green leaves, and waxy-white, tinted violet-rose flowers. Dwarf of habit and blooms early.

A. glandulosa.—Requires a position in partial shade, in deep, moist soil composed of loam, peat, and sand. Dwarf-growing, with large, handsome blue flowers, with a white centre, borne on slender stems 9 to 12 inches high in May and June. Another gem, but, unfortunately, is rather apt to go off unexpectedly. It greatly dislikes disturbance, so it is advisable to grow from seed.

The above are the most suitable kinds for the rock garden, others being of rather too tall a habit, but should, when possible, be naturalised in woods or planted amongst shrubs. The following are the best kinds for that purpose :—

A. californica.—Thriving in a half-shady position in deep, moist loam. Deep orange, with slender, bright orange spurs. Liable to perish after flowering, so seed should be saved. Seedlings usually come "true."

A. chrysantha.—Half-shady situation in almost any soil. Grows as high as 4 feet. Golden-yellow, long-spurred variety.

A. Stuartii.—Moist loam, half shade. Large blue and white flowers in May. Grows about 2 feet high. A fine plant.

There are also many hybrids, most of which are pretty.

ARABIS (CRUCIFERAE), Rock Cress

This genus contains some useful varieties, but none can be called choice plants. All are of easy culture and will grow in almost any aspect or soil.

A. albida.—Any soil or aspect. Trailing plant, covered in early spring with a profusion of snow-white flowers. This well-known plant needs no further description ; there is no rockery or rock garden from which it is absent.

A. albida, fl. pl.—A double variety of the above and an improvement. Flowers last longer, though coming in a little later. There is also a variegated form of this.

A. androsacea.—Warm position in gritty soil. Tufts of silvery leaves. Flowers white. An attractive and rare species, and well worth growing.

A. aubrietoides.—Of compact habit, only growing about 3 inches high. Pale pink flowers in May. Quite a pretty plant. It should be grown in rather a dry position, as it is apt to go off in a damp spot.

A. Billardieri rosea.—Likes a dry soil in sun. It is a compact grower, with small pink flowers in April.

A. Sturii.—Any position or soil. Compact grower, with little, hard, dark green leaves and pretty, pure white flowers. A garden hybrid, and perhaps the choicest of the family.

The following varieties are of little value except in a botanical collection :—

A. procurrens.—Dwarf habit and small whitish flowers. Rather pretty.

A. Ferdinandi Coburgi.—Very dwarf-growing, with white flowers.

A. purpurascens.—Grows about 6 inches high, with pale purple flowers in May.

ARCTOSTAPHYLOS (ERICACEAE)

Very pretty, trailing, mostly evergreen shrubs, for moist, peaty soil.

A. alpina (Black Bearberry).—Moist, peaty loam in half shade. A deciduous shrub with small-toothed leaves, white or flesh-coloured flowers in terminal racemes, and bluish-black berries. A rare native plant.

A. californica.—Peaty loam and half shade. Evergreen shrub of vigorous growth and trailing habit, with spatulate, leathery leaves and white flowers in July and August. A useful plant for covering rockwork.

A. Uva-ursi (Bearberry).—Almost any soil, but prefers that of a peaty nature. Half shade. Dwarf, prostrate-growing shrub, with dark leathery leaves and pretty rose-coloured flowers clustered at extremities of the branches. Blooms in July and August, followed by scarlet berries. One of the best of trailing shrubs, evergreen, and of easiest culture in almost any soil. Propagated by layers.

ARENARIA (CARYOPHYLLACEAE), Sandwort

A family giving us several very pretty species. Most are of easy culture and increased by division in early spring or July and August.

A. balearica.—The only thing this plant needs is a cool and shady spot ; it is indifferent as to soil. A quick-growing, diminutive little plant coating the surface of rock with an emerald-green mantle not a quarter of an inch high, from which in summer spring countless upright, tiny, star-shaped white flowers borne on thread-like stems about an inch long. The daintiest little plant imaginable, which in a moist climate becomes a veritable weed. But, frail as it looks, do not allow it to encroach on other diminutive treasures, for it will smother them to death.

A. caespitosa (syn. *A. verna caespitosa*).—A neat little plant growing about 4 inches high, with very leafy stems. White flowers during the early summer.

A. gothica.—Very poor, stony soil in sun. A trailing plant with dark green glossy leaves and pure white flowers. A lovely little plant, which is apt to perish in any soil but the poorest and stoniest.

A. Huteri.—Requires very sandy, light soil and sun. Only grows about 3 to 4 inches high, with large white blossoms. Top dress with sand and leaf-mould. A delightful little plant.

A. laricifolia.—Likes a high ledge in sandy loam. Dwarf-spreading plant about 4 inches high, with very narrow leaves arranged in clusters and pretty bell-shaped white flowers. Increased by division. A charming little plant.

A. montana.—Light sandy loam in partial shade. A fairly quick-growing plant of trailing habit. Narrow dark green leaves and a profusion of large pure white flowers in early summer. Seed and division. One of the most attractive flowers of early summer, and should be grown so as to fall over the face of a rock.

A. m. grandiflora.—Very similar to the above. Flowers larger. Flowers in June.

A. purpurascens.—Ordinary soil in sun. Prostrate habit. Densely tufted, narrow, pointed, glossy leaves, with pale purplish, star-shaped flowers in May. A free bloomer. Propagated by division or seed. A very pretty little plant.

A. verna.—Light sandy soil in sun. Grows in neat, prostrate tufts of emerald-green leaves, awl-shaped, with numerous small, starry white flowers in April. Also an attractive little plant, readily propagated by seed.

A. multicaules.—Like *A. balearica*, but larger flowers and more ovate leaves.

A. tetraquetra.—White flowers and prostrate habit. A pretty little plant.

Other varieties grown, but of more botanical than garden interest.

ARETHUSA BULBOSA

Shady position in very wet soil, composed of spongy peat and sphagnum moss. Hardy American orchid with solitary rose-purple flowers, sweet-scented and very lovely. A very difficult plant to cultivate.

ARMERIA (PLUMBAGINACEAE), Thrift

Well-known plants of easy culture and much beauty.

A. caespitosa.—Well-drained crevice in rocks in sun. The dwarfest of the genus, only growing 1 to 2 inches high. Forms tufts of grassy foliage. Pale pink flowers in June. Very pretty.

A. cephalotes (syns. *A. latifolia* and *A. formosa*).—Sandy loam in sun. Grass-like leaves about 8 inches high in dense tufts, from which spring tall stems 15 to 20 inches high, each bearing round, dense heads of closely packed flowers of a bright rose colour. Quite easy of cultivation, and readily increased by division or seed. Colour liable to variation when grown from seed. There is a white form, *alba*, also a handsome plant.

A. maritima (syn. *A. vulgaris*).—The well-known Sea Pink of Great Britain, growing in very sandy soil. There are several varieties :—A white form, *alba* ; a pink form, *rosea* ; and *laucheana*, a bright rosy-pink.

A. setacea.—Sunny position in vertical crevice. Narrow, acute leaves in dense rosettes. Distinct. Grows 3 inches high, and rosy-pink flowers from April to June.

Other varieties are advertised in catalogues, but all are very similar to *A. maritima*, only with flowers of different shades of pink.

ARNEBIA ECHIOIDES, The Prophet Flower

Partial shade in rich, well-drained loam. A compact-growing and well-known plant, with its primrose-yellow flowers, which open with five black spots on the corolla, gradually fading away. The spikes of flower are about 15 inches high and continually produced. A very charming plant, and well worthy of a spot in the rock garden. Propagated by cuttings in the autumn.

ARNICA (COMPOSITAE)

Hardy, dwarf perennials allied to the Groundsel. Increased by seed or division in spring.

A. montana.—Deep, peaty soil. A pretty plant, growing about 12 inches high. Tufted habit, with large heads of composite flowers of a rich golden-orange colour.

A. Pallens.—A sulphur-coloured form.

A. Chamissonis.—Rather smaller in habit and flowers ; neither so brilliant in colour nor as large as *montana*. Also requires deep, peaty soil.

ARONICUM GLACIALE (syn. DORONICUM GLACIALE)

Requires rather heavy loam and half shade. Grows about 6 to 8 inches high, with big broad leaves, and large, clear, yellow flowers about 2 to 3 inches across, borne on short leafy stems. The flowers are rather like the Doronicums in appearance.

ARTEMISIA (COMPOSITAE), Southernwood, Wormwood

Dwarf-growing, half-shrubby perennial plants with silvery-grey leaves, but only of secondary value for the rock garden. The following are a selection :—

A. Baumgartenii.—Sun, in ordinary sandy loam. Silvery foliage growing about 6 inches high.

A. brachyphylla splendens.—Sun and loam. Silvery leaves, and of creeping habit. A nice little plant.

A. sericea.—Suitable for a hot spot. Silky white leaves, and of dwarf habit.

16

ASARUM (ARISTOLOCHIACEAE)

A family of plants more curious than pretty, and of no great value. They are all dwarf-growing and form mats of cyclamen-like leaves and brownish flowers. Their chief beauty lies in their foliage. They are useful for a cool, damp, shady corner and easily propagated by division in spring. The following are the best-known varieties :—

A. europaeum, canadense, and *Sieboldii.*—This latter has variegated and marbled leaves.

ASPERULA (RUBIACEAE), Woodruff

Pretty little plants of easy culture in any soil or position. Propagated by division of the roots in spring or early summer.

A. ciliata.—Ordinary soil in sun. Compact-growing, with myriads of little white flowers.

A. hirta.—In sunny position, in light gritty soil. Forms compact tufts with small white flowers changing to pink. Grows about 3 inches high.

A. nitida (syn. *A. Gussonii*).—Sandy soil. Compact dwarf-grower, only about 4 inches high, and very pale pink flowers.

A. odorata. — Light soil. Neat-growing, with small, fragrant flowers.

A. suberosa (syn. *A. Athoa*).—Likes a dry, sunny spot. Has rather downy foliage about 4 inches high, and small, pink, trumpet-shaped flowers. A very pretty little plant, which dislikes damp.

ASTER (COMPOSITAE), Michaelmas Daisy

A very large genus, including many lovely plants, but mostly of too tall a growing habit to be suitable for the rock garden. There are a few, however, which should be included in every collection. They are all hardy and quite easily cultivated, and propagated by division in spring or autumn.

A. alpinus.—Ordinary loam in half shade. Forms sturdy tufts about 6 inches high of rather downy leaves. The daisy-shaped flowers, which are about 2 inches across, are of pale blue, with a golden-coloured eye. It is a fairly rapid grower, and easily increased by division. A good plant, to which slugs and mice are much devoted. This may be taken as the type, for there are many forms, giving a variety of colours.

A. al. albus.—A white form.

A. al. altro-violaceus.—Deep violet in colour.

A. al. ruber.—Deep red flowers.

A. al. roseus.—Pink flowers.

A. al. speciosus.—Rather deeper-coloured than the type.

A. al. superbus.—A good, deep, violet-blue form.

A. al. himalaicus.—Deep blue. One of the best.

A. al. subcoerulea.—Flowers 2 inches across; of a most lovely shade of blue. A choice form.

A. acris.—Likes sun and loam. Grows about 2 feet high, and is in late summer smothered with a cloud of small, soft, purple flowers. Of easiest culture and readily divides. A lovely and dainty plant, which should be freely grown in bold masses.

A. "Pattersoni."—Dwarf-growing, rather similar to *alpinus*, with pale blue flowers.

Astragalus (Leguminosae), Milk Vetch

A numerous genus of the Vetch tribe, of which there are few suitable species. Increased by division or seed. The latter is the best method.

A. alpinus.—Ordinary soil in sun. Prostrate habit. Flowers bluish-purple, in summer. A good plant.

A. hypoglottis (syn. *A. danicus*).—Likes sunny aspect in calcareous, well-drained soil. Trailing habit, with heads of blue flowers in July and August. Very easily grown, and a useful plant There is also a white-flowered form of this, which is pretty.

A. monspessulanus.—Sunny aspect in rich, moist, calcareous soil. Trailing habit. Only some 4 inches high. A vigorous grower. Should be planted to fall over the face of a rock. Flowers pale rosy-lilac, with bars of white on upper petals; the unopened buds a deep crimson. A useful plant, of easy culture. There is also a white form, *albus*, of this.

A. onobrychioides.—A handsome, strong-growing variety, with purple-crimson flowers in profusion in capitate spikes. A good plant for the rougher parts of the garden.

A. purpureus.—Prostrate-growing plant, rather hairy. Bright purple flowers in June.

A. pannosus.—Ordinary soil. Tufts of woolly, pinnate leaves about 9 inches high. Flowers rose-coloured, in compact, globose heads. Blooms in July.

Aubrietia (Cruciferae)

An indispensable genus of trailing plants, so well known that a description is unnecessary. They are all most accommodating, thriving in any soil, and quite indifferent to aspect. Readily grown from seed, cuttings, or division. They are practically all of the same type, though varying much in colour of flower. The following are the best varieties, and mostly garden hybrids :—

"*Bridesmaid.*"—Large flowers, rosy pink. A good variety.

"*Craven Gem.*"—Good purple.

"*Dr Mules.*"—Best habit of growth of any Aubrietia, being very compact. Deep violet-purple flowers. Better grown in shade, as in sun the flowers fade.

"*Fire King.*"—Of rather straggling habit. Flowers crimson, with a trace of magenta, so will require care in grouping, but is all the same a very desirable plant.

Lloyd Edwards.—About the best purple aubrietia yet raised.

A. Moerheimi.—Flowers pale rose, rather like, but not so large as, "*Bridesmaid.*"

Prichard's A1.—Deep violet-coloured flowers of large size, but of rather loose growth.

A. Wallacei.—Deep violet-blue flowers, blooming both in spring and autumn.

There are also two with variegated foliage—*A. argentea*, silvery white ; *A. aurea*, gold variegation ; both tidy, compact growers, and quite pretty.

A. tauricola.—A distinct deciduous species, which forms compact tufts and has deep blue flowers.

AURICULA (*see* PRIMULA)

AZALEA (ERICACEAE)

A very large genus of lovely shrubs, many of which are evergreen. They are typically mountain bushes, growing only to a moderate height and very free-flowering, and are most eminently suitable for planting in the rock garden. They also have the advantage of being easier to grow than the Rhododendrons, to which family they are very closely allied. Although supposed to grow only in peat, they will be found to thrive and flower well in ordinary loam, provided it is fairly free from lime, which, like all other peat-lovers, they detest. There are a vast number of named kinds, all of which are lovely and most suitable for planting amongst rocks. But as space will not permit me to enumerate them all, I shall only give a few of the more distinctive types.

A. amoena.—Peat or ordinary loam ; any aspect. Forms a compact little evergreen bush about 12 to 18 inches high. Small dark green leaves and rosy-crimson flowers. Blooms in May in the greatest profusion. A delightful little shrub, which should be freely planted in masses.

A. procumbens (syn. *Loiseleuria procumbens*).—Deep, sandy peat in half shade. A small, trailing shrub with wiry branches, not growing more than from 2 to 3 inches high, and forming a compact mass. Bears small, pink, bell-shaped flowers in spring. Very difficult to grow, and rarely seen in health in the garden. Good young plants with perfect roots to start with are essential. A little gem, and worthy of some trouble to grow.

A. rosaeflora. — Peaty soil. A compact-growing little bush rather similar to *A. amoena*, with salmon-rose-coloured flowers in spring. Quite hardy, of easy culture, and very attractive.

A. serpyllifolia.—Peaty soil and half shade. Of compact growth, with narrow leaves and a profusion of small pink flowers.

A. s. latifolia.—A stronger-growing form of the above. Other lovely kinds, but of taller habit, are—

A. calendulacea.—Orange flowers.

A. nudiflora, of which there are endless hybrids.

A. mollis.—Shades of orange and orange-red.

A. viscosa.—Fragrant white flowers.

A. Vaseyi.—Lovely delicate pink flowers.

BELLIS (COMPOSITAE), Daisy

Few forms of the Daisy are worth growing in the rock garden. The following are a selection :—

B. perennis.—Numerous named and unnamed double varieties. Great favourites with some people.

B. rotundiflora coerulea.—Requires sheltered, sunny position and protection in a severe winter. White, daisy flowers tinged with lavender. A charming little plant.

BELLIUM (COMPOSITAE)

A genus closely allied to the common Daisy; neither very beautiful nor very hardy. They all require a warm, sunny spot and sandy loam.

B. bellidioides.—Very dwarf habit, with small, white, solitary flowers.

B. crassifolium.—Flowers whitish-yellow, rather downy. Blooms in June.

B. minutum.—Very small, like a miniature Daisy. Pale white and yellow flowers from June to September.

BERBERIS (BERBERIDEAE), Barberry

A handsome genus of shrubs, of which there are a few kinds suitable for the rock garden. They are all of easy cultivation.

B. buxifolia nana.—Evergreen dwarf species, growing only 12 inches high. Small yellow flowers in abundance.

B. Darwinii nana.—A dwarf form of the well-known evergreen species. Orange-coloured flowers.

B. stenophylla Irwinii.—A delightful little shrub.

B. Thunbergi minor.—A miniature of *Thunbergi*, and well worthy of a place.

B. empetrifolia.—Likes rather peaty soil. Grows 18 inches to 2 feet, with bright orange-coloured flowers. Most charming and useful.

BLETIA HYACINTHINA

A hardy orchid. Requires peaty soil in a half-shady spot. Flower-stems about 12 inches high, bearing deep, rosy-purple flowers. A pretty plant for drier parts of the bog garden.

BORAGO LAXIFLORA (BORAGINACEAE)

Dark-green hairy leaves. Lovely pale blue flowers on hairy branching stems freely produced throughout the summer. Loam in open position. Quite hardy.

This is a plant that deserves to be more freely used, as the flowers are an exquisite shade of blue ; but, being somewhat coarse in habit, it should not be planted in the choicer parts of the rock garden.

BRACHYCOME (COMPOSITAE)

A genus of beautiful little half-hardy plants, closely resembling the daisy.

B. Sinclairii.—Requires a sunny aspect, where it can get ample moisture. Grows in a compost of loam, leaf-mould mixed with small stones. A very dwarf-habited plant, only about 2 inches high, spreading moderately. Leaves deep bronzy-green, and rather downy, arranged in tufts. Small, white, daisy-like flowers all the summer. A delightful wee plant.

B. iberidifolia.—The Swan River Daisy, though an annual, may be used to temporarily fill bare spaces.

BRUCKENTHALIA SPICULIFOLIA

Half-shady position in dry, peaty loam. A dwarf-growing plant of the Heath family, only some 9 inches high, with pale purple flowers in July.

BRYANTHUS (ERICACEAE)

A genus of small trailing shrubs of Heath family.

B. empetriformis (see *Menziesa empetriformis*).

B. erectus.—Small alpine shrub, said to be a hybrid (*Kalmia glauca* × *Rhododendron Chamaecistus*).—A half-shady position in sandy peat. A neat evergreen shrub, about 8 to 10 inches high, with pale green leaves and large red campanulate flowers. A delightful little shrub of fairly easy culture.

B. glanduliformis.—Sandy peat. A very dwarf shrub, only some 3 to 4 inches high, with bright magenta-red flowers, rather like a pentstemon in shape, and about 1½ inches long.

BUXUS (EUPHORBIACEAE), BOX

Dwarf-growing forms of the common Box may be used for giving evergreen effects. Quite hardy.

CALAMINTHA (LABIATAE)

A small genus of hardy plants of easy culture in ordinary soil. Readily increased by seed, or division of the roots in spring.

C. alpina.—Sandy loam. Only grows some 4 inches high. Freely branched, tufted habit, with purplish flowers in whorls in June.

C. grandiflora.—Rather larger form.

C. glabella.—Tubular, lilac-coloured flowers, sweet-scented. Suitable for growing with the very dwarfest plants.

CALANDRINIA UMBELLATA

Requires a very hot and dry position in poor sandy loam. Neat little shrubby plant growing about 6 inches high. Narrow, rather hairy leaves, and dazzling magenta-crimson flowers freely produced. Hardy only in dry soils. Very easily raised from seed. The flowers will only open in full sun, and for brilliancy are equalled by few ; but having a shade of magenta in their colouring, care should be taken as to what plant it is associated with. It very much dislikes disturbance, and young plants are the best. It is a succulent plant, and the hottest, driest spot is the best place for it. It should be treated as biennial.

Other varieties, *C. grandiflora, C. Menziesii,* and *C. nitida,* have purple-rose-coloured flowers, and should be treated as half-hardy annuals.

CALCEOLARIA (SCROPHULARIACEAE)

There are three varieties of this genus well worth growing ; they are quite different from the well-known and, I think, ugly greenhouse kinds.

C. plantaginea.—Raised parts of the bog garden and peaty loam. Rosettes of plantain-like leaves, pubescent. Bright yellow flowers borne on stems about 12 inches high from June to August. A good plant.

C. polyrhiza.—Moist peat and loam in half shade. Dwarf-growing, with spikes of incurved and spotted canary-yellow flowers in July, borne in profusion. Quite hardy, and a good plant.

C. violacea.—Sheltered position in sandy loam. A shrubby plant, growing 18 inches to 2 feet, with pale blue flowers, spotted violet. Is hardy only in favourable localities. Easily increased by division. A lovely plant, and well worth giving protection to during the winter.

CALLIRHOË (MALVACEAE), Poppy Mallow

Dwarf plants of the Mallow tribe.

C. involucrata.—Hot, dry position in very light sandy loam. Grows about 6 inches high, with trailing stems, cut leaves, and crimson-magenta-purple flowers, rather like a Mallow. Blooms in June. Easily raised from seed. Colour of the flowers is brilliant, but merging on the magenta shade, so care should be taken with what flowers they are associated.

CALTHA (RANUNCULACEAE), Marsh Marigold

Lovely and showy plants for the waterside. The single form, though lovely, is so common that it is hardly worth while giving it a place, but there are some very good double forms which should be grown. All are of easy culture.

C. biflora.—Compact grower, with white flowers.

C. monstrosa, fl. pl.—A fine double form.

C. palustris, fl. pl.—A double form of the common Marsh Marigold.

C. polypetula.—Large leaves and yellow flowers.

C. polysepala.—Enormous leaves and flowers, said to have been obtained from the Vatican.

C. purpurascens.—Rather distinct species, with purplish stems and the outside of bright orange-coloured flowers of a purplish tinge.

C. parnassifolia.—Yellow flowers in April and May.

CAMPANULA (CAMPANULACEAE), Bell-flowers

A large genus varying greatly in habit, height, and colour. Many are too coarse and tall-growing for the rock garden, but amongst the dwarfer-habited kinds will be found some of the choicest plants for the garden. They mostly like a sunny aspect and sandy loam, and are all very partial to limestone, except *Allionii, pulla,* and *pulloides,* which all three dislike extremely. there are so many varieties and hybrids, some scarcely distinguishable from one another, that it would be impossible to give anything like a complete list; but the following kinds are the best and most distinct forms, dwarf of habit, and well suited for the rock garden. Unless otherwise stated, it may be understood that sandy loam and sun are what they require.

C. Abietina.—Close green mats of leaves, 2 inches high. Lovely open, star-shaped, purple flowers in May, on slender, erect stems about 6 inches high. Increased by division, which it requires occasionally. One of the best kinds.

C. Allionii (syn. *C. alpestris* and *C. nana*).—Small stone chips, with a dash of peaty soil, in sun, are the needs of this plant, which hates lime. Long, narrow, hairy leaves and blue, bell-shaped flowers on slender stems about 6 inches high. Blooms in July. One of the loveliest and most difficult Campanulas. Requires abundant moisture during growing season.

C. alpina.—Rather long leaves covered with a greyish down. Of erect habit, growing from 6 to 10 inches high. Spikes of fine dark blue flowers, pendulous, tubular-shaped, about 1 inch long. Blooms in July. Division or seeds.

C. barbata.—Compact tufts of shaggy leaves. Lovely pendulous, pale blue, bell-shaped flowers nearly 1 inch long, all fringed at the mouth. These are borne four or five on a spike, in May. Unfortunately not always perennial. Dislikes excessive damp in winter, so should be planted in a dryish spot.

C. b. alba is a lovely form; requiring same treatment.

C. caespitosa.—A dwarf, spreading little plant. Tufted habit, 4 to 6 inches high. Round glossy leaves and a cloud of pale blue flowers in summer. Too strong a grower for association with choice plants; but for planting between steps and clothing odd corners there is no better or more lovely little flower. Readily increased by division. There is a white form, which is difficult to distinguish from *pusilla alba*.

C. carnica.—Rather of the type of the native Harebell. Flowers long, narrow, and tubular, and lilac-purple in colour. Quite hardy and a good grower.

C. carpatica.—Erect, deep blue flowers, funnel-shaped, growing in loose panicles about 9 to 18 inches high, according to the richness of the soil, and very freely produced during the summer. Stems leafy and branched. This is the type, but there are an endless number of hybrids and varieties; of the latter the best and most distinct are—

C. car. alba.—A pure white form, very lovely.

C. car. pallida.—Palest of blue flowers.

C. car. riverslea.—A good and very free-blooming and vigorous variety, with deep blue flowers.

C. car. pelviformis.—A more distinct variety, and one of the best. Grows as high as 18 inches, and bears a profusion of large, rather flat, saucer-shaped flowers of a pleasing shade of pale blue. Not quite as robust as some of the other kinds. Slugs, therefore, are rather devoted to it.

C. car. " White Star."—Large, saucer-shaped flowers, nearly 2½ inches across, white, with just a trace of blue in them, which, if anything, rather enhances their beauty.

C. cenisia.—Deep, very gritty, sandy soil. Spreads vigorously underground, and above makes compact rosettes of light green leaves. Grows only about 3 inches high, with funnel-shaped, solitary blue flowers. Division.

C. collina.—Likes a hot, stony bank. Greyish, downy leaves of medium growth. Pendulous, long, funnel-shaped flowers of the most beautiful violet colour, rivalling *C. pulla* in intensity. A lovely and uncommon plant of the easiest culture. Quite one of the gems of the genus.

C. Elantines.—Of trailing habit, with hairy leaves and blue starry flowers, rather flat-shaped. Dislikes damp, and should be planted in a crevice or moraine in full sun. Slugs are very devoted to this species.

C. elatinoides.—Very similar to the above, but of taller habit.

C. excisa.—Open position in gritty peat and loam. A rapid-growing little plant of spreading habit. Thin, erect stems, 3 to 6 inches high, and drooping, bell-shaped flowers of pale violet. It derives its name from having a small round hole at the base of every lobe. A charming little plant. Does not like lime. Increased by division.

C. fragilis.—Requires well-drained, sandy loam, as it dislikes excessive moisture. Prostrate, trailing habit, barely 5 inches high. Rather large, pale, clear lilac-blue, bell-shaped flowers, with a white centre, borne on half-prostrate stems. The stems of this plant are very brittle, from which it derives its name. A very pretty little plant.

Other Campanulas very nearly allied to and requiring much the same treatment as *fragilis* are *Barrelieri, Balchiniana, rupestris,* and *Tenorii.* These are all so much alike that to the ordinary gardener, at least, it is very hard to distinguish them apart.

C. garganica.—Prostrate, compact habit, and free-growing. Toothed, heart-shaped leaves. Plant covered in summer with a profusion of bluish starry flowers, with a white centre, rising about 3 inches. One of the best and easiest-growing Campanulas. Should be planted in crevices in vertical parts of the rock garden to show it at its best. Easily increased by division or seed. *Alba* is a white and lovely form.

C. g. hirsuta.—This is a very hairy form of the above, and of rather coarser growth. A gem amongst the Campanulas. *Hirsuta alba* is a white, rare, and very beautiful form.

C. grandiflora (syn. *Platycodon*).—Good, well-drained loam in partial shade. " The balloon Campanula," so named from the shape of its large inflated blossoms just before they fully open ; when fully expanded, they are about 3 inches across, of a deep, rather slaty-blue, borne on stalks about 15 inches high. There is a white form, *alba*. Also a dwarfer-growing variety, *Mariesii*, which also has a white form. All these balloon Campanulas have fleshy root-stocks, very liable to decay in undrained situations. They all come readily from seed, and vary much in shades of white and blue.

C. " G. F. Wilson."—A hybrid, *C. carpatica × pulla.* Very free grower, spreading underground rapidly. Quite dwarf habit. Deep blue, semi-pendulous, bell-shaped flowers, with a lighter centre. A charming plant, of the easiest culture. Increased by division.

C. glomerata.—Sun, in ordinary soil. Grows 12 to 18 inches high. Flowers bluish-violet-coloured, borne in terminal heads. There are many varieties of this species.

C. g. acaulis.—Is a dwarf form of *C. glomerata*, which bears its flowers on stems a foot or so high ; but in this case the deep violet clusters of flowers nestle close to the downy foliage, which slugs much appreciate.

C. g. daharica (syn. *speciosa*).—This plant is true to the type, bearing on stems about 9 inches high flowers of the most brilliant blue. It is a striking plant, very easily grown, and readily increased by division.

C. haylodgensis.—This is a hybrid between *pusilla* and *carpatica.* Yellowish-green leaves and pale blue, open, bell-shaped flowers in summer and autumn. It is of easy culture and a useful plant.

C. hederacea (syn. *wahlenbergia*).—Requires a moist, boggy spot, or by the edge of a stream. A fragile, creeping plant, with delicate leaves on thread-like stems, and small, pale bluish-purple flowers. A pretty little plant for a wet spot, and a native.

C. Hendersoni.—Forms a pyramid 10 inches high, of large saucer-shaped, showy purple flowers. A handsome plant, but rather inclined to go off. Probably a variety of *carpatica.*

C. hostii.—Very nearly allied to *C. rotundiflora*, but is somewhat stronger in habit, growing about 12 inches high, and has flowers of a deeper shade of purple.

C. isophylla.—Sunny position in well-drained, sandy loam. Of trailing habit, free-growing. Roundish, toothed leaves. Lovely pale blue, salver-shaped flowers, with a lighter centre. It flowers in July and August. A well-known plant, generally grown in the house, and a familiar object in cottage windows, with sheets of blossom from some hanging basket. In the rock garden there can be no more beautiful sight than a good plant of it, when in full bloom, falling over the face of some sunny rock. It is not very hardy, and dislikes excessive damp, so will need a little care in any but very favoured localities. *C. isophylla alba* is a white, and, if possible, more attractive form.

C. lanata (syn. *velutina*).—Requires the hottest, driest, sunniest crevice to be found. Large woolly leaves. Flower-spikes short, with large, hairy, bell-shaped flowers. Primrose-coloured, and tinged with pink. A lovely and attractive plant, but not easy to keep, as it is very liable to damp off. It should be planted in a vertical fissure and protected from moisture overhead. Flowers in July. Grows readily from seed.

C. macrorrhiza.—Likes a vertical fissure in full sun and calcareous soil. It has a thick, woody root-stock and numerous light, drooping stems, with clusters of fine blue flowers during the winter. A perfectly hardy and easily grown species, and one that should be more frequently used, not only on account of its hardiness, but also because of its blooming in winter.

C. Mayli.—Warm, sunny position in light gritty loam. Roundish hirsute leaves. Lovely pale blue salver-shaped flowers. This species is of the *isophylla* type, and should be protected in winter from damp. A very beautiful and well-known basket plant.

C. mollis.—Forms a spreading carpet of glossy leaves about 6 to 8 inches high. Flowers dark blue, and freely borne in May and June. Quite hardy, and a useful plant.

C. muralis.—Smooth, dark green leaves, forming a carpet some 6 inches thick, with deep blue, bell-shaped flowers. Of the hardiest constitution, and one of the best dwarf-growing Campanulas. Some authorities claim this species as being synonymous with *Portenschlagiana*, while others say the latter is a more robust and distinct form. There is also in catalogues *Portenschlagiana Bavarica*, which claims to have larger flowers. But there is a form of *C. muralis* of rather taller habit, with larger and deeper-coloured flowers, and if anything more floriferous.

C. pulla.—Open, level, sunny spot in peaty soil. Spreads underground fairly rapidly, sending up shoots of bright green leaves, and on hairy stems about 3 inches long a solitary, pendulous, bell-shaped flower of the deepest violet-blue in July and August. Of easy culture so long as there is no lime in the soil. It is said to die off during the winter, so it is advisable to keep a stock of it in pots to replace casualities. One of the gems of the genus, and indispensable.

C. pulloides.—A chance hybrid, probably between *carpatica* and *pulla*. The same parentage as " *G. F. Wilson,*" which its flowers resemble in shape and size, but they have the deep purple of *pulla*. It is of the same habit, but taller and stronger-growing than *pulla*. Blooms very freely in July and August. A glorious Campanula, than which there is none better grown, and very few, if any, as good. Readily increased by division. There is a variety of it named *Kewensis*, which claims to be larger and of a more gorgeous violet-purple, and altogether a superior plant. I have not seen it myself, but if it answers the description it must indeed be something to rave about.

C. punctata.—Ordinary soil in partial shade. Grows about 12 inches high and has long, drooping, white, bell-shaped flowers spotted with dark red. Not long-lived, but easily raised from seed. Quite a handsome plant.

C. pusilla.—Very like *C. caespitosa,* but of rather dwarfer habit. Pendulous, pale blue, bell-shaped flowers. Leaves glossy, toothed, and heart-shaped. Blooms in June and July. There is a white form, *alba,* and *pallida,* a variety with even paler blue flowers. All three are of easy culture and very pretty plants. Increased by division.

C. p. "*Miss Willmott.*"—A recent introduction bearing larger and paler blooms than the type, and in greater profusion. Well worth growing.

C. raddeana.—A beautiful new species from the Caucasus. Leaves deep green. Stems about 6 to 8 inches high, from which spring numerous semi-pendent cup-shaped flowers of a rich purple. Ordinary light soil in sun or half-shade. Grows and spreads rapidly. Quite one of the best.

C. Raineri.—Needs a sunny chink in strong, gritty loam. Rare, dwarf-growing species, with large, erect, dark blue, funnel-shaped flowers. Easily grown, and a very good plant for a dry spot. Slugs are very fond of it.

C. rhomboidalis.—Nearly allied to *C. rotundifolia.* It has deep blue flowers, and grows 10 to 12 inches high. Ordinary light soil in sun. Increased by seed or division.

C. rotundifolia.—The common native Harebell, but, though common, is well worthy of a spot in the less choice parts. There is a white form, *alba,* which is a good thing, and *C. r. soldanelli flora plena,* which is particularly attractive.

C. r. alpina.—Deep blue colour, and is very fine.

C. rupestris.—Very gritty, well-drained soil in full sun. Dwarf habit. Greyish silvery leaves and large pale blue flowers, a very attractive plant. Increased by seed and division.

C. sarmatica.—Ordinary soil in any position. Grows about 10 inches high. With pale blue flowers. Somewhat similar to *C. barbata.*

C. Stansfieldi.—Likes rather a shady or half-shady spot in well-drained loam. Forms compact little plants with hairy, yellow-tinted foliage, and clear blue, bell-shaped flowers. Quite hardy, and easily grown. It dies down during the winter. Readily increased by division. Quite in the front rank of dwarf Campanulas.

C. Steveni nana.—Ordinary light soil in sun or half-shade. Very similar in habit to *C. Abietina.* Forms a carpet of narrow, glossy leaves, from which rise large pale blue flowers on slender 6-inch stems. A recent introduction from the Caucasusana. One of the best and most attractive of the genus.

C. S. alba is also a good white form, rare and very beautiful.

C. tridentata.—Of tufted habit, with large purple flowers. Requires light, very gritty soil in full sun. A really *attractive* plant, which should be more often grown.

C. Tommasiniana.—Rather a bushy-growing little plant, about 8 inches high, with spikes of pale blue, pendulous, tubular flowers. A particularly good species, of which slugs are very fond.

C. turbinata.—Dwarf-growing plant, with greyish-green leaves and solitary, salver-shaped flowers $1\frac{1}{2}$ inches across, of a deep blue colour, borne on erect stems about 6 inches high. Quite hardy, and easily grown. A good plant. Also known as *C. carpatica turbinata.*

C. t. Isabel.—Is a good variety, with large rich blue flowers.

C. Waldsteiniana.—A neat little plant, growing about 6 inches high. Flowers star-shaped and bright blue, with a white eye, borne on wiry stems clothed with narrow leaves. One of the easiest to grow and best of Campanulas.

C. Zoysii.—Forms dense little tufts, about 3 inches high, of tiny ovate leaves. Flowers drooping, bright blue, tubular, and curiously contracted at the mouth. Blooms in June, and very freely. Quite easy to grow in a sunny chink in gritty loam. A most delightful little plant, but beware of slugs and snails, for they will come any distance to feast off *Campanula Zoysii.*

CAMPHOROSMA MONSPELIACA (CHENOPODIACEAE)

A curious and little-known half-shrubby plant, like a silvery grey cedar. Should be planted so that its branches can hang over a rock. Ordinary soil in any position.

CARDAMINE, syn. DENTARIA (CRUCIFERAE), Ladies' Smock

Vigorous-growing plants for a half-shady position in damp loam and leaf-mould. They are more useful than choice plants for associating with the coarser-growing kinds in the bog garden. The following are the best varieties :—

C. bulbifera.—Fern-like foliage and pale purple flowers in loose spikes. Flowering in spring and growing 1 to 2 feet high.

C. digitata.—Grows only about 12 inches high. Rich purple flowers in flat racemes. Blooms in April.

C. enneaphylla.—Creamy-white flowers in clusters in April and June. Grows about 12 inches high.

C. trifolia.—Forms a neat mass of dark green leaves about 3 inches high, of rather creeping habit, from which rise spikes about 6 inches long of large, pure white flowers. This variety is about the choicest of the genus.

CARLINA ACAULIS

An everlasting. Requires full exposure to the sun in the poorest of soil, otherwise it loses its brilliant appearance and grows coarse. Thorny rosettes of leaves, on each of which lie silvery-white, thistle-like flowers. Propagated by seed.

CASSANDRA (see ANDROMEDA)

CASSIOPE (see ANDROMEDA)

CASTILLEJA ACUMINATA

Peaty soil. Spikes of labiate yellow flowers; with the enveloping bract are a most brilliant vermilion. Quite hardy, but difficult to cultivate. Grows 18 inches to 2 feet high.

CATHCARTIA VILLOSA

Requires a sheltered nook in light, rich soil. Of the Poppy tribe, and nearly related to the Meconopsis. Grows about 12 inches high, with silky, vine-shaped leaves, and large yellow flowers with brown anthers. Hardy, but only a biennial. Increased by seed, which is freely produced.

CERASTIUM (CARYOPHYLLACEAE), Mouse-ear Chickweed

Tufted plants of spreading habit and silvery leaves. Useful, but by no means choice rock plants. All grow freely in hot, dry positions in ordinary soil.

C. alpinum. — Dwarf-tufted plant, about 2 to 4 inches high. Leaves ovate, lanceolate, densely covered with whitish down. Large white flowers in early summer. Does not like excessive moisture on its foliage, otherwise quite hardy. Increased by division or cuttings inserted after flowering.

C. Biebersteinii.—Silvery-white leaves, ovate, lanceolate, and small white flowers in early summer. Grows 6 inches high.

C. grandiflorum.—Very soon forms large tufts of hoary, narrow leaves. Bears large pure white flowers in the greatest profusion in the summer. Grows anywhere, and freely increased by cuttings or by division. A well-known and showy plant for the rougher parts of the rock garden, but too rampant in growth to put near anything choice.

C. tomentosum.—A form similar to *grandiflorum*, but with smaller flowers and more compact habit.

The above are the only varieties of Cerastium worth growing except in botanical collections, to which might be added *glaciale*, a large and handsome variety, and *repens*, useful dwarf carpeter.

CHAMAEBATIA FOLIOLOSA (ROSACEAE)

A little-known, dwarf, evergreen, shrubby plant of the Rose family. Pretty fern-like leaves and bramble-like flowers ¾ inch across. Quite hardy, and worth a spot in the less choicer parts of the rock garden in light loam.

CHAMAELIRIUM CAROLINIANUM (LILIACEAE)

Raised parts of the bog garden. A pretty plant with wand-like spikes of white flowers.

CHAMAEMELUM CAUCASICUM (syn. MATRICARIA)

Dry position. Trailing habit, with fern-like leaves and white flowers. Nearly allied to the Camomile family, and not of much value.

CHEIRANTHUS (CRUCIFERÆ), Wallflower

Wallflowers are very useful for the wall garden. Besides the well-known bedding varieties, there are a few of a rather distinct habit. All are of the easiest culture.

C. alpinus.—In old walls and dry banks. Forms neat little tufts of dark green foliage, covered during the summer with a profusion of small sulphur-coloured leaves. A very pretty little plant, of the easiest culture, and well worth a spot in the rock garden.

C. Cheiri.—The old-fashioned flower, with its shades of yellow, orange, and purplish-red, both double and single. In ordinary garden soil these grow rank and coarse, but on the tops of walls they form stout, dwarf little bushes, covered with flower during the summer.

C. mutabilis.—Old walls and dry banks. A shrubby plant, growing 2 to 3 feet high. Orange-purple-coloured flowers and buds deep red. Quite hardy, and of easy culture. A pretty and distinct little plant. Increased by division. Other varieties: *Allionii*, hybrid growing 12 inches high; flowers deep orange. *Marshalii*, another hybrid with orange-coloured flowers.

CHIMAPHILA (ERICACEAE)

Low-growing evergreen shrubs of the Heath order, from North America.

C. maculata (syn. *Pyrola maculata*).—Sandy, peaty soil in shady, but not wet position. Grows only 3 to 6 inches high. Small, glossy, leathery leaves, upper side variegated with white, under surface red. White pendulous flowers in June. Rather difficult to grow. Increased by division.

C. umbellata (syn. *Pyrola umbellata*).—Same soil and position. Reddish-coloured flowers, rather larger than the last, and leaves unvariegated. Both increased by careful division.

CHIOGENES HISPIDULA (syn. GAULTHERIA SERPYLLIFOLIA), Creeping Snowberry

Wet, peaty soil in a shady, cool spot. A creeping evergreen plant like a small Cranberry. Small white flowers and round white berries. A plant for the bog garden.

CHRYSANTHEMUM (COMPOSITAE)

The section of this genus, better known as Marguerites, though as a rule more suitable for the herbaceous border, gives a few varieties of dwarfer habit which would look well in the rock garden.

C. alpinum (syn. *C. Leucanthemum*).—Likes poor, gravelly soil. Grows only about 4 to 6 inches high, with small, deeply cut, hoary leaves and pure white flowers, with a golden eye, a miniature of the common one-eyed daisy. Blooms in summer.

C. arcticum.—Grows about 9 inches high. Rosy-white flowers from May to July. A pretty little plant.

17

C. hybridum coronopifolium.—Dwarf habit. Finely cut leaves. Numerous white, daisy-like flowers.

C. Tchihatchewii.—Dry, stony banks. Rapid-growing dwarf carpeter, with evergreen, fern-like foliage. Small, whitish, daisy flowers with yellowish-coloured eyes. A very useful plant. Will quickly clothe the most arid and hopeless-looking spots, where nothing else would grow.

CHRYSOGONUM VIRGINIANUM

A plant of the Compositae order, of neat branching habit, growing 6 inches high in loamy soil. Has yellow flowers, freely produced during the whole summer. Will grow under trees. A useful, if not brilliant, little plant.

CHRYSOPSIS VILLOSA (COMPOSITAE)

Ordinary soil in any aspect. Dwarf-growing plant with downy leaves and golden-yellow flowers from July to September. Of easy culture, and increased by division in spring.

CISTUS (CISTINEAE), Rock Rose

This genus may be included amongst the most beautiful of our flowering shrubs. They all love hot, dry, sandy banks ; some varieties are not hardy in a cold, wet climate. The flowers, though lasting but one day, are borne in such profusion that a constant succession is kept up for a considerable time during the summer. The dwarfer kinds can be used amongst the rockwork, while the taller-growing varieties may be associated with other shrubs. All grow readily from cuttings and seeds.

C. albidus.—Compact-growing bush, 2 to 4 feet high. Leaves and young shoots covered with a white pubescens. Large purplish-rose-coloured flowers with yellow at the base.

C. algarvenses (syn. *Helianthemum ocymoides*).—Neat shrub, growing about 2 feet high, with narrow grey-green leaves. Rather small, bright yellow flowers, with a crimson-purple spot at base of each petal. Increased by division. Requires shelter from strong winds, as its branches are rather brittle. A lovely little shrub, and quite one of the best of the family. Other names of this variable plant are *Helianthemum algarvense, candidum,* and *rugosum.*

C. Bourgaeanus.—Grows about 12 inches high, with prostrate branches and narrow dark green leaves like Rosemary. Flowers white, about 1 inch across.

C. Clusii (syn. *C. rosmarinifolius*).—Leaves and flowers the same as the last, but of more erect habit, growing about 2 feet high. Not very hardy.

C. Corbariensis (*Salvifolius* × *populifolius*).—Forms a compact bush about 2 feet high. Leaves glutinous ; margins fringed. White flowers about 1½ inches across, with a yellowish centre, in June and July.

C. crispus.—Grows about 2 feet high, with large flowers of 2 to 3 inches across, of rosy crimson, flowering from June to November. One of the best.

C. cyprius.—Grows up to 5 feet high. Dark green leaves, smooth above and hoary beneath, which in winter assume a glaucous tint. Flowers borne in clusters, white, with a dark base and petals, and 4 inches across. Flowers in July. A very good shrub, often sent out as the Gum Cistus.

C. florentinus (*monspeliensis* × *salvifolius*).—Grows from 12 to 18 inches high. Compact habit. Dark green leaves and large white flowers, with base of petals yellow, borne in the summer in the greatest profusion. Quite one of the best of the dwarf kinds.

C. formosus (syn. *Helianthemum formosus*).—Rather a loose habit. Grows up to 3 feet high. Small hoary leaves and yellow flowers, with a dark purplish-brown blotch at the base of each petal. Very pretty, but liable to succumb in a hard winter. As it strikes easily from cuttings, a stock should be kept to replace casualties.

C. glaucus.—Grows about 2 feet high. Dull green glabrous leaves, downy underneath. Large white flowers with a yellow blotch. Pretty.

C. hirsutus.—Leaves downy on both sides. Flowers white, with yellow base. Rather smaller than the last, which it otherwise resembles. Grows up to 2 feet high.

C. ladaniferus (Gum Cistus).—Grows about 3 feet high. Dark glossy leaves, white and woolly underneath. Large white flowers, 4 to 5 inches across. Blooms in June to August. A well-known and handsome shrub, not very hardy everywhere.

C. l., var. *maculatus.*—Flowers white, with a maroon blotch at base of petal. Otherwise the same as above, of which it is a variety.

C. laurifolius.—Flowers white, with a yellowish mark at the base of each petal, but otherwise similar to the above, except that it is very hardy, standing any amount of cold and wet. Grows readily from seed or cuttings. Blooms in June.

C. lusitanicus.—Grows about 18 inches high, of rather prostrate habit. Dark green, slightly viscous leaves, and large white flowers, each petal having a yellow base, with a dark green maroon blotch above it. A lovely little shrub, and quite one of the best.

C. purpureus.—Growing about 2 feet high, with large reddish-purple flowers, with a dark purple spot at base of petal, in the summer. Leaves rather hairy. Not common.

C. rosmarinifolius (see *C. Clusii*).

C. salvifolius.—Slender habit, growing some 2 feet high, with sage-like leaves and white flowers ; very hairy. The above are the most distinctive kinds, but others are also well worth growing.

C. Gauntlettii.—Crimson flowers.

C. obtusifolius.—White flowers, yellow eye.

C. monspelienses.—Flowers white.

C. recognitus.—Dwarf-growing. White, crimson-spotted flowers.

CLAYTONIA (PORTULACEAE)

Rather uninteresting little plants for damp spots in loam and leaf-mould. Some varieties are only biennials. Rather fleshy, obovate leaves in compact tufts about 3 inches high, and loose racemes of small flowers, rose-coloured, with deeper veins. The following are the best varieties :—*C. Asarifolia*, *C. siberica*, and *C. virginica*.

CLEMATIS (RANUNCULACEAE)

The following varieties can be used to clothe large masses of rock or waste banks.

Many species are known under the name of *Atragene*.

C. alpina.—With large violet-blue flowers.

C. tangitica.—Yellow flowers and fluffy seed-pods.

C. Viticella.—Large blue, purple, or rose-coloured flowers.

C. Douglasi.—Non-climbing variety, only growing about 1 foot high. Flowers deep purple inside, lilac outside. Leaves hairy.

COCHLEARICA ALPINA (CRUCIFERAE)

A native. Forms neat rosettes of glossy, heart-shaped leaves. Dwarf-growing. White flowers. Of no great value. Should be planted in poor soil to prevent its growing coarse.

CODONOPSIS (CAMPANULACEAE)

A genus of plants of the bell-flower order, growing from 1 to 2 feet high. They should be planted high up on the rock garden, so that the curiously veined markings inside the pendulous bells can be seen. All are of easy culture in a warm corner.

C. Bulleyi.—Of trailing habit, large lavender-blue flowers. Of recent introduction, and should become popular.

C. ovata.—The best known. Pendulous, pale blue flowers with white and yellow markings inside the bells. Partially erect stems 6 to 12 inches long. Not very hardy.

C. rotundifolia.—Large yellowish-coloured flowers with dark purple veining. Climbing habit and an annual.

Other varieties :—

C. ussuriensis.—Blue flowers of more climbing habit, and distinct.

C. Clematidea.—White flowers tinged with blue. Grows 2 to 3 feet high.

COLCHICUM (LILIACEAE), Meadow Saffron

Very closely allied to the Crocus family. They are, however, rather larger than the true Crocus. They should be grown in light sandy loam, enriched with manure, in rather a moist spot. As the flowers come before the leaves, they look better when appearing through a carpet of Sedums, which also protect their bloom from being splashed with the earth. Being mostly autumn flowers, they give a bit of colour to the rock garden at a time when it is much needed. They also look well planted in masses on grassy slopes. There are a great many varieties, but the following is a good selection :—

C. alpinum.—Deep rosy lilac.

C. autumnale.—Bright purple. There are several varieties :— *Roseus*, rosy lilac ; *Striatium*, rosy lilac, striped white ; *album*, pure white ; *atropurpureum*, deep purple ; and others.

C. crociflorum.—Flowers white, striped purple. Spring flowering.

C. libanoticum.—Rosy-white flowers in February.

C. Parkisoni.—Purple flowers netted with white; blooms in October.

C. Sibthorpii.—As large as *C. speciosum*, but richer in colour, and of a more compact form, netted with crimson lines.

C. speciosum.—Large, rosy-purple flowers, nearly a foot high. Blooms in October.

C. s. album.—A magnificent, pure white form with golden anthers. As large as the type. Quite the pick of the family.

C. s. atrorubens.—A very much deeper and richer-coloured variety of the type.

CONANDRON RAMONDIOIDES (GESNERACEAE)

Shade, in vertical fissures in deep, moist, peaty, and gritty loam. Forms flat tufts of thick, wrinkled leaves, from which rise pale purple and white flowers on wiry stems about 5 inches high. Of doubtful hardihood, at least it is a difficult plant to keep. It is very closely allied to the Ramondias, and should receive similar treatment.

Convallaria majalis (Liliaceae)

The well-known Lily-of-the-valley, and a universal favourite. Although of suitable habit, is better confined to the beds in the kitchen garden than in the rock garden proper, but can be made use of for planting amongst low shrubs or in half-shady spots in the woods.

Convolvulus (Convolvulaceae), Bindweed

Climbing plants of graceful habit. Many of them, however, far too vigorous to be allowed into the rock garden. The more moderate growers will be found useful for draping rocks or covering banks. They are mostly indifferent to soil, but prefer it light, and in sun. The following are the better kinds, easily increased by division of roots or seed:—

C. althaeoides.—Dry banks. A non-climbing variety, with large pale red or blue flowers, variable both in leaves and colour. Increased by seed or division. Hardy and deciduous.

C. arvensis.— White or rose-coloured flowers, wide, trumpet-shaped, very pretty, but an awful weed. This variety should only be planted in the wildest part of the wild garden, where it can run riot without doing any harm.

C. Cantabricus.—Grows about 12 inches high. Pink flowers in clusters during August. Hardy and deciduous.

C. Cneorum.—Warm, sunny bank, sheltered. A very distinct shrubby kind, growing about 18 inches to 2 feet. Leaves covered with silvery tormentum, and white, shaded pink, flowers. A beautiful plant, and should be freely grown when possible, but it is not very hardy in cold climates. Easily struck from cuttings.

C. lineatus.—Dry, warm position in sandy soil. Very dwarf-growing, only about 6 inches high. Tufts of small, silvery, pointed leaves, amongst which appear pale reddish-purple-coloured flowers an inch across, in June. A choice deciduous plant for covering arid slopes in the rock garden.

C. mauritanicus.—Requires warm, sunny position in sandy loam. A trailer, though not of rampant growth, with lovely, clear, pale azure-blue flowers, with a white throat and yellow anthers. A lovely plant, but not of renowned hardihood. Increased by seeds or cuttings.

C. soldanella.—The native Bindweed of our seashores. Pale pink flowers on trailing stems. Very sandy soil will suit it well.

Coris monspeliensis (Primulaceae)

Dry, sunny spot in well-drained, light, sandy, and peaty soil. Branching and dwarf habit, growing about 6 inches high. Small purple flowers with yellow anthers, 6-inch spikes. Hardy only in warm and sheltered position. Doubtful perennial. Increased by seed, sown as soon as ripe in a cold frame.

CORNUS (CORNACEAE), Dogwood

Genus of hardy shrubs, but only two are suitable for rock garden. Readily increased by cuttings or suckers.

C. canadensis (Dwarf Cornel).—Deep, sandy, peaty soil in half shade. Very dwarf-growing, with whorled, ovate leaves, dark green turning red in winter. Flowers greenish-white and insignificant.

C. suecica.—Similar position and soil as last. Flowers dark purple, in terminal umbels, produced in June. Red berries. Grows about 6 inches high.

CORONILLA (LEGUMINOSAE), Crown Vetch

Plants and shrubs of the Peaflower order, some of which are worth growing. The Coronillas are all deep-rooted.

C. iberica (syn. *cappadocica*).—Sunny position in light sandy loam. Neat, prostrate habit, with foliage not rising more than 3 or 4 inches from the ground. Bright golden-yellow flowers, freely produced during the summer. Fairly rapid grower. Hardy in dry position. A most attractive plant, which should be freely grown. Division.

C. minima.—Warm, sunny position in deep, light soil. Very dwarf and prostrate-growing, and bright yellow flowers in June and July. Is of easy culture, and well worth a place in some hot corner. Increased by division or cuttings.

C. montana.—Light soil in full sun. Trailing habit. Bright golden-yellow flowers in the greatest profusion in June and July. This species deserves to be more widely cultivated.

C. varia.—The well-known Coronilla of railway banks, with its rosy-yellow flowers, which, however, vary considerably. It may be found useful for covering some sun-baked waste corner of the rock garden where little else will grow.

CORTUSA MATTHIOLI (PRIMULACEAE), Bear's-ear Sanicle

Nearly allied to the Primulas. It requires moist, sandy peat and loam in half shade and sheltered from the wind. Large rather hairy leaves about 6 inches high. Pendulous, deep purplish-crimson flowers, with a white ring at base, are borne in umbels on stems about 8 inches high. Increased by seed or division. A very pretty plant for the bog garden.

C. grandiflora.—Is a larger form and of more vigorous habit.

C. Pubens.—Has flowers of a magenta-purple colour. A dwarfer-growing plant than *C. Matthioli.*

CORYDALIS (PAPAVERACEAE), Fumitory

Nearly all the Fumitories are pretty and attractive, and increased by division after flowering ; they are a large family, of which only a selection of the best is here given.

C. bracteata.—In ordinary soil. Sulphur-yellow flowers and rather thin foliage. Very easy of culture.

C. cheilianthifolius.—Ordinary soil, rather light. Very pretty fern-like foliage, and clear Naples yellow flowers. Grows about 12 inches high. Is of the easiest culture, seeding itself about. A new species, and one of the best.

C. nobilis.—Likes light, rich soil. Grows about 18 inches high. Fern-like foliage and stout leafy stems with large heads of rich yellow flowers. A handsome plant, easy to grow, but slow to increase. Propagated by division and seeds.

C. thalictrifolia.—Requires a sheltered position in light soil. Tufted and spreading habit. Distinctive foliage, which in autumn assumes a reddish hue. Grows only about 10 inches high. Large pale yellow flowers borne in racemes. A handsome and new introduction, flowering from spring to autumn. Less hardy than some of the other kinds.

C. Wilsoni.—Sunny position in ordinary soil. Handsome, divided glaucous leaves and yellow flowers. Grows about 8 inches high. Quite hardy. A recent introduction from China, and likely to prove an addition.

Other species :—

C. capnoides.—Creamy-white flowers, very pretty.

C. lutea.—The common yellow Fumitory.

C. ochroleuca.—Pale yellow flowers.

C. exima.—Bright rose-coloured flowers.

C. formosa.—Bright rose.

COTONEASTER (ROSEACEAE), Rock Spray

A very large genus of trees and shrubs ; but a few of the dwarf-growing kinds are charming for covering rocks and banks. The following are the most suitable for that purpose :—

C. adpressa.—Ordinary soil. A very compact, close, and fast-growing prostrate shrub. Rosy-pink flowers, followed by red berries. Deciduous. A new Chinese species, very attractive, and a valuable addition.

C. congesta nummularia.—Close, prostrate habit.

C. horizontalis.—Branches grow fan-shaped, and lie close to a wall or face of a rock. The small, dark green, ovate leaves take a brilliant orange-red tone in the autumn, with vermilion-coloured berries. A fairly fast grower. A charming and valuable shrub. Deciduous.

C. humifusa.—Long trailing shoots and dark green leaves. Useful for covering rocks.

C. microphylla.—Handsome evergreen species of trailing habit, but too strong and rapid a grower for any but the rougher parts of the rock garden, where it should make a pretty picture with its sheets of white flowers in summer and crimson-red berries in winter, which show up so well against its dark green foliage.

CROCUS (IRIDACEAE)

These well-known little bulbous plants look well in masses in the wild garden, or in groups in the less choice parts of the rock garden. There are a great number of varieties, a selection of which can be made from any bulb catalogue.

CYANANTHUS LOBATUS (CAMPANULACEAE)

Sunny position in sandy soil mixed with peat and leaf-mould. Trailing habit, and small dark green foliage. Flowers deep purplish-blue, with a whitish centre. Deciduous plant, flowering in late autumn. Requires moisture during growing season. A very pretty and distinct plant, and well worth growing.

C. incanus.—Dry, sunny position in well-drained, peaty loam. Flowers not as large as *C. Lobatus*, but of a most beautiful shade of blue, with a tuft of white hairs at the throat of the corolla. A most exquisitely lovely and rare plant, and not easy to cultivate.

CYCLAMEN (PRIMULACEAE), Sowbread

Besides the greenhouse varieties, there are a large number which are quite hardy, and may be used with good effect in the garden. They do best when planted beneath low bushes, which gives them shelter. They require half shade in loam and leaf-mould and perfect drainage to ensure success. The corms should be planted just below the surface of the ground, and should not be allowed to become exposed. A light top dressing of leaf-mould when at rest is advisable. Amongst many others the following are well-known varieties :—

C. Coum.—Crimson flowers.

C. hederæfolium.—Crimson flowers and prettily marked leaves.

C. vernum.—Various colours.

CYDONIA JAPONICA SIMONI

A dwarf and creeping form of *Pyrus Japonica*, with blood-red flowers in early spring. A handsome and useful shrubby plant.

C. Pygmaea.—Compact habit and brick-red flowers. Also a charming little shrub for the rock garden.

CYPRIPEDIUM (ORCHIDACEAE), Lady's Slipper

Most interesting and beautiful hardy orchids.

C. acaule (syn. *C. humile*).—Deep, moist loam, peat, and sand, in half-shady position. Large rose-coloured flowers blotched with purple. Very pretty, but not easy to grow.

C. Calceolus.—Half-shady position in fibrous loam; likes limestone. Flowers, reddish-brown sepals and petals; lip yellow. A very pretty native plant.

C. macranthon.—Good fibrous loam and limestone. Rich purple flowers about 12 inches high. A very handsome species.

C. parviflorum.—Full shade in very moist peat, loam, and sand. Flowers rather small. Sepals and petals brown and purple; lip yellow, spotted red. One of the best.

C. pubescens (syn. *C. hirsutum*).—Rather heavy loam and limestone, well drained, in half shade. Sepals and petals yellow, streaked brown; lip yellow; stems and leaves pubescent.

C. spectabile. — Half shade in moist, loamy peat and sand. Flowers large, white-pink, tinted with crimson-veined lips. The handsomest and freest blooming of the family. A good mass of these hardy orchids is indeed a gorgeous sight.

All the Cypripediums need a well-drained position, though at the same time requiring moisture. They like to get their roots into decaying leaves, so choose a well-drained, low-lying spot in half shade.

CYTISUS (LEGUMINOSAE), Broom

A genus of very graceful and extraordinarily floriferous shrubs. Some of tall-growing habit, while others are quite prostrate; but they are all suitable for the rock garden, and can be used in different parts; they are typically rock shrubs. They are all of the easiest culture, and mostly indifferent to soil, and many kinds come readily from seed. The brooms are so closely allied to the Genistas that much confusion arises.

C. albus (White Spanish Broom).—Growing 4 or 5 feet in a few years. White flowers borne in long racemes in the greatest profusion. A grand shrub for bold masses. Cut back after flowering.

C. a. durus.—A prostrate, weeping variety of more moderate growth.

C. Ardoini.—Forms a low trailing mass 4 to 6 inches high,

covered in April and May with deep yellow flowers. A lovely plant for growing over a rock.

C. Carlieri.—Forms compact bush about 3 feet high. Erect spikes pale yellow flowers from July to October. One of the choicest Brooms.

C. Kewensis.—A hybrid raised at Kew. Prostrate, trailing habit. Creamy-white flowers in May in the utmost profusion. One of the most beautiful of dwarf Brooms.

C. praecox.—Grows about 5 feet high, but slowly. Another lovely Broom. Covered in May with pale primrose-coloured flowers, it is indeed a beautiful sight. Cuttings strike freely. There is a white form equally good.

C. schipkaensis.—Dwarf habit. Quantities of creamy-white flowers. A good plant.

C. scoparius.—The common yellow Broom has many lovely varieties: *andreana*, *pallidus*, *Firefly*, all lovely and completely smothering the bushes with the profusion of their flowers. There are many other varieties, but the above selection includes the best and dwarfer-growing kinds.

DALIBARDA (syn. RUBUS) REPENS (ROSACEAE)

Deep peaty soil in shade. Tufted, creeping plant, about 2 inches high. White shaded rose-coloured flowers in June. Slow growing. Hardy. Division.

DAPHNE (THYMELACEAE)

Shrubs of the highest value, some tall-growing, while others are quite dwarf. Beautiful and fragrant flowers. Not easy to keep in health.

D. alpina.—Loam and sand, shaded from mid-day sun. Low-branching shrub, seldom growing over 2 feet high. Fragrant yellowish-white flowers, borne in clusters on the sides of the branches from April to June; red berries in the autumn. This species does not dislike lime as much as some of the others do. Deciduous.

D. blagayana.—Peat and loam, cool, well-drained soil, in a rather shaded position. Prostrate habit and straggling growth. Leaves form rosettes at end of branches and encircle the dense clusters of creamy-white, most deliciously fragrant flowers. Blooms in April and May. Evergreen. Not very hardy, and, except in favoured localities, should have protection during the winter. Stones should be placed on all the prostrate branches to encourage them to layer, for, like all other Daphnes, it is liable to go off without any apparent reason. A most lovely plant, and worth considerable trouble to grow.

D. Cneorum.—Peaty and sandy soils. Spreading habit, growing only 10 to 12 inches high. Rosettes of small leaves and clusters of rosy-red flowers in the summer, and also very fragrant. Hardy Propagated by layers. This delightful evergreen shrub should also have stones placed on its prostrate growths. Difficult to keep in health, suddenly dying off without any apparent cause, but a gem amongst dwarf, shrubby plants. There is also a white form, *alba*, which is very lovely.

D. fioniana.—Loam and half-shady aspect. Compact evergreen shrub 2 to 3 feet high. Dark glossy leaves and rosy-coloured, sweet-scented flowers. Hardy, and not difficult to grow.

D. Genkwa.—Peaty loam and half shade. A small deciduous shrub of straggling growth. Greyish-coloured leaves and violet-coloured flowers in clusters before the leaves come. A rare plant, not hardy in cold districts.

D. Mezereum.—Light, warm soils. Erect habit, growing some 3 to 4 feet in height. Deciduous. Rosy-coloured, sweet-scented flowers in early spring before the leaves appear. A fairly common shrub in gardens. There is a white form which is prettier.

D. rupestris.—Peat and stones and silver sand in half-shady position. Compact, very slow-growing little shrub. Waxy-pink flowers in profusion. Hardy. One of the very choicest miniature shrubs.

Other varieties of Daphne, but of no special note, are—

D. Houtteana.—Grows 3 feet high. Small, dark purple flowers. Quite hardy.

D. striata.—Trailing habit. Sweet-scented, rosy-purple flowers in clusters. Quite hardy, and a useful and attractive shrub.

DARLINGTONIA CALIFORNICA (SARRACENIACEAE)

The Californian pitcher plant. Requires a wet bog in fibrous peat and sphagnum moss in sun. Pitchers rise as high as 2 feet. Not very hardy. Should be sheltered from cold winds.

DELPHINIUM (RANUNCULACEAE), Larkspur

A genus of tall-growing, herbaceous plants, of which there are few kinds suitable for the rock garden.

D. grandiflora.—In ordinary soil. Grows about 18 inches high, with very large, brilliant blue flowers. Easily raised from seed, which produce a variety of shades of blue. There is also a white form. They are very attractive plants, and should be used in masses.

D. nudicaule.—Dry, sunny position, and well drained. Beautiful orange-scarlet flowers, growing about 18 inches high. Not easy to grow, except in a fairly dry climate. Seed germinates freely.

D. tatsienense.—Light sandy loam in full sun. Grows about 12 to 18 inches. Numerous bright blue flowers on branching stems A most attractive plant of recent introduction.

DENTARIA (*see* CARDAMINE)

DIANTHUS (CARYOPHYLLACEAE), Pink

A large genus of neat-habited plants essentially suited for the rock garden. With few exceptions they are quite easy to grow. They mostly like sunny, open positions in light soil, with a little lime rubbish added. The wire-worm is a great enemy of this genus, and should be guarded against.

D. alpinus.—Open position in rather moist, light soil, but will not stand baking by the sun, so a half-shaded spot suits it best. It requires plenty of moisture during the growing season. Forms neat, compact tufts of dark glossy leaves. Large, handsome, carmine-rose-coloured flowers spotted with crimson, about 3 inches high, in June. Very floriferous. Easily raised from seed. A lovely little plant, and one of the best of the genus, but a little uncertain, going off suddenly without any apparent cause.

D. al. alba.—A white form of the above, but not as pretty as the original, the colour being rather a dirty white. Also a very free bloomer.

D. al. grandiflorus.—Is a new form of the type, claiming to have larger and deeper-coloured flowers and to be of more robust constitution.

D. Atkinsoni.—Light sandy soil. This is a hybrid, and about the most brilliant-coloured of the genus. Spikes of flowers of the richest crimson imaginable, and so very floriferous that it generally blooms itself to death, putting all its vigour into the flower-spikes and making no "grass." It is advisable, therefore, to keep a stock plant, cutting off all bloom-spikes, or to group several plants together in the garden, only allowing some of them to flower in the same season.

D. arenarius.—Requires a very dry, sandy, and sunny position. A compact little plant, with numerous white, deeply fringed flowers, with a carmine blotch at the base of petals. Blooms in May and June.

D. arvenensis.—Delights in a sunny chink amongst rock, in sandy loam. Compact little cushions of glaucous leaves and rose-coloured flowers. A diminutive form of *D. caesius*, and very pretty.

D. caesius.—Old walls or sunny fissures in limy, sandy, poor soil. Compact tufts of glaucous leaves and clouds of rosy-pink flowers, on stems about 6 inches long. Blooms in the summer. The native cheddar pink, growing freely from seed, which should be sown on old walls and amongst rocks. One of the prettiest and easiest grown.

D. callizonus. — Rather cool, very well-drained, sandy loam, amongst stone and rocks. Dwarf-growing, with broad, greyish leaves, and of rather spreading habit. Large, brilliant pink flowers, with a dark belt of crimson at base, about 4 inches high. A most lovely and difficult plant to grow, going off in that unaccountable manner so characteristic of many of the alpine pinks. Easily raised from seed when it can be obtained ; but it ripens it but sparingly. Keep well watered during growing season.

D. cal. alpinus.—Is a hybrid of the above with *alpinus*, and is of more robust constitution.

D. cruentus.—Light gritty, sandy loam, in sun. Foliage rather sparse. Deep crimson flowers in crowded heads on stems about 12 inches high. Very easily grown and raised from seed.

D. deltoides.—Will grow almost anywhere in light sandy soil. Forms spreading mats, about 2 inches high, of smooth, blunt leaves. Flowers very numerous, on branching stems about 8 inches high, either rosy-pink or white, with a crimson base and petals. Comes very freely from seed. Easily grown, and apparently not affected by the wire-worm. Flowers nearly all the summer. Young plants are best, as when old they are apt to get ragged in growth. Very pretty and useful species. *Superbus* is a bright ruby-red variety and very pretty.

D. Fischeri.—Half-shady position in rather moist, gritty loam. Light, rose-coloured, solitary flowers, 3 to 4 inches high, freely produced in the summer.

D. Freynii.—Peaty, gritty loam, without lime, in a cool, well-drained corner. Glaucous foliage and large rosy-purple flowers. Dwarf of habit, and difficult to grow.

D. fragrans.—Light sandy loam, in sun. Fragrant white flowers, deeply fringed. Pretty and compact-growing.

D. glacialis.—Crevices of rockwork in half-shady corner. It requires cool, peaty, and leaf-mould soil mixed with granite chips. It very much dislikes lime. Forms compact tufts of narrow leaves, and during the summer numerous pink flowers rather smaller than *D. alpinus*. A pretty and attractive little plant, very difficult to cultivate. Requires plenty of moisture during the growing season.

D. g. gelidus.—Of much the same habit, and requires similar treatment as *D. glacialis*. Pure pink flowers, white spotted at the throat.

D. Knappii.—Light sandy soil and lime rubbish. In position not fully exposed to the sun. Heads of sulphur-coloured flowers on prostrate stems, about 12 inches long. Distinct on account of the colour of its flowers, but is a ragged and weak-growing plant of but secondary beauty and little value. Grows freely from seed.

D. monspessulanus.—Sandy loam in sun. Pink fringed flowers on slender stems about 12 inches long, rather similar to *D. superbus.* A pretty and useful plant. Varieties of above are *albus* and *dependens.*

D. neglectus. — Light sandy loam and lime rubbish, in sun. Compact tufts of grass-like, wiry, glaucous leaves about 2 inches high, from which rise on slender stems, about 3 inches long, numerous bright rosy-pink flowers, having the undersides buff-coloured. Blooms from June to September. Comes very readily from seed, though by this means the colour of the blooms is apt to vary somewhat as to shade. *D. neglectus* is the gem of the genus. Lovely and dainty in appearance, and of the easiest culture, it should be freely grown, and can be associated with the choicest plants.

D. petraeus.—Dry, sunny position in sandy, limy loam. Compact, hard tufts of narrow, sharp-pointed leaves, 1 to 2 inches high. Rosy-white, solitary flowers. Hardy, and of easy culture.

D. plumarius.—Sandy soil on sloping bank. The original from which many of the garden pinks were raised. It has pink and fragrant flowers, is easily grown, and is useful for massing in the less choice parts.

D. Robinsonii.—Sandy loam, in sun. An attractive hybrid, bearing, on 12-inch stems, large double salmon-pink flowers of a most delicate shade. A most persistent bloomer, being in flower for about nine months of the year. Of easy culture, and quite hardy.

D. sylvestris.— Open, sunny position in dry, stony, and sandy loam. Flat tufts of rather sparse leaves, and on stems 6 to 8 inches long two or three rosy-pink flowers. A lovely species, but having the same characteristic of some of the alpine pinks of dying off without warning.

D. suavis.—Sandy loam, in any situation. Should be planted to fall over the face of a rock. Forms rapidly spreading, compact mats of stiff, grass-like leaves, from which spring countless small white, rather flat-shaped flowers, borne singly on slender stems, and about 6 inches long. Quite hardy, and easily increased by rooted layers. Quite one of the best, although not as brilliant as some. Its delightful habit of growth would give it a place in the front rank.

These comprise about the best and most distinctive varieties of Dianthus, for although there are many others, they have more a botanical than garden value. New hybrids are constantly being advertised in catalogues, some of which are acquisitions. There are also numerous garden hybrids, pinks rather stronger-growing than most of the above, but in the larger rock gardens should be used in big masses. The following are some good kinds :—" *Her Majesty*," large white ; " *Mrs Simkins*," well known, fragrant white pink ; " *Nellie* " ; " *Edmond Matthewii*," crimson, with a darker crimson blotch, very handsome ; " *Princess May*," apricot pink ; and many others.

DIAPENSIA LAPPONICA (DIAPENSIACEAE)

A rare little evergreen shrub of very dwarf habit. Requires damp, peaty, and gritty soil in open position. It grows in dense, rounded tufts, with narrow leaves, 1 to 2 inches high. Cup-shaped, solitary flowers, pearly-white, with yellow stamens, in the summer. Hardy, but not easy to cultivate. Easily raised from seed.

DIASCIA BARBARA (SCROPHULARIACEAE)

The only representative of the genus. Ordinary soil in any position. Grows about 4 to 6 inches high. Flowers salmon pink, freely produced. Spreads freely underground. It is in flower practically the whole year. It is reputed to be only half-hardy, but I have never found it suffer in the least, although it has been exposed to very hard frosts. Increased readily by division. A most attractive and uncommon plant.

DICENTRA (syn. DIELYTRA) (PAPAVERACEAE)

A genus of graceful-growing plants, useful for wilder part of the rock garden. The following are a selection of the best kinds :—

D. canadensis.—Grows about 6 inches high. Flowers white, in May. Leaves glaucous.

D. eximia.—Shady position, rich, sandy soil. Pretty, fern-like foliage. Grows 12 to 18 inches high. Reddish-purple flowers, borne in long drooping racemes.

D. formosa.—Dwarfer-growing form of the above, with lighter-coloured flowers. Requires same treatment and position.

D. spectabilis.—A well-known plant, with its pink heart-shaped blooms, which give it the popular name of " the bleeding heart."

DIPHYLLEIA CYMOSA (BERBERIDACEAE), Umbrella Leaf

A dwarf plant, growing about 9 inches high, of the Barberry family. It likes very moist peat and is suitable for edges of streams or in the bog garden. Large, umbrella-like leaves, arranged in pairs, and loose clusters of white flowers, in June, succeeded by dark blue berries.

DODECATHEON (PRIMULACEAE), American Cowslip

Attractive and distinct plants, very closely allied to the Primulas. They are all of easy culture in cool, half-shady, and rather moist, sandy, and leafy soil. They all have clusters of flowers like Cyclamens, borne on the top of upright stems.

D. Hendersoni.—Clusters of Cyclamen-like, rich, deep, crimson flowers, on stems about 12 inches high.

D. integrifolia.—Moist, peaty loam and stone chips in half shade in the bog garden. Tufts of small, rather oval, and entire leaves. Clusters of rosy-crimson flowers, on stems 4 to 6 inches high, in early summer. This is the best of the genus and the most difficult to cultivate. Easily raised from seed, which it ripens freely.

D. Jeffreyi.—Has larger and thicker leaves than the type, and of a darker green. Flowers rich, dark rose colour, borne on stems 18 inches to 2 feet high. The largest of the genus, and a good plant for a sheltered spot in the bog garden, where its big leaves will not be torn by the wind.

D. Meadia (Shooting Star).—Varies a good deal in the colour of its flowers, in shades varying from lilac to purplish-rose. Quite hardy, and of easy culture and readily grown from seed. This well-known plant should find a place in every bog garden.

DONDIA EPIPACTUS (syn. HACQUETIA)

A dwarf-growing plant about 4 inches high, very distinctive on account of the bright yellow involucre which surrounds its rather insignificant greenish-yellow flowers. It is quite hardy, and easily grown in stiff loam, and is one of our earliest plants to flower.

DOUGLASIA LAEVIGATA (PRIMULACEAE)

Gritty loam in open position. Closely allied to the Androsaces. Of dwarf and tufted habit, bearing bright carmine flowers. One of the gems for the rock garden.

DRABA (CRUCIFERAE), Whitlow Grass

A genus of minute plants, with white or yellow flowers, requiring sandy soil in full sun, and should be associated with the dwarfest-growing plants.

D. aizoides.—Sandy soil on a sunny bank. Forms dense little tufts about 3 inches high. Slow to increase. Flowers freely produced, and of a bright yellow colour, in March. Increased by division and seed.

D. Aizoon.—Sun, in sandy soil. Forms compact rosettes of dark green, stiff little leaves, with small, bright yellow flowers, on 3-inch stems. A pretty and very early-flowering little plant, of easy culture, and readily raised from seed, which it ripens freely.

18

D. alpina.—Well-drained chinks in the rock garden, in light soil, and sun. Grows about 2 inches high. Dark green leaves and bright golden flowers. A delicate and difficult plant to grow. The attacks of slugs should be guarded against. Nearly allied to this is *D. aurea*, with taller-growing flowers, and less compact habit.

D. ciliata.—Has white, diminutive flowers. Growth only about 2 inches high.

D. cinerea (syn. *D. borealis*). — Good white flowers, and dark green leaves, of free-growing habit. Seeds and division. Biennal.

D. cuspidata.—Very small tufts of dark green ciliated leaves, and yellow flowers, in March. Increased by seed.

D. grandiflora.—The largest-growing of the genus, with white flowers.

D. imbricata.—Forms dense green carpet from which rise tiny yellow blossoms on threadlike stems 3 inches high. Flowers in spring. Very dainty.

Other varieties, all of very diminutive growth, are—*D. bruniæfolia, ciliaris, Kotschyi, Olympica,* and *rigida,* all bearing yellow flowers. Those with white flowers are — *D. bryoides, Mawii, nivalis,* and *salamoni.*

DRACOCEPHALUM (LABIATAE), Dragon's Head

This genus, though generally considered herbaceous plants, give a few varieties suitable for the rock garden. They can all be increased by seed or division.

D. grandiflorum (syn. *D. altaicense.*)—Requires very well-drained, sandy loam. Of rather compact, shrubby habit, growing only about 8 to 12 inches high. Narrow, greyish leaves, and handsome blue flowers, in early summer, in whorled spikes not very easy to grow in any but a dry climate. Young plants should be protected from the attacks of slugs. Increased by division.

D. Ruyschiana.—Light sandy soil, well drained, on elevated spots. Spreading, rather prostrate habit, of fairly rapid growth. Rosy-purple flowers, freely produced in late summer. Increased by seed or division. *Japonica* is a deeper and better-coloured form of this, and altogether a finer plant.

Other suitable varieties, all requiring the same conditions as to soil and position, are—

D. austriacum.—Large blue flowers, in whorled spikes.

D. botroides.—Purple flowers in June.

D. speciosum.—Grows about 18 inches high, with pink and blue flowers, in July.

DROSERA (DROSERACEAE), Sundew

Interesting little sundews for the bog garden, growing them in wet sphagnum moss. Besides our native kinds, *D. intermedia*, *D. longifolia*, and *D. obovate*, we should try the North American sundew, *D. filiformis*, with its rose-purple-coloured flowers, and glandular, hairy leaves. It is quite hardy, but difficult to cultivate even in wet sphagnum moss.

DRYAS (ROSACEAE)

A small genus of woody, spreading plants of much beauty and value.

D. octopetala (syn. *D. integrifolia*).—Mountain Avens. Sunny slopes, peaty loam, well drained, yet rather moist. Likes limestone. Of close, prostrate, creeping habit, free-growing, and forming a carpet of dark green leaves, which in winter turn brown, looking as if the plant had died. Large creamy-white flowers, with yellow stamens like the Burnet rose. Profusion of blooms in summer, followed by fluffy-headed seed-vessels, like those of the "traveller's joy" clematis. A native, and quite hardy, and of easy culture. Increased by layers and seed. One of the gems for the rock garden, which should be freely grown, not alone on account of its flowers, but also for the fluffy seed-vessels.

The variety *minor* is dwarfer and more dense in growth ; also a treasure.

D. Drummondii.—Requires same treatment as above, which it exactly resembles, except that it has pale yellow flowers, which, however, have the reputation of not opening.

D. lanata.—Poor stony soil on sunny slopes. Small silvery leaves. Creamy-white flowers, smaller and in greater profusion than *D. octopetala*, of which it may be regarded as practically a miniature form. A really good plant.

D. tenella is a rare species from Labrador, rather similar to *octopetala*.

EDRIANTHUS (*see* WAHLENBERGIA)

EMPETRUM NIGRIUM (EMPETRACEAE), Crowberry

Dwarf evergreen shrub, growing about 12 inches high. Like a heath, it has black berries. *Rubrum* has red berries. Both of easiest culture in damp, peaty soil, and may be used with the dwarfer shrubs. Evergreen.

EPIGAEA REPENS (ERICACEAE)

A small, trailing evergreen shrub. Requires shelter from cold winds in a shady position, in peaty, fibrous loam and sand. Very pretty, fragrant, rose-coloured flowers in terminal racemes in early spring. Difficult to grow. Grows wild in parts of North America in sandy, rocky soil, under the shade of pines.

EPILOBIUM (ONAGRACEAE) "Willow Herb"

Few of this genus are suitable, being generally of too coarse and rank a growth. Increased by seed and division.

E. Dodonaei (syn. *E. Fleischeri*).—Sandy, gritty soil. Of rather shrubby habit, with rosy-red flowers in July. Pretty and useful.

E. nummularifolium.—Of creeping habit and very rapid growth. Pale pink flowers. As it spreads rapidly, it should be given plenty of room.

E. obcordatum. — Also of creeping habit and rapid growth. Cherry-pink flowers. Looks well planted to fall over a stone. Requires a moist, well-drained spot.

EPIMEDIUM (BERBERIDACEAE), Barrenwort

A genus of perennial plants, with pretty foliage, and suitable for associating with the dwarfer shrubs. They all grow about 12 inches high, with pretty, though not striking flowers, which are half hidden by the foliage. They should be grouped together in peaty soil in shade, in which position they should thrive well and give a pleasing effect. The following are a good selection :—

E. alpinum.—Flowers crimson and yellow.

E. coccineum.—Red flowers ; foliage turns red in autumn.

E. niveum.—White.

E. roseum.—Rose-coloured.

E. rubrum.—Dark red.

E. sulphurium.—Yellow.

EPIPACTIS PALUSTRIS (ORCHIDACEAE)

A hardy orchid, with handsome, slightly drooping flowers, whitish, tinged crimson. Spreads fairly rapidly underground. Thrives in any moist, peaty soil. A good plant for the bog garden. Blooms in July.

ERANTHIS HYEMALIS (RANUNCULACEAE), Winter Aconite

This well-known "harbinger of spring" needs no description. Patches of it, if planted in odd corners, will brighten our rock garden with its yellow blossoms in January.

ERICA (ERICACEAE), Heath

A large genus of well-known shrubs, some growing into almost trees, while others are prostrate, shrubby plants. They all require peaty soil and hate lime in any form. The following are the dwarfer kinds suitable for the rock garden :—

E. carnea.—Prostrate-growing, delightful little plant, gladdening our hearts with its rosy-pink flowers in January. A well-known plant, which should be freely grown. There is a white form, *E. c. alba*, equally attractive, blooming at the same time. It also goes by the name of *E. herbacea*.

E. cinerea.—Rather taller-growing than the last. Flowers vary considerably in shades of white and pink. Amongst its varieties are *alba, bicolor, coccinea, purpurea*, and *rosea*.

E. lusitanica (syn. *E. codonodes*).—A lovely shrub, often growing 4 feet high. White flowers tipped with pink, borne in wreaths during the winter. Perfectly hardy, and a precious shrub, and quite one of the prettiest and best.

E. mediterranea.—A lovely, peat-loving shrub, growing 3 to 5 feet high, flowering in spring.

E. Tetralix.—The well-known bell-heather, growing in moist, boggy places on our moors. It will also do in ordinary garden soil.

E. vulgaris (syn. *Calluna vulgaris*).—The well-known common "Ling," and, being quite indifferent to soil, may be used for the wilder parts of the rock garden. There are many varieties, some of which are of little value. The best are *E. v. alba, pilosa, Alportii rubra* and *rosea, serlei, hypnoides, pygmea, tenella*, and *tomentosa*.

E. dabaecia (syn. *Menziesia polifolia*).—A lovely shrub, growing 18 inches to 2 feet high, and found wild in the west of Ireland. It does best in a partially shaded position in peaty loam. Bears during the summer and autumn a profusion of large drooping bells, borne in racemes of a crimson-purple colour. There are few more beautiful shrubs grown. There are several varieties : *alba*, a white one, even prettier than the type. A deeper-coloured form, *atropurpurea* ; and one with purple and white flowers, called *bicolor*.

E. Veitchii is a cross between *E. lusitanica* and *arborea*, and is well worth growing and quite hardy.

ERIGERON (COMPOSITAE)

A genus of plants with large daisy-like flowers, resembling the Michaelmas daisies. Only the dwarfer kinds are suitable for growing in the rock garden. The following are a selection, all of which are of easy culture in a half-shady position in good loam.

E. alpinus.—Like an inferior *Aster alpinus*. Pale blue flowers.

But the variety, *grandiflorum*, is good, with large, deep blue, daisy-like flowers.

E. aurantiacus.—Large orange-coloured flowers. Floriferous and pretty.

E. Coulteri.—Large white flowers, with golden centres. Blooms late into the autumn. A handsome plant.

E. glaucus.—Smooth glaucous leaves. Large deep lavender-coloured flowers, from July to October.

E. leiomerus.—Small tufted species. Narrow grey-green leaves, and lovely pale violet-blue flowers. Quite one of the best of the genus and quite hardy and easily grown.

E. mucronatus (syn. *Vittadenia triloba*).—Prostrate and much-branched habit, bearing a profusion of white, small, daisy-like flowers the whole summer. A very charming plant, of rapid growth. Easily raised from seed. Quite indifferent to soil or aspect. Not very hardy.

E. Roylei.—Dwarf tufted habit. Bluish-purple flowers, with a yellow centre. Very pretty.

E. trifidus.—Small blue flowers. Dwarf habit, only growing 3 to 4 inches high. Rather a distinct plant.

Of the taller-growing kinds, the following are all good :— *E. glabellus*, lilac flowers ; *E. salsuginosus*, pale lilac flowers ; and *E. speciosus splendens*, with deep lilac-coloured flowers.

ERINUS ALPINUS (SCROPHULARIACEAE)

A pretty little plant, admirable for growing in old walls and in any odd chink, or for crevices between steps. Forms very dwarf tufts of downy, toothed leaves. Rosy-purple flowers in racemes the whole summer. There is a white form, and also a very hairy form, *hirsuta*.

ERIOGONUM UMBELLATUM (POLYGONACEAE)

Small shrubby plant. Requires a sunny position in sandy loam. Forms a dense, spreading tuft, with numerous yellow flowers in umbels, borne on stems 4 to 8 inches high. Quite hardy, and blooms profusely during the autumn. Seed or division.

Eriogynia Pectinata

A distinct plant, nearly allied to the Spiraeas. It is an evergreen of trailing, tufted habit, spreading by means of slender stolons. Bright green, ferny foliage. White flowers in terminal spikes. Likes a shady corner in good sandy loam. A pretty little plant.

Eritrichium nanum (Boraginaceae)

An alpine gem, which so far has defeated all efforts to cultivate with any degree of success. Its needs, though few, are difficult to supply. No moisture during the winter, while during the spring and summer it requires moisture at its roots, but none on its leaves. This, though it may sound simple, is not so easy to supply. The following method may be tried. Plant in a mixture of coarse sand, grit, and granite dust, and a little fibrous peat, under some overhanging rock fully exposed to the sun. Round the neck of the plant sink pieces of slate in such a way that the moisture from the overhanging ledge is directed towards the roots of the plant, and also place stones on the surface of the ground to keep its leaves dry. It makes tufts of tiny little woolly leaves, from which in spring rise, in the greatest profusion, diminutive flowers of the most dazzling azure-blue, with a yellow eye. A gem indeed, and worth any amount of trouble to obtain success.

Erodium (Geraniaceae), Heron's Bill

Dwarf-growing plants of the Geranium order, requiring warm, dry, sunny spots. All very lovely, and worth growing in the choicer parts of the garden.

E. guttatum.—Pretty silvery, fern-like foliage, forming a neat tuft, with pure white flowers veined with purple, borne on slender, branching stems. A dainty and attractive plant, but not very robust.

E. macradenum.—Dwarf-growing. Violet-pink flowers with deep purple markings, borne on stems about 4 inches high, in June and July.

E. cheilanthifolium.—Fern-like leaves, with dark veining on its white petals.

E. chrysanthum.—Has sulphur-coloured flowers.

E. corsicum.—Dwarf habit. Soft round leaves. Flower pink. Gritty soil in dry position.

E. olympicum.—Of rather bushy habit. Silvery foliage. Loose heads of delicate pink flowers. Very lovely.

E. pelargonifolium.—Sunny position in light gritty soil. Of rather prostrate habit. Flowers white, marked with purplish-red. This species rather resembles the greenhouse Pelargoniums both as to flower and leaf. Rather a tender plant, liable to die off in the winter, and possibly for this reason is not as much used as it deserves to be.

E. petraeum.—Warm and dry chinks. Grows about 5 inches high, with smoothish, pinnate leaves, and purple flowers in June.

E. Reichardi (syn. *E. chamaedryoides*).—Very dwarf-growing, making flat tufts of little heart-shaped leaves, and solitary white flowers, very faintly veined with pink. Likes moist, sandy soil. A wee, dainty plant.

E. supracanum.—This plant has hoary leaves and bright pink flowers. Very lovely.

ERYSIMUM (CRUCIFERAE), Hedge Mustard

Very similar, but not so good as Wallflowers. The best of the genus are—

E. comatum.—Narrow, silvery foliage and yellow flowers.

E. linifolium.—Lilac flowers. Very profuse bloomer, and free grower. About the best of the genus.

E. pulchellum (syn. *E. rupestre*).—Blooms profusely in spring and autumn, and has bright golden-yellow flowers.

E. rhaeticum.—Densely tufted, covered with clear yellow flowers in early summer. They all like dry and sunny positions in well-drained, gritty soil. Increased by seed.

ERPETION RENIFORME (syn. VIOLA HEDERACEA)

A small and delicate little plant, only half hardy, covering the ground with a mass of small leaves, and has slender, creeping stems. Blue and white flowers, very pretty, and only about 2 inches high. It likes a shady position in good sandy loam. Except in a warm climate, it will require to be lifted in the autumn and taken into a cold house.

ERYTHRAEA (GENTIANACEAE)

A genus of pretty, dwarf-growing plants with pink flowers. They like a partial shady position. Increased by seed. The two best are—

E. diffusa.—A rapid grower, with pink blossoms in summer in great profusion.

E. Muhlenbergi.—Grows about 8 inches high, with a profusion of flowers, about 3½ inches across, of a deep pink colour, with a greenish-white star in the centre. Blooms in the spring.

ERYTHRONIUM (LILIACEAE)

The " Dog's-tooth " Violet, a well-known genus of bulbous plants of the easiest culture, and may be planted in odd nooks in the rock garden. A selection can be made from any bulb catalogue.

FRAGARIA MONOPHYLLA (ROSACEAE), Alpine Strawberry

This form of the wild strawberry, with its large white flowers, is a pretty plant for the rock garden, to cover some waste bank.

F. indica.—Is a pretty trailer, flowering later, and has golden-yellow flowers and red, insipid fruit.

FRITILLARIA (LILIACEAE), Fritillary

These distinct and graceful bulbous plants, though not strictly rock plants, can be grouped with good effect in shady corners, in rich, well-drained soil. There are a great number of species, of which a selection should be made.

FUCHSIA (ONAGRACEAE)

A genus of shrubs which are hardy only in a warm climate or near the sea. There are many lovely varieties, but, being so delicate, cannot be generally used.

F. procumbens.—Sunny position in light sandy soil. A trailing species, with erect, yellowish-green flowers and large purple berries. Only half hardy.

F. pumila.—A dainty, dwarf, erect-growing shrub, bearing a profusion of crimson flowers in the summer. Needs protection in the winter.

GALAX APHYLLA (DIAPENSIACEAE)

An evergreen perennial plant with a creeping rootstock. It should be planted in moist, sandy, peaty loam, in partial shade. The round, shiny leaves, on slender stalks, in autumn and winter, assume a brilliant crimson colour if planted in a position exposed to the sun. In June appears a wand-like spike of small white flowers about 12 inches high. Hardy, and easily grown in the raised parts of the bog garden. Increased by division. A very pretty subject.

GAULTHERIA (ERICACEAE)

A large genus of low-growing, evergreen shrubs for the peat bed. The following are the most suitable :—

G. procumbens (Creeping Wintergreen).—Moist peat or loam, in half shade. A pretty, very dwarf-growing evergreen shrub. Procumbent habit, forming dense masses, about 6 inches high, of shining leaves, and in June small, pendulous, white flowers, succeeded by red berries. Quite hardy, and increased by division. An attractive little shrub for a moist spot.

G. nummularioides.—Moist peat and sand, in half shade. A small, evergreen, creeping shrub, about 4 inches high, with wiry stems. White, Lily-of-the-valley-like flowers, tinged pink, in summer, succeeded by scarlet fruit.

G. tricophylla.—Moist, peaty, and stony soil, in half shade. Compact grower, forming tufts of box-like dark green leaves margined with minute hairs. Pinky-white, small, bell-shaped flowers, in summer, followed by large, indigo-blue berries. Quite hardy, and propagated by division. A very pretty little creeping shrub. It is a good plan to plant it in a slight saucer-shaped hollow amongst stones. The berries are most attractive.

G. Shallon.—A coarse-growing, evergreen shrub, with dark green leaves, so not particular as to soil. Useful for planting under trees in the wilder parts, but too rampant a grower for the choicer parts. White flowers and purple berries.

GAZANIA (COMPOSITAE)

A genus of very handsome plants, which unfortunately are not quite hardy, but can easily be propagated by cuttings, made from the side shoots near base of plant. These should be taken in July or August, never in the spring, and inserted in sandy loam in a close frame.

They all require a position in full sun, in light sandy loam and peat.

G. bracteata (syn. *G. nivea*).—Leaves 5 to 8 inches long, grown in the form of a rosette. Flowers 2 inches across, white, with a yellow disk.

G. b. grandiflora.—A hybrid, *G. bracteata* × *G. splendens.*

G. montana.—Prostrate habit. Flowers pale yellow.

G. pygmaea.—Dwarf habit. Flowers small, white, with a purplish band.

G. Pavonia. — Grows about 18 inches high. Leaves hairy. Flowers yellow, with a brown spot at base, with a green tinge. Blooms in July. A handsome plant.

G. rigens.—Grows about 12 inches high. Leaves spatulate and hairy. Flowers of a brilliant golden colour, in June.

G. splendens.—Trailing habit. Leaves a silky white beneath. Flowers brilliant orange colour, with a black and white spot at the base of each ray-floret. Blooms July to October.

G. uniflora.—Decumbent habit, shrubby growth. Leaves downy beneath. Flowers yellow. Blooms July and August.

There are also several hybrids of garden origin, some with variegated leaves.

GENISTA (LEGUMINOSAE)

A genus of shrubs very nearly allied to the Cytisus ; in fact it is not easy to distinguish one from the other. They all grow easily in any dry, sandy loam, and are very useful and attractive. They are a numerous genus, and the following is a selection of the dwarfer and most suitable kinds. The tall-growing varieties can be used with good effect for massing with other shrubs.

G. anglica.—A dwarf-growing, native shrub, seldom reaching 2 feet in height. The yellow flowers in leafy racemes appear in June and July.

G. anxsantica.—Very similar to the native *G. tinctora.* Its yellow flowers appear in late summer.

G. germanica.—Grows about 18 inches to 2 feet, with arching branches and yellow flowers produced in summer and autumn. A useful shrub. Very pretty.

G. hispanica (Spanish Gorse).—A most useful, very compact, dwarf, evergreen shrub, only growing some 12 to 18 inches high, with a profusion of yellow flowers the whole summer.

G. pilosa.—A dense, prostrate-growing shrub for dry, gravelly soils, and yellow flowers very freely borne in May and June.

G. prostrata.—A creeping shrub, scarcely more than 2 inches high. Yellow flowers very freely produced during the early summer. A very useful and attractive evergreen shrub for growing over stones or banks. One of the best.

G. radiata.—Evergreen, much-branched spiny shrub, growing 3 to 4 feet high, and a wealth of yellow flowers during the summer. Hardy, and one of the best and most useful of the genus.

G. sagittalis.—A creeping shrub about 6 inches high. Very distinct, with peculiar winged stems and a profusion of rich yellow flowers. A shrub more peculiar than attractive.

G. tinctoria, fl. pl.—A compact, dwarf-growing, deciduous shrub, about 12 inches high, of spreading habit and fairly rapid growth. Profusion of yellow flowers in the summer. Very useful and attractive. There is a single form, but the double is the better of the two.

GENTIANA (GENTIANACEAE), Gentian

A very numerous genus of mountain plants, amongst which are some gems for the rock garden. I shall deal only with the perennial, for although there are many annual and biennial kinds, their beauty is of too fleeting a nature to be suitable for our purpose. The perennial kinds are, unfortunately, all somewhat unreliable in cultivation, growing like weeds in some places, while in others, under apparently similar conditions, unaccountably pining away in a short time. They all exceedingly dislike disturbance, and drought at certain times of the year is fatal to them.

G. acaulis (" Gentianella ").—South-east or south-westerly aspect, on slight slope. Loam, plentifully mixed with limestone and gravel, and well drained, though not so as to render the soil very dry. It forms a dense carpet of compact tufts of glossy green leaves, from which rise large tubular, deep blue flowers, in the spring and summer. Quite hardy, and increased by division. This plant is the well-known "Gentianella," than which no more lovely plant can be found in the rock garden. It is, however, very uncertain in cultivation, for while in some places it will grow and flower freely without the least trouble, in others no amount of care will make it thrive. One thing specially to observe is to plant it deep and as firmly as possible : to this particular attention should be paid. With me, a gravel walk is what it revels in. It is also a good plan to put chips of stones over the surface of the ground, which helps to retain the necessary moisture, and amongst which its shoots like to ramble. If the weather be very dry during the spring and summer, it should be watered freely. It is difficult to lay down any rules for its cultivation, for what appears to suit it in one garden will not do so in another ; but if the above directions are carried out, there is every reason to expect success. There is also a white form, which is not so pretty as the type.

Very nearly akin to *G. acaulis*, and which may almost be taken as varieties of it, are *alpina*, which is rather smaller. *Angustifolia*, deep blue throat and spotted with green. *Clusii*, very similar to *alpina*, has lanceolate leaves and very dark blue flowers. *Coelestina*, sky-blue, with interior of throat white. *Kochiana*, elliptic-shaped leaves and flowers spotted with black. All like a limestone soil, except the last-named, which requires a soil free of it.

G. altiaca.—Ordinary soil. Open position. Head of blue flowers. Prostrate habit. A new species from Altai Mountains. Easily increased by seed.

G. angulosa.—In form very similar to *G. verna*, though more robust and having rather taller-growing flowers. A very persistent bloomer.

G. asclepiadea (Willow Gentian).—Rather moist loam. Sheltered position in partial shade. A tall-growing, deciduous species, reaching 3 feet. Numerous large deep blue flowers on willow-like spikes. Quite hardy, and easily cultivated. This is rather more of a herbaceous than a rock garden plant. There is a very handsome white form.

G. bavarica.—Requires sunny position in sandy peat, very wet, though thoroughly drained. Such a spot as the banks of a tiny stream should suit it. Forms close, dense tufts, with very small, box-like leaves of a yellowish-green. Deep sapphire-blue flowers, rather larger than *G. verna*, borne in profusion. It is a very difficult plant to grow, but a gem withal.

G. brachyphylla.—Likes limestone soil in sun. Tufted, compact habit, with flowers slightly paler in shade than *G. verna*. Fairly easy to grow.

G. ciliata.—Sunny, well-drained position in fibrous loam mixed with broken limestone. Grows about 12 to 18 inches high, with large, solitary flowers deeply fringed, and of a fine azure-blue colour. Requires to be kept rather dry during the winter. It is not an easy plant to cultivate.

G. decumbens.—Should have a sunny position in rather moist, gritty loam. Prostrate stems with numerous flowers of a fine blue colour, borne in terminal spikes. Blooms in July and August. It is of comparatively easy culture and quite hardy. There is also a white form of good colour.

G. Favrata.—Sun in moist, stony peat and loam. Forms compact tufts, and has large deep blue flowers. It is a natural hybrid between *bavarica* and *verna*, and is of fairly easy culture.

G. freyniana.—Sandy loam in half shade. The clusters of brilliant blue flowers are freely borne in July. Rather an uncommon species, but very lovely, and not specially difficult to grow.

G. Kurroo.—Sunny position ; sandy peat and leaf-soil mixed with pieces of stone. Rosettes of smooth leaves about 4 inches high. Branching stems, with flowers of brilliant azure-blue, in July and August. Fairly easy to cultivate.

G. ornata.—Cool gritty loam or moraine. Forms a fairly compact carpet of dark green leaves. Flowers a lovely shade of pale blue inside, the outside of the corolla tube a rich chocolate purple striped with ivory yellow. A recent introduction from the Himalayas. A glorious plant, which does not appear difficult to grow and should prove a valuable acquisition.

G. Pneumonanthe.—Moist, peaty loam, in sun. Grows about 6 inches high, of a fine blue colour. A native, and of easy culture. It is well worth a spot in the rock garden.

G. Przewalskii.—Moist loam and peat. Sun. Forms loose tufts of long, narrow leaves. Prostrate stems and deep blue flowers in clusters. Not very free-flowering. Easy to cultivate and readily raised from seed. A delightful plant, which should be freely grown. It blooms in July.

G. pyrenaica.—Full sun, in moist peat and loam. Procumbent habit. Forms tufts of narrow, sharp-pointed leaves. Dark violet, almost stalkless flowers. It is a difficult species to grow, but one of the best.

G. septemfida.—Requires full sun, in moist, sandy peat and loam. Bears flowers in clusters on stems about 9 inches high. Blue and white inside, and brown outside. Of fairly easy culture in a cool, moist position. A very lovely plant, flowering in August.

G. verna.—Requires sun, in moist, peaty loam and limestone chips. Forms compact tufts about 1½ inches high, from which spring flowers about 3 inches high, of the most dazzling azure-blue. Seed and division. A lovely little gem, and one of the choicest rock plants, but, though a native, is not easy to keep when grown in the garden. Good tufts of it, to start with, are essential, and copious waterings during the spring and early summer. It likes very fibrous loam, so a good plan is to half bury a sod of turf, grass side down, and plant the Gentian in it. Firm planting is also very important ; after the winter's frost it is well to go round and press the plants firmly home. Protecting the plants with glass during the winter has proved effective in promoting growth and flowers. It is so lovely that no trouble should be spared to endeavour to grow it, trying it in different positions. South-east is a good aspect.

This completes the selection of the dwarf choicer varieties of Gentians. There are many others also of low-growing habit, but they are either very nearly akin to *G. acaulis* or *G. verna*, without having their brilliancy of flower, so are scarcely worth growing, except in a botanical collection. Of the taller and coarser-growing varieties, most of which, though easy of culture, are only suitable for the rougher parts, the following are the most showy of this description :—*G. Andrewsii, Burseri, lutea, saponaria,* all require moist loam and bear blue flowers, with the exception of *lutea,* which has yellow blossoms, and is the strongest-growing of the genus, reaching 3 feet in height.

GERANIUM (GERANIACEAE), Crane's Bill

A genus of showy perennials, but too strong-growing for the rock garden, with the exception of the following. They are all of easy culture in sandy, well-drained loam, and are not particular as to aspect, provided they get a fair amount of sun. Propagated by seed and division.

G. argenteum.—Grows about 6 inches high, with silvery-grey leaves and large, pale rose-coloured flowers. A charming, compact-growing plant, flowering in June ; it should have a place amongst the choicest plants.

G. cinereum. — A dwarf, compact-growing plant, with silvery leaves and pink flowers veined with red. Quite a vigorous grower, easily increased by seed or division. A very good plant for a choice spot in the sun.

G. Endressi.—A useful plant, growing 9 to 12 inches high, with rose-pink flowers freely produced during the summer.

G. Traversii.—Of prostrate habit, forming, by means of trailing stems, a dense carpet of grey hairy foliage from which rise large rose-pink flowers on slender stems ; these are very freely produced during the summer. A recent and valuable introduction from the New Zealand Alps, and one that should be found in all rock gardens.

G. sanguineum.—A close-growing plant, about 18 inches high, of vigorous habit. Deep crimson-purple flowers, about $1\frac{1}{2}$ inches across. A handsome and striking plant. The white form, *alba*, is even more lovely. Both of these are of such strong growth that they should not be associated with the more diminutive plants, but are so lovely and of such easy cultivation that a place should be found for them where they can have room to spread and form large bold masses.

G. s. lancastriense.—Grows about 4 inches high, and has pink flowers veined with red. It is a valuable and attractive little plant of spreading, though not encroaching, habit, compact in form and of easy culture. It is a rare British native found on the coast of Lancashire. Readily increased by seed or division.

G. sessiliflorum.—Forms compact little tufts, with whitish flowers almost hidden by the foliage. More curious than pretty. Seed and division.

G. subcaulescens.—Grows about 9 inches high, with large, rosy-crimson flowers, and a dark eye. Pretty.

G. tuberosum.—Large, rosy-purple flowers. Grows about 9 inches high.

G. wallichianum.—Grows about 6 inches high, of compact habit, with large violet-blue flowers freely produced during the summer. An attractive species of easy culture.

For massing in woods, or growing in the wilder parts of the rock garden, the following will be found suitable :—

G. armenum.—Purplish-rose-coloured flowers of a large size. Free-flowering and of vigorous habit.

G. grandiflorum.—Grows about 12 inches high with large rose-purple-coloured flowers. An attractive and showy plant.

G. macrorhizum. — Large crimson flowers freely produced. Grows 9 to 12 inches high, a vigorous and effective plant.

G. sylvaticum.—A vigorous-growing species with pink flowers freely produced during the summer.

G. s. alba.—A white form of the above, and equally vigorous in habit, free-flowering and attractive.

G. ibericum (syn. *G. platypetalum*).—A very handsome plant, with large blue flowers, and of vigorous habit.

GERBERA JAMSONII (COMPOSITEAE), Transvaal Daisy

Sandy loam and peat. Hot, dry, and sunny aspect. Large leathery leaves in a rosette. Tall, daisy-like flowers, 3 inches across, of a most brilliant orange-scarlet colour. Scarcely hardy, and, even in the most favoured climate, will in this country need protection in winter. It requires to be kept dry during the winter. Raised from seed, when fertile seed can be obtained. A great number of lovely hybrids, between this plant and *G. viridifolia*, have been raised, which are rather more robust.

GEUM (ROSACEAE)

Though a fairly numerous genus, only a few are suitable for the rock garden. They all like good sandy loam, in sun. Propagated by seed or division.

G. Heldreichii.—Forms a compact tuft, with brilliant orange-red flowers, on stems about 12 inches high.

G. montanum.—Forms very compact rosettes, growing close to the ground, and of a spreading habit. Large bright yellow-coloured flowers, borne singly on stems about 5 inches high, and succeeded by feathery seed-vessels. A very pretty plant for the rock garden, and of easiest culture. Increased by seed or division. There are two varieties, *aurantiacum*, with rather deeper-coloured flowers, and *grandiflorum* (syn. *Maximum*), which has larger flowers ; both are good plants and should be grown.

G. *reptans*.—Requires rather a dry position, in full sun. Forms compact tufts of greyish-green leaves, which are velvety and rather deeply cut. Flowers are large and of a beautiful pale yellow colour. The plant spreads rather quickly by means of slender runners, which often extend as far as 8 or 10 inches. Is rather a shy bloomer, and it would be well to grow it in poor and very stony ground. Quite the best of the genus. Division.

G. *rivale*.—Forms spreading tufts, increasing fairly rapidly. Flowers rather a reddish colour, borne on stems about 9 inches long. Increases very readily from seed. In bloom the whole summer.

GLOBULARIA (SELAGINACEAE)

Creeping plants for dry, sunny positions in moist, light, sandy loam. Not of very great value for rock garden. Increased by seed and division.

G. *cordifolia*.—Forms a dense carpet, only about 3 inches high, with round, terminal clusters of blue flowers in early summer. Of easy culture, and readily increased by seed or division.

G. *nana*.—Only grows about 1 inch high, forming a dense carpet with compact heads of light blue flowers from May to August. Is a pretty plant for growing over stones. Easily increased by seed or division.

Other varieties are G. *bellidifolia*, *nudicaulis*, and *trichosantha*, all of which are much the same and carry heads of bluish-white flowers in early summer.

GNAPHALIUM (*see* LEONTOPODIUM AND ANTENNARIA)

GOODYERA PUBESCENS (ORCHIDACEAE)

A pretty little hardy orchid for a moist, peaty spot in shade. Its flowers are white but insignificant, but its attraction lies in its leaves, which lie close to the ground and are veined with silver. It likes pieces of sandstone in the soil for its roots to cling around.

GUNNERA MAGELLANICA

Very prostrate, creeping plant for covering some moist corner ; it spreads rapidly. Pretty leaves, not rising more than a couple of inches from the ground. *Dentata* is an even smaller form.

Gypsophila (Caryophyllaceae), Chalk Plant

The dwarf-growing species of this genus are indispensable rock plants, of the easiest culture. Although chalk-loving, they do quite well in ordinary, well-drained soil in full sun.

G. cerastoides.—Only grows about 3 inches high, and of spreading habit. It is a fairly rapid grower, forming a good tuft in a couple of years. In very sandy soil. Flowers are white, with violet streaks, and are freely produced during the summer. A first-class plant, and easily increased by division or seeds.

G. prostrata.—A rapid-growing, trailing plant, forming mats of glaucous, succulent-looking foliage, and myriads of small white flowers. Of easiest culture, and readily increased by layers or seeds. A delightful plant for growing over a rock or bank. *Rosea* is a variety, having pink flowers equally floriferous.

G. repens.—Of creeping habit. Leaves glabrous. Flowers white or rose-coloured. Shy bloomer. *G. repens Monstrosa* is a variety, larger in all its parts and rather coarse-growing.

G. Sundermanni.—Has glaucous foliage and pink flowers.

Habenaria (Orchidaceae)

A genus of hardy orchids charming for the bog garden. They all require a moist soil composed of equal parts of sand, peat, and leaf-mould, in partial shade. In order to protect the roots from the sun, mulch the plants with mown grass. The following are the best kinds to grow :—

H. blepharoglottis. — Beautifully fringed white flowers in June and July.

H. ciliaris.—Golden-yellow flowers, with a fringed lip, borne in spikes about 12 inches high, in July.

H. fimbriata.—Beautifully fringed lilac-purple flowers, borne in long spikes.

H. psycodes.—Fragrant rosy-crimson flowers, borne in spikes 9 inches long. Very pretty.

Haberlea rhodopensis (Gesneraceae)

A shade-loving plant, forming rosettes of leaves very like *Ramondea pyrenaica,* from which spring slender stalks about 4 inches long, each bearing three to four flowers exactly like a *Streptocarpus,* of a bluish-lilac colour, with a yellow throat. It requires to be grown in fibrous peat, and should be planted in vertical fissures in a northern aspect, where the sun never reaches. It can also be planted on the level, but in such a way that rain cannot lie in the rosettes, which would be likely to cause them to damp off. There is a white form, *virginalis*, even more lovely than the type. Both increased by seed and careful division.

HABRANTHUS PRATENSIS (AMARYLLIDEAE)

A bulbous plant of much beauty and brilliancy. The flowers, which are of the brightest scarlet, and feathered at the throat with yellow, are borne on upright stems about 12 inches high. It is easily grown in loam, leaf-mould, and sand, and is readily increased by division. The variety *fulgens* is the best form, and is a very choice plant.

HEDYSARUM (LEGUMINOSAE)

A very numerous genus of plants belonging to the Vetch family, some of which are good for the rock garden. They are quite easily grown in sandy loam, in open, sunny spots. Increased by seed.

H. multijugum.—A shrubby plant, growing about 2 feet, of graceful habit, and having long panicles of crimson-purple flowers. Propagated by seed or division.

H. neglectum.—Very pretty flowers of a brilliant rosy-purple colour. Blooms in June, and grows about 12 inches high.

H. obscurum.—A creeping plant, growing from 9 to 12 inches high, with brilliant purplish-crimson flowers in long spikes, in August. It has silky leaves, and is a good rock plant, of free growth. Seed and division.

HELIANTHEMUM (CISTACEAE), Sun Rose

A genus of shrubby plants, mostly dwarf-growing, and of the greatest beauty and value for the rock garden. They are of the easiest culture, all they require being a light, rather poor soil, fully exposed to the sun. They all strike readily from cuttings. There are an endless number of hybrids, both single and double, giving all shades of yellow, pink, and crimson, any of which are well worth growing. The blossoms, though only lasting the day, are borne in such profusion that the flowering season lasts a long time. They all require to be cut hard back after flowering, which induces them to grow more compact ; for if this were not done, they would become rather leggy and straggling. They all grow rapidly. Not including the various named hybrids, the following are the most distinctive kinds :—

H. canum.—A native plant only growing about 3 inches high, with small pale yellow flowers.

H. Tuberaria (syn. *H. globulariaefolium*).—Quite a distinct plant, not having woody branches, but from the root sending up hairy, plantain-like leaves. On stems about 9 inches high, yellow flowers, about 2 inches across, are borne ; these droop when in the bud. It blooms during the summer, and likes a warm aspect in good light loam. Increased by seed or division.

HELICHRYSUM (COMPOSITAE), Everlastings

Hardy perennial plants requiring a hot, sunny position in loam.

H. arenarium.—Has grey, downy leaves. Flowers bright yellow, borne on stems 4 to 8 inches high, which are furnished with narrow, hoary leaves. Blooms in July.

H. bellidioides.—Gritty soil in sunny position. Prostrate habit with small ovate silvery leaves. Pure white daisy-like flowers with a yellowish eye. A dainty little plant from New Zealand and an acquisition for the rock garden.

H. microphyllum.—A small bushy plant, with narrow, silvery-coloured leaves and yellow flowers, in the summer.

HELLEBORUS (RANUNCULACEAE)

The well-known Christmas Rose and its varieties are so essentially border plants, that I do not think it necessary to do more than allude to them. In rock gardens of some size they can advantageously be used.

HELONIAS BULLATA

A marsh plant, requiring moist, fibrous, peaty soil, in a shady position. Rosettes of long, narrow leaves, and oval-shaped spikes of small, rose-coloured flowers. A pretty, though not showy plant.

HEPATICA (*see* ANEMONE)

HERNIA GLABRA (ILLECEBRACEAE)

Carpeting plant of dense creeping habit, pretty deep green foliage, and inconspicuous flowers. It will grow in any soil. Of no value except for carpeting purposes. *Aurea* is a golden-leaved variety.

HESPEROCHIRON PUMILUS (HYDROPHYLLACEAE)

A very dwarf-growing plant, for a well-drained position, in light loam. Forms a tuft of slender-stalked leaves. Flowers bell-shaped, white, with a purple tinge, and half an inch across.

H. californicus.—Has white flowers with dark stripes, and requires similar treatment.

HEUCHERA (SAXIFRAGACEAE), Alum Root

Of the Heucheras, though described in such glowing colours in all catalogues, the best is *H. sanguinea splendens*, which is a handsome plant, with its graceful sprays of coral-red flowers. They all are easily cultivated in any ordinary, well-drained soil. They require to be divided and replanted every few years, as they grow out of the ground.

HIERACIUM (COMPOSITAE), Hawkweed

A very large genus, very few of which are suitable, being mostly of too coarse and rank-growing a habit. They are all of the easiest culture in any soil. Propagated by division in spring.

H. rubra.—Dwarf-growing and spreading habit, very vigorous, forming a carpet, only about 1 inch high, of dark green leaves. The flowers, which are borne in great profusion on stems about 3 inches high, are of a brilliant, deep orange-red colour. It is in bloom all the summer. A very pretty plant, but too strong-growing to associate with the choicer rock plants. Increased by division.

H. villosum.—Forms good tufts, about 6 inches high. Flowers bright yellow, on stems about 12 inches long. The leaves and stems are clothed with long, white, silky down, which gives it a very attractive appearance. A good plant. Grows very freely from seed.

Other kinds are : *H. aurantiacum*, which is similar to *rubra*, but flowers orange-yellow. Good for the wild garden, but too rampant in growth for the choicer parts.

H. gymnocephalum.—Yellow flowers and silvery foliage. Grows about 9 inches high.

H. lanatum.—Yellow flowers and evergreen, downy, leaves.

HIPPOCREPIS COMOSA (LEGUMINOSAE), Horseshoe Vetch

A prostrate-growing native plant, of trailing habit. Light, chalky soil in sun. Small pinnate leaves, and deep yellow flowers in clusters. A pretty and useful little plant for draping the face of a rock. Hardy, and of easiest culture.

HORMINUM PYRENAICUM (LABIATAE)

Forms dense tufts of thick, crinkly leaves, from which rise spikes of purplish-blue flowers in July and August. Not of easy culture. Not a plant of much value or interest. Increased by seed and division.

HOUSTONIA (RUBIACEAE)

Delicate and dainty-growing little plants, which are difficult to succeed with, but they are worth some trouble. They like a soil composed of peat, sand, leaf-mould, and fibrous loam, in an open, but well-drained ledge. Require plenty of moisture during summer, but in winter should be kept dry, by placing a piece of glass over them. Propagated by careful division in the autumn, or by seed.

H. caerulea (*Bluets*).—Forms dense cushions of bright green leaves about half an inch high, which from May to July is thickly studded over with lovely little pale sky-blue flowers, on thread-like stems about 2 inches high. A most dainty little gem, and should find a place among the choicest rock plants.

H. c. pallida has paler blue flowers, and *alba*, white. Both lovely.

H. purpurea.—Has purple flowers.

H. serpyllifolia.—Is even of dwarfer habit, and has white flowers.

HUTCHINSIA ALPINA (CRUCIFERAE)

A dainty, neat-growing little plant, forming dense little cushions of dark green leaves about 3 inches high, which in summer are covered with small pure white flowers in clusters. Grows readily in any sandy soil, is of vigorous habit, and can easily be raised from seed. In fact the trouble is to prevent it seeding itself over the rock garden. A very charming little plant.

H. rotundifolia (see *Æthionema cepeaefolium*).

HYPERICUM (HYPERICACEAE), St John's Wort

A large genus of shrubs, some quite tall-growing, while others are little more than trailing plants. They are all of easy culture in ordinary, light sandy loam, in an open position. Of the dwarf-growing kinds.

H. Coris.—Makes little tufty bushes about 9 inches high, with small, blue-grey foliage, and numerous golden-yellow flowers. A very pretty and amenable little plant, and one of the best of the genus. Evergreen.

H. empetrifolium.—A half-hardy, evergreen, shrubby plant, growing 6 to 12 inches high. Numerous small, golden-coloured flowers in the summer.

H. fragilis.—A prostrate-growing evergreen plant, forming very compact tufts, about 8 to 10 inches high, of slender branches, clothed the whole length with small, bright green, ovate leaves. Large, golden-yellow flowers borne in the greatest profusion the whole summer. Of easy culture and quick growth, in any warm, well-drained position, and readily increased by division. A very gem for the rock garden ; the best of the family.

H. Kotschyanum.—Gritty loam in sun. A dwarf trailing species. Flowers buff-coloured. Very pretty.

H. repens.—A dwarf, trailing plant, with small, heath-like foliage.

Flowers, borne in terminal racemes, are of a bright golden-yellow. It is a pretty plant, but not nearly so good as *H. reptans*, with which it must not be confused.

H. reptans.—Forms a close mat, some 2 inches high, of long, trailing stems. Small leaves and large golden-yellow flowers in the greatest profusion from July to October. A very quick grower. There is no better plant for covering a rock. Second only to *H. fragilis* in value and beauty, and by some, in fact, considered better.

The above represent the best trailing kinds. The following are the choicest of the shrubby type :—*H. ægyptiacum, balearicum, olympicum, Hookerianum,* and *moserianum.*

IBERIDELLA ROTUNDIFOLIA (CRUCIFERAE)

A charming little plant, found at very high altitudes in the Alps. It requires light shingly loam, well drained, and makes dense mats only about 3 inches high. The glaucous, olive-green leaves are thick and leathery. The flowers are bright rosy-lilac, and sweet-scented. They are borne in some profusion from April to June. A very delightful little plant, of easy culture, and coming freely from seed. It should be grown among the choicest rock plants, and should find a place in every garden.

IBERIS (CRUCIFERAE), Candytuft

A genus of evergreen, dwarf-growing plants, of the easiest culture in any light loamy soil, in an open situation. With one or two exceptions, they are all quite hardy. Propagated by seeds, division, or cuttings.

I. correaefolia.—Grows about 12 inches high, making quite a shrubby little plant. Compact, flat heads of large, pure white flowers. It blooms rather later than the other kinds, not coming into flower until about the beginning of June. Of free and vigorous growth, and easily increased by seed or cuttings. It is one of the best.

I. gibraltarica.—A somewhat straggling-growing plant of some 12 inches high, with larger flowers and leaves than the other kinds. The flowers, which are very [freely produced, are borne in close heads and of a rosy-lilac colour. It blooms about May. Not very hardy, and, except in a favoured climate, should be protected during the winter. Easily propagated by cuttings. A most attractive plant, which is well worth taking some trouble about.

I. petraea.—Of very dwarf and prostrate habit, and a great profusion of white flowers. Very pretty species, of fairly easy culture in good loam. It is given by some as a variety of *I. Tenoreana.*

I. sempervirens.—A dwarf-growing and well-known little ever-green, shrubby plant. It bears a profusion of white, sweet-scented flowers in April and May. Readily increased by cuttings and seeds. It is hardy and of easy culture. Varieties of this plant, which are rather better, are: "*Little Gem*," more compact and dwarfer in habit, with smaller flowers. "*Snowflake*," an improved form of *sempervirens*. More compact growth, and larger flowers of a purer white. The best white of the family, blooming in April and May.

I. stylosa (syn. *Noccaea stylosa*).—A very dwarf-growing plant, with pale lilac flowers, sweet-scented. Blooms in spring.

INCARVILLEA (BIGNONIACEAE)

A genus of plants of rather recent introduction, of which only a few kinds are at present in cultivation.

I. Delavayi.—Requires a very deep root-run in good loamy soil, plentifully mixed with sand and leaf-mould. It likes a half-shady position. Handsome leathery leaves about 12 inches long. Flowers trumpet-shaped, and of a rosy-purple colour, borne in racemes on stout stalks from 1 to 3 feet high. Quite easy to grow, provided the crowns are kept fairly dry during the winter. It is a herbaceous rather than a rock plant, and can easily be raised from seed.

I. grandiflora.—This is of dwarfer habit, with smaller leaves and rather larger and better-coloured flowers. It requires the same treatment and position as the last named. It comes equally freely from seed.

I. Olgae.—Tall-growing, reaching about 3 feet. Pinnate leaves. Rose-pink, trumpet-shaped flowers. Not a very hardy kind, nor a very free bloomer.

I. variabilis.—Slender stems and loose panicles of rose-coloured flowers. Also of doubtful hardiness, and a shy bloomer.

INULA (COMPOSITAE)

A genus of plants chiefly suitable for the herbaceous border, but a few kinds can be used for the rock garden. These should be associated with the more robust-growing plants. They are all of easy culture in ordinary loam. They have large, composite flowers, and are easily increased by seed or division.

I. acaulis.—Dwarf foliage, and large yellow flowers on stems about 6 inches high.

I. ensifolia.—Is of compact habit, and has yellow flowers, one or more, on erect stems 9 inches high.

I. montana.—An early flowering species, growing about 9 inches high.

Ionopsidium acaule (Cruciferae), Violet Cress

This, though only an annual, may be included, being such a dainty little plant, which, when once established, sows itself, and causes no further trouble. It likes rather a damp spot, and only grows from 1 to 2 inches high, with small, pale violet-coloured flowers, borne in endless profusion the whole summer. It often comes into flower a couple of months after being sown. One of the very few annuals admissible into the rock garden.

Iris (Iridaceae)

A very large genus of plants, wonderfully varied, both in habit and flower. They are mostly too coarse-growing for the rock garden, but a few of the dwarfer kinds are suitable. The following are some of the best :—

I. arenaria.—Sandy soil in sun. Grows 3 to 4 inches high. Flowers bright yellow, striped purplish-brown. Blooms in May.

I. cristata.—Light sandy, stony soil on a level spot, in sun. Of dwarf habit, spreading freely by means of rhizomes. Flowers a lovely blue, and of a large size. A beautiful plant, of which the slugs are inordinately fond. There is also a white form, *alba*, which is very lovely.

I. gracipiles.—Requires a partial shady position in fibrous loam, well drained, and plentifully mixed with leaf-mould. A dwarf-growing and very lovely little plant, with clear blue flowers shaded with lilac. It is quite hardy and not difficult to grow.

I. lacustris.—This is a miniature form of *I. cristata*, with flowers pale blue and gold. It requires similar treatment. A charming and dainty plant.

I. verna.—Requires sandy peat and shady position. Only grows about 4 inches high. Flowers a rich violet-blue, and sweet-scented.

Other species suitable for growing in the rock garden, in light soil and sunny position, are—*I. alata*, *I. aphylla*, *I. Chamaeiris* and its varieties, *I. pumila* and its varieties.

Isopyrum thalictroides (Ranunculaceae)

A graceful and dwarf-growing little plant for a half-shady position in light, rather poor soil. It has greyish-green leaves rather like a maiden-hair fern, and panicles of small white flowers. It is quite hardy, and easily propagated by seed or division.

Jankaea Heldreichi (Gesneriaceae)

A plant very nearly allied to the Ramondias, but most difficult to grow. It requires a northern aspect, in such a position that no moisture can fall on its leaves, while at the same time it likes a moderate amount at its roots. The best way to achieve this is to plant in a miniature cavern, so arranged that no drip can fall on it, though soaking the ground around. It requires sandy peat. It forms flat rosettes of thick leaves, coated with white silvery down. Lovely, pale violet-blue flowers, and shaped rather like a Soldanella. One of the gems for the rock garden.

Jasione (Campanulaceae), Sheep's Scabious

A genus of plants bearing flowers resembling a scabious. They are not of much interest for the rock garden.

J. numilis.—Requires a dry, well-drained position in sandy loam. Of spreading, tufted habit, growing about 6 inches high. Flowers small and of a bright blue colour, borne in July and August. It is not very hardy and needs protection from damp and cold during the winter. Propagated by seed sown in the autumn.

J. Jankea.—Requires light sandy soil in sunny position. Forms rosettes of a deep green colour, from which rise stems about 9 inches high, bearing heads of deep blue flowers in July. Increased by seed.

J. perennis.—Sunny position in light loam. Bears dense heads of bright blue flowers in July. Of taller habit than either of the preceding. Often over 12 inches in height. Increased by seed sown in autumn.

Jeffersonia diphylla (Berberidaceae)

A plant for a shady spot in the raised parts of the bog garden, in sandy peat. Leaves large and two-lobed. Flowers white, with yellow stamens, and about an inch across, freely produced in April. Increased by division during the winter, or by seeds sown as soon as ripe.

Kalmia (Ericaceae), American Laurel

Evergreen shrubs, and among the most beautiful grown. They are of the greatest value for the rock garden. They all require a peaty soil.

K. angustifolia.—Rather damp, peaty soil. It grows about 18 inches high, and of graceful habit. Clusters of rosy-pink flowers towards the end of May. Quite hardy, and easily grown. There are several varieties, bearing flowers of different shades of pink.

K. glauca.—Moist, peaty soil. Of dwarf habit, growing 1 to 2 feet high, with smooth leaves, silvery below, and purplish-pink flowers. A good rock garden shrub.

K. hirsuta.—Moist, peaty soil. Leaves rather hairy. Of dwarf habit, growing 1 foot high, and not very hardy.

K. latifolia.—Moist, peaty soil. The largest-growing of the family, reaching a height of 8 to 10 feet. Leaves are broad. Waxy pink flowers in clusters. A very handsome shrub of slow growth, having several varieties, the best being *maxima*, which has larger and deeper-coloured flowers. *Myrtifolia* is a dwarf-growing variety with flowers as large as the type. A lovely little shrub. They can all be propagated by cuttings or layers.

Lapeyrousia (*see* Anomatheca)

Lathraea Clandestina (Orobanchaceae)

A very curious little parasitic plant, living on the roots of willow, poplar, and beech trees, provided they are in boggy ground. Only the flowers, which are of a lilac-purple colour, appear over the ground, the stems and small white leaves remaining underground.

Lathrus (Leguminosae), Pea

In large rock gardens some of the rarer species of the everlasting pea will be useful, for in no way are they more effective than when falling over the face of a large rock. Some of the following kinds are suitable for this purpose :—

L. cyaneus (syn. *Platystylis cyaneus*).—Likes a light soil in a sunny position. Grows about 9 inches high. Blue flowers in April and May. Hardy, and of easy culture. This is an upright, not trailing species.

L. latifolius.—Indifferent to soil or position. A vigorous-growing and trailing species, with rosy-coloured flowers. There are also white varieties which are good.

L. hirsutus (syn. *Orobus hirsutus*).—Quite hardy in any soil or position. Of trailing habit. Bears a profusion of purple flowers the whole summer. An attractive plant.

L. rotundifolius.—Of easiest culture in any soil or position. It is of trailing habit. Flowers very numerous, and of a bright rose-pink colour. Useful for draping a rock.

L. Sibthorpi (syn. *L. undulatus*).—Light soil in sunny position. Trailing habit, but not so vigorous as some of the other kinds. Purplish-red flowers, borne in spikes. It blooms in May.

L. magellanicus.—Ordinary soil. Trailing habit. Leaves and stem covered with a bluish bloom. Lovely sky-blue flowers in bunches, freely produced during the summer. A beautiful, though not very hardy, almost evergreen plant. Grows readily from seed.

L. variegatus.—Ordinary soil. A compact plant, growing about 1 foot high. Bears rather small flowers ; upper petal rose-coloured and veined with purplish-crimson, and points of the wings blue. A pretty plant, quite hardy, and easily grown. Propagated by seed or division.

L. varius (syn. *Orobus varius*).—Ordinary soil. Of erect and graceful growth, about 1 foot high. Flowers white and very pale rose-coloured, borne in loose spikes. Blooms in early summer. Quite hardy, and of easy culture.

L. vernus.—Ordinary soil. Erect growth, about 12 inches high. Flowers purple and blue, very freely produced in April. A charming, spring-flowering plant, and of easiest culture and quite hardy. Readily increased by division or seed.

LEDUM (ERICACEAE), Labrador Tea

Dwarf-growing shrubs for moist, peaty, and sandy soil, well drained. Propagated by layers. When transplanting any of the Ledums, care should be taken that the ball of earth around the roots remains intact.

L. buxifolium (syn. *Leiophyllum buxifolium*), Sand Myrtle.— Moist, peaty soil in partial shade. Very dwarf-growing, with tiny, box-like foliage, and numerous heads of small pink-and-white flowers in the summer. A pretty little shrub for a choice spot.

L. latifolium.—Peaty loam. Grows 2 to 3 feet high. Of compact habit, with small, dull-green leaves, brown beneath. Numerous clusters of small white flowers in April and May. Quite hardy, and a useful, if not striking, shrub.

L. Lyoni.—Is of very dwarf habit, with numerous clusters of rosy-pink flowers. Likes a peaty soil. A pretty shrub.

LEONTICE ALTAICA (BERBERIDACEAE)

Ordinary soil in an open position. Grows 3 to 6 inches high. Flowers yellow, in terminal racemes. Forms tuberous rhizomes, and may be increased by offsets or seeds. Not very hardy, or of any special merit.

LEONTOPODIUM ALPINUM (COMPOSITAE)

The well-known "Edelweiss" needs no description. It should be planted on an exposed position in the rock garden, in full sun, and in very poor, gritty soil, with plenty of lime rubbish added. If grown in rich soil, its flowers become greenish, and it is liable to die from over-feeding. An old wall is a good spot for it. There are several varieties: *L. maximum*, a larger form, and *L. Lindauicum*, flowering in late summer.

LEUCANTHEMUM ALPINUM (*see* CHRYSANTHMEUM ALPINUM)

LEUCOJUM (*see* ACIS)

LEUCOTHOË (ERICACEAE)

Pretty evergreen shrubs, liking a peat or leaf-mould soil. Propagated by seeds or layers.

L. acuminata (syn. *Andromeda acuminata*).—Grows about 2 feet high. Long, pointed leaves on arching stems, which in summer are wreathed with small, bell-shaped, white flowers. A very choice shrub, easy of culture, and quite hardy.

L. axillaris, *L. Catesbaei*, and *L. racemosa*, all known under the generic name of Andromeda, are very similar to the above.

L. Davisiae.—Forms a neat evergreen bush, 2 to 3 feet high, Small leaves on slender stems, on the ends of which dense clusters of small white flowers are produced in May. A very choice and attractive little shrub, and though not as hardy as some of the other kinds, it should be cultivated.

LEWISIA (PORTULACACEAE)

Pretty plants, allied to the Mesembryanthemums.

L. cotyledon. — Full sun in light well-drained gritty soil or moraine. Large delicate pink flowers. A beautiful species.

L. Howellii.—Same soil and position as above. Rosettes of crinkled leaves from which rise panicles of large pale salmon-coloured flowers. A very beautiful and attractive species.

L. rediviva.—Wants a sunny, dry, and very well-drained spot in gritty loam. Forms rosettes of rather long leaves on a woody stalk. The flowers are large, about 3 inches across, rose-coloured on the outer edge, shading to nearly white at the centre. They are borne in the summer in such profusion as nearly to hide the plant. A delicate plant, disliking much moisture in the winter, so it is advisable to protect it with a sheet of glass during that time.

L. Tweedyi. — Lovely salmon-pink flowers. Is even more beautiful and also more delicate. The least excess of damp seems to prove fatal, so, unless in an exceptionally favoured climate, it should be kept as a house plant. Soil and treatment same as the last.

LIBERTIA (IRIDACEAE)

A genus nearly allied to the Irises.

L. formosa.—Light peaty soil, well drained. It forms tufts of grass-like leaves, and bears on spikes about 18 inches long, large, pure white flowers. A beautiful plant, and the best of the genus. It is easy to grow and hardy.

L. ixioides, white flowers with yellow stamens, and *L. Magellanica*, white flowers. These are both very similar to *L. formosa*, only with much smaller flowers, and require the same soil and treatment.

LILIUM (LILIACEAE)

Some of the Lilies are amongst the choicest plants for the bog garden, while the smaller ones can be grown in damp spots in the rock garden. A selection should therefore be made from some catalogue. Those for the bog garden like cool, moist, well-drained slopes in very rich soil, in partial shade. The following are a few of the best :—*L. auratum, Platyphyllum, Martagon* and varieties *alba* and *dalmaticum, monadelphum, Krameri, longiflorum* and varieties, and *giganteum*. These fairly represent the various types, and are mostly of easy culture, but all Lilies are somewhat uncertain.

LINARIA (SCROPHULARIACEAE), Toadflax

Of this genus only a few should be grown in the rock garden. The following are a selection of the most suitable :—

L. alpina.—Any soil or position. A dwarf, spreading plant of rather dense habit. Bluish-violet-coloured flowers with orange throat, in the greatest profusion. It is, strictly speaking, only a biennial, but it sows itself about so freely that it does not matter. It should only be planted on a spot in which it can be allowed to run wild, and not smother out choicer plants.

L. antirrhinifolia (syn. *Cavanillesii*).—Any aspect in light soil. Is of neat spreading habit, only growing about 6 inches high, and is not so rampant a grower as some of the other kinds. Bright purple flowers throughout the summer. Most easily cultivated and raised from seed. A good plant, though an annual.

L. compacta.—Tiny little, creeping species, with minute, mauve flowers. Dainty little plant for clothing steps, etc.

L. pallida (syn. *Cymbalaria maxima*).—Attractive foliage, and large flowers of a pale violet colour, with a white throat. A most rampant grower, spreading under stones, etc., by means of under-ground stems. It should only be planted in the wilder parts, where it can do no harm. A decidedly pretty flower.

LINNEA BOREALIS (CAPRIFOLIACEAE)

A trailing evergreen plant. It requires a shady position in moist, sandy peat. It forms long, rather straggling stems, on which are borne graceful, pale pink flowers in the summer. A pretty plant, which looks well falling over the face of some rock.

L. canadensis.—Is a larger form of the above ; more brilliant in colour and stronger in growth. It is not particular as to aspect or soil, but thrives everywhere. It is altogether a more desirable plant.

LINUM (LINACEAE), Flax

A genus of lovely and graceful plants, which should be freely massed in the rock garden.

L. alpinum.—Light sandy loam and peat, in any open position. Of quite dwarf habit, growing only 3 to 6 inches high, with large, dark blue flowers in summer. A very dainty and choice plant.

L. arboreum.—Requires a warm, sheltered position in light sandy loam. Forms a small, shrubby bush. Large flowers of a clear yellow colour. Not hardy, and needs some protection.

L. campanulatum.—Requires an open position in sandy loam. Grows about 12 inches high. Flowers yellow, freely produced in summer. A very desirable plant.

L. flavum.—Dry, sandy loam in sun. A shrubby evergreen plant, growing about 18 inches high, with bright yellow flowers in branched heads in the greatest profusion. Fairly hardy, and very easily raised from seed. A most attractive and useful plant.

L. monogynum.—Likes a sunny position in sandy loam. Grows about 18 inches high, of slender habit. Large, pure white flowers in summer. Hardy, except in cold districts, where it is said to need some protection. Grows freely from seed. A very beautiful plant, which should be boldly massed.

L. narbonense.—Sunny aspect in good, light soil. A very graceful plant, growing from 15 to 20 inches high, and during the whole summer a profusion of light blue flowers, veined with violet-blue. Quite hardy, and of easy culture. Makes a lovely and strik-ing picture when planted in a bold mass. Increased by seed or division.

L. perenne.—Ordinary soil, in a sunny aspect. Grows 12 to 18 inches high, in dense tufts, and bears a profusion of clear cobalt-blue flowers during the summer. Also a beautiful plant, readily increased by seed or division, and of easiest culture. Quite hardy. There is also a white form which is good. *L. Leonii, L. sibiricum,* and *L. provinciale* are considered forms of *perenne.*

L. salsoloides.—Likes a sunny aspect in well-drained, sandy soil. A dwarf, half-shrubby species, growing about 12 inches high, with rather heath-like foliage. Large, pure white flowers, with a purple centre, freely produced in June and July. Quite hardy, and of easy culture, and readily raised from seeds. A very choice plant.

L. viscosum.—Well-drained, sunny position in sandy loam. A dwarf, half-shrubby plant, growing about 12 inches high, with rather hairy stems. Large, pale purple-coloured flowers, veined with a deeper shade, are borne during the summer. Of easy culture, and can be readily propagated by division or seed. A handsome, showy species for the rock garden.

LIPPIA NODIFLORA (VERBENACEAE)

A plant of the Verbena order, growing 6 to 12 inches high. It bears, during the summer, heads of pretty white or pink flowers It is useful for covering waste spaces, and will grow in any ordinary soil. Half hardy.

LITHOSPERMUM (BORAGINACEAE), Gromwell

A genus of dwarf, half-shrubby plants of the greatest beauty and value for the rock garden. Some of them, unfortunately, are not quite hardy. Propagated by seed, cuttings, or division.

L. canescens.—Requires a dry, sunny position in sandy and gritty loam, mixed with a very little lime rubbish. It forms a compact little bushy plant about 12 inches high, with greyish, hoary foliage. The flowers, which are of a good size, are orange-coloured, and borne in clusters from April to June. A hardy, deciduous plant, and very choice.

L. Gastoni.—Likes a sunny position between rocks, in sandy peat and loam, mixed with grit. Grows about 9 inches high, and bears, during the summer, lovely azure-blue flowers, with a white eye, in terminal clusters. Fairly hardy, but rather difficult to cultivate. When planting, care should be taken not to disturb or break any of its roots ; if grown in a pot, do not break the ball of earth, but plant intact. One of the choicest of the whole family. They are lucky indeed with whom it will thrive.

L. graminifolium. — Likes a sunny position in sandy loam. Forms rather a compact tuft, about 9 inches high, with rather long and narrow foliage. The flowers, which are small, and of a deep blue colour, are borne in drooping terminal clusters. Hardy, and of comparatively easy culture. It requires top dressing occasionally. A very choice species, flowering from June to August.

L. hirtum.—A sunny, dry position in gritty loam. Rather similar to *L. canescens*, but of dwarfer habit. Clusters of orange-yellow flowers from May to September. It is difficult to keep in any but a dryish climate.

L. petraeum (syn. *Moltkea petraea*).—Very sandy peat and loam in a sunny position. It grows from 9 to 18 inches high, forming compact little bushes, with clusters of lovely deep blue flowers, very freely produced during the summer. Fairly easy to cultivate, and one of the choicest of the family. Easily raised from seed or cuttings.

L. prostratum.—A warm, sunny aspect in sandy peat and loam. It has a great aversion to lime. A prostrate-growing, half-shrubby plant; evergreen. Beautiful deep blue flowers nearly the whole year. Quite hardy, but rather uncertain, in places growing most freely, while in others it barely exists. It should be planted so that its prostrate stems can fall down the face of a rock or bank. A lovely and indispensable plant, of the greatest value for the rock garden. It can be increased by cuttings. There is a new variety, known as " Heavenly blue," which is lighter in colour and very choice, but in no way superior to the type.

L. purpureo-coeruleum.—Likes a little lime in the soil. Grows in sun or shade. Of rather rampant habit, sending out runners which ought to be removed, as otherwise it will not bloom. The flowers open red, soon change to a deep blue. Of very easy growth, but should not be allowed in the choicer parts of the rock garden. It is a native plant.

L. rosmarinifolium.—Likes a sunny position in a rather moist soil of peat, loam, and grit. A compact-growing plant, rather similar to *graminifolium*, but with longer and narrower leaves. Deep blue flowers very early in the year; it is sometimes in full bloom by the end of January. A very good plant, but not very hardy, and needs protection during hard frost.

LOBELIA (CAMPANULACEAE)

Some varieties of the Lobelia look very fine grown in masses in a large bog garden. In any but fairly mild climates, they require a little protection from hard frosts, and though requiring a great deal of moisture during the spring and summer, in the winter months they should be kept fairly dry.

L. cardinalis and *L. fulgens*, and the numerous hybrids raised

20

from these species, are the best kinds to grow. They give many shades of colour, from the most dazzling vermilion to almost salmon-pink.

LOISELEURIA DECUMBENS (see AZALEA PROCUMBENS)

LONICERA (CAPRIFOLIACEAE), Honeysuckle

The various species of Honeysuckle will be found useful for clothing large rocks or banks, and when grown in this manner will look far better than in their usual position, stiffly trained against some wall.

LUPINUS (LEGUMINOSAE), Lupine

A genus of shrubs of rapid growth and very floriferous. They will grow in any soil.

L. arboreus.—Of very rapid growth in any good soil ; it will reach a height of 4 to 5 feet in a few years. It should be sheltered from the wind. Flowers yellow and very fragrant, abundantly produced. Easily raised from seed. " *Snow Queen*" is a lovely white form. There are also numerous hybrids.

L. decumbens.—Has pale lilac flowers borne in spikes, and silky leaves.

LYCHNIS (CARYOPHYLLACEAE), Rose Campion

A genus of showy plants, of which a few kinds are suitable for the rock garden.

L. alpina.—Should be grown in rather moist, sandy loam. Grows only a few inches high, and has rose-coloured flowers in compact heads. Of quite easy culture, and readily propagated by seeds.

L. Lagascae (syn. *Petrocoptis pyrenaica*).—Likes a sunny position in sandy loam, and looks best planted in a fissure. Of slightly spreading habit, though neat and compact. Leaves rather glaucous. Bears a profusion of bright rose-coloured flowers, with white centres, and blooms in early summer. Not difficult to grow, and quite one of the best of the genus. Propagated by seed.

L. pyrenaica.—Sunny position in light soil. Grows 3 to 4 inches high. Flowers pale pink, borne in forked clusters during the summer.

L. Viscaria.—Any light soil. Forms compact tufts, about 4 inches high, of long narrow leaves. Heads of rosy-red flowers, on stems about 10 to 12 inches long. The variety of this, named *splendens*, is more worthy of culture, being of a brighter colour. There is also a white and a double variety, both of which are good plants. All are of the easiest culture, and readily propagated by seed or division.

LYSIMACHIA NUMMULARIA, Creeping Jenny

A native plant of creeping habit and very rapid growth. It likes a shady position in moist soil. Bright yellow flowers in the greatest profusion all along its trailing stems. Too rampant a grower for any but the wilder parts. There is a golden-leaved variety, *aurea*, which is well worth cultivating, and is not nearly so encroaching.

L. henryi.—Trailing habit. Flowers old gold. A good recent introduction from China.

The other varieties of Lysimachia are too coarse-growing.

MACROTOMIA ECHIOIDES (*see* ARNEBIA ECHIOIDES)

MAGNOLIA (MAGNOLIACEAE)

Of this genus there is only one kind which is suitable for growing in the rock garden : this is *M. stellata.* It likes a sheltered position in good loam. It is a deciduous shrub, growing 3 to 4 feet high, covered in March, before the leaves appear, with waxy white, star-shaped flowers, about 4 inches across. It is quite hardy, but requires to be well established before flowering.

MAIANTHEMUM BIFOLIUM (syn. CONVALLARIA BIFOLIA)

It is very like, and closely allied to, the Lily-of-the-valley. It prefers rather a damp, shady spot. The flowers are small, and not fragrant. It is of quite easy cultivation.

MALVASTRUM (MALVACEAE), False Mallow

Prostrate, growing plants, with flowers very like the Mallows. They all require a warm, well-drained position, in light sandy loam, and are not very hardy.

M. Munroana (syn. *Sphaeralcea Munroana*).—Flowers reddish-pink, tinged with brown, in June.

M. coccinium.—Scarlet-coloured flowers. Six inches high.

M. lateritium.—Has flowers of a brick-red colour. Prostrate habit. A handsome plant.

MARGYRICARPUS SETOSUS (ROSACEAE), Pearl Fruit

A pretty evergreen, creeping plant, which in winter is covered with white berries, which look well against the dark green foliage. It likes an open position in peat and loam.

MAZUS PUMILIO (SCROPHULARIACEAE)

A very dwarf-growing plant, spreading underground very rapidly. Likes a warm, dry position in partial shade, and should be planted in sandy loam. It quickly forms dense tufts, scarcely an inch high. Flowers are a pale violet colour, with a white centre, which barely rise above the leaves. Hardy, and easily increased by division.

M. rugosus.—Light soil in any position. Trailing habit, spreading rapidly. Violet labiate flowers with orange spots.

MECONOPSIS (PAPAVERACEAE)

These glorious poppies, of comparatively recent introduction, some of them at least, grow to a considerable height, but, being truly mountain plants, should find a home in the rock garden. Being little more than biennials, should be raised annually from seed. The seedlings, which require great care in handling, should be grown in pots during the first winter, and planted out the following spring. They all require a partially shady position, in a moist, very deep, rich, and gritty soil of peat, loam, and sand, with very quick drainage.

M. aculeata.—Grows from 18 inches to 2 feet. The leaves are cordate and covered with brownish hairs. Flowers, borne in a pyramid shape, are of a beautiful violet-blue colour. A singularly handsome and striking plant.

M. cambrica.—Our native Welsh Poppy, the only representative we have of the family, is of the easiest culture in any dry spot, and is of such vigorous habit, that it should not be allowed into the choicer parts of the garden. It has handsome, fern-like foliage, and bright yellow flowers. The double form is rather a better plant, and not so rampant a grower. The gem of the species, however, is *M. c. aurantiaca, fl. pl.*, a double form, with beautiful orange-yellow flowers.

M. integrifolia.—Grows 2 to 3 feet high. Woolly leaves and pale primrose-coloured flowers. Lovely.

M. nepalensis.—Grows 3 to 5 feet high. Soft, yellow-green leaves, and flowers of a lovely pale yellow colour.

M. punicea. — Grows 2 to 3 feet high. Bears drooping, crimson flowers. Distinct.

M. simplicifolia.—Only grows about 9 to 12 inches high, and bears clear blue flowers.

M. Wallichii.—Grows 4 to 5 feet high. Divided leaves, covered with silky hairs. Lovely blue flowers, with yellow stamens. A glorious plant.

These poppies do not always come true to seed, varying considerably in shade, which is all the more unfortunate, as seed is the only means of propagating them.

MEGASEA (*see* SAXIFRAGA)

MELITTIS MELISSOPHYLLUM (LABIATAE), Bastard Balm

A plant of the *Salvia* order, growing about 18 inches high. Leaves ovate and slightly hairy. Flowers rather pretty, of a creamy-white colour, and spotted purplish-rose. A useful plant for growing amongst the shrubs adjoining the rock garden. Increased by seed or division.

MENTHA REQUIENI (LABIATAE), Mint

A pretty little creeping plant, with tiny, pale purple flowers. Smells strongly of peppermint.

MENYANTHES TRIFOLIATA (GENTIANACEAE), Buckbean

An aquatic plant with pale pink flowers. A pretty plant, which can also be grown on the edges of ponds or streams.

MENZIESIA (ERICACEAE)

Dwarf and compact-growing shrubs, for moist peat.

M. caerulea (syn. *Phyllodoce taxifolia*).—Grows only 4 to 6 inches high, with pinkish-lilac flowers. It blooms in autumn.

M. empetrifolia (syn. *Bryanthus empetriformis*).—A tiny shrub of neat habit, thriving in moist, sandy peat. Heath-like foliage. Flowers borne in clusters, bell-shaped, and of a rosy-purple colour. A very choice and pretty little shrub.

M. ferruginea.—Has brown flowers, and only grows about 6 inches high.

M. f. globularia.—Grows 2 to 5 feet high, and has pink flowers in May.

M. polifolia (see *Erica polifolia*).

MERENDERA BULBOCODIUM (LILIACEAE)

A pretty bulbous plant bearing erect flowers of pale rosy-purple, blooming in the autumn. Increased by seed or division.

MERTENSIA (BORAGINACEAE)

Very beautiful plants of the Borage order, of graceful habit.

M. alpina (syn. *M. lanceolata*).—Requires a cool spot, in moist, peaty soil. Grows from 6 to 10 inches high, with bluish-green

leaves. On each stem is borne one to three terminal drooping clusters of pale blue flowers, in spring. A rare and beautiful
plant.

M. dahurica (syn. *Pulmonaria dahurica*.)—It should be planted
in a mixture of peat and loam, and in a sheltered nook, to save its
leaves from being broken by the wind. It grows from 8 to 12
inches high. The bright azure-blue flowers are borne in panicles
on erect, branching stems. It blooms in June. Quite hardy, and
of easy culture. It is a choice plant for the rock garden, and
propagated by seed and division.

M. echioides.—Requires peat and leaf-mould soil, in a cool spot.
Grows about 12 inches high. The flowers, which are produced in
spring and autumn, are of a lovely rich blue colour.

M. elongata.—Cool, peaty loam. Grows about 9 inches high.
Narrow, blue-grey leaves. Buds rosy-red, opening to pale blue. It
blooms in the spring. It is not difficult to grow, and can be raised
easily from seed. About the best of this lovely genus.

M. lanceolata (*see M. alpina*).

M. maritima.—Requires a light, very sandy soil of good depth.
It forms long trailing stems, and has bluish, glaucous leaves.
Flowers are of a lovely turquoise-blue colour. Quite easy to grow.
Slugs have a great love for this plant. It blooms in the summer.
It can be increased by seed or division.

M. oblongifolia.—Cool spot, in peat and leaf-soil. Grows only
3 to 4 inches high. Fleshy, dark green leaves, and clustered heads
of pale blue flowers.

M. primuloides.—Cool, light, peaty loam. Heads of lovely
flowers, changing from ruby to a deep blue colour as they open. It
grows from 6 to 9 inches high. It is of easy culture, and a very
choice and lovely plant.

M. p. var. *Chitralensis* has larger flowers and deeper colouring.

M. sibirica.—Light loam, in a cool spot. Grows 12 to 18 inches
high. Small, bell-shaped flowers, in loose, drooping terminal
clusters. They vary in colour from the rosy-pink of the half-opened
bud to the purple-blue of the fully expanded flower. It is in bloom
from May to June. Of easy culture, and may be increased by
division. There is also a white form.

M. virginica.—Likes rather a moist soil of rich, light loam. It
should be planted in some sheltered spot where the wind cannot
affect its lovely glaucous leaves. The trumpet-shaped flowers,
nearly an inch long, and of a lovely purple-blue colour, are disposed
in drooping terminal clusters from stems 12 to 18 inches high. It
is of easiest culture in any but stiff or dry soils, and can be
increased by division. A most lovely and attractive plant, blooming in April.

Mesembryanthemum (Ficoideae)

A genus of succulent plants, some of which are fairly hardy in a very dry, sandy position in a favourable climate. They are mostly of a trailing habit, and of very rapid growth. The flowers, which only open in the sun, are extraordinarily brilliant and of every colour and shade. Anybody enjoying a warm, dry climate should certainly try a selection of them. They strike with the greatest ease from cuttings inserted in pure sand.

Micromeria (Labiatae)

A large genus, of which the following are the only suitable kinds. Easily grown in ordinary soil in an open position, and are useful for planting in chinks. Increased by cuttings.

M. croatica.—Grows 3 to 6 inches high. Flowers pale rose-violet. Summer.

M. graeca.—A pubescent shrubby plant, growing 9 inches high, with pink flowers, in June.

Other species are *M. Juliana*, with pink flowers, and *M. rupestris*, with white or purple flowers.

Mimulus (Scrophulariaceae), Monkey Flower

A numerous genus, of which a few of the named varieties may be planted in the bog garden, and will give a good patch of colour during the summer. *M. Brilliant* and *M. Model* are the two best for this purpose.

M. radicans.—A tiny, creeping plant, with brownish, rather hairy leaves lying close to the ground. Small white flowers, with a violet-coloured blotch. It requires to be planted in a very damp spot. Quite hardy, and of easiest culture in any moist, boggy position. An interesting and charming little plant. Propagated by division.

M. primuloides.—Is also a minute, creeping species, for a wet spot, and has pretty yellow flowers. Easily propagated by division.

Mitchella repens (Rubiaceae), Partridge Berry

A charming little evergreen, trailing plant, for a damp spot in shade, and planted in light peaty loam and sand. It has roundish, shiny leaves, and white flowers tinged with purple, followed by red berries in the autumn.

Mitella (Saxifragaceae)

Hardy perennials of no special merit.

M. diphylla.—Likes a partially shaded position in light peaty soil. Serrated leaves in tufts, growing about 6 inches high. Slender racemes of white-fringed flowers from April to June.

M. pentandra.—For a shady spot in peaty soil. Forms a good tuft of palmate leaves, and spikes of yellowish flowers on slender stems. Sows itself about freely.

MODIOLA GERANIOIDES (MALVACEAE), syn. MALVASTRIUM GILLIESII

A trailing plant, growing 4 to 6 inches high, with rosy-purple flowers, with a dark line in the centre, borne singly on slender stalks. Quite hardy, and of easy culture in light, well-drained soil. Increased by division.

MOEHRINGIA MUSCOSA (CARYOPHYLLACEAE)

A dwarf evergreen plant for a damp spot in fine sandy loam. It grows 2 to 3 inches high, with prostrate stems clothed with very narrow leaves. Small white, solitary flowers, produced in May and June. Increased by seed or division.

MOLTKIA PETRAEA (*see* LITHOSPERMUM PETRAEA)

MONESES GRANDIFLORA (syn. PYROLA UNIFLORA)

Hardy perennial plant for a half-shady position in moist, spongy peat and sandy loam. Forms flat rosettes of leaves about 6 inches high. Solitary pink or white flowers about ¾ of an inch across. A very difficult plant to cultivate.

MORISIA HYPOGAEA (CRUCIFERAE)

One of the most charming little rock plants. It likes a very well-drained, sandy soil in an open position. I find it does best in a fairly cool spot not baked by the sun. It forms flat little tufts of glossy leaves, and the flowers, which bloom in April, are of a bright clear yellow and about 1 inch across, borne singly on very short stalks. Quite hardy, and a little gem for association with the choicest rock plants. Increased by seed and careful division.

MUEHLENBECKIA NANA (POLYGONACEAE)

A dwarf evergreen shrub of trailing habit, forming a carpet only a few inches high. Sunny position in well-drained, sandy soil. The leaves are small and of a dark green colour, and borne on slender, wiry stems. Other varieties, suitable only for clothing very large rocks or for growing amongst shrubs, are *M. complexa* and *adpressa*, both of which bear rather inconspicuous white flowers.

MUSCARI (LILIACEAE), Grape Hyacinth

Little bulbous plants commonly known by name of Grape Hyacinth. Only one or two species are really distinct. They are early flowering, and valuable on that account. They like a sunny spot, and increase fairly rapidly.

M. conicum.—"Heavenly blue" is the best coloured, having deep blue flowers very freely produced.

M. moschatum.—Rather ugly flowers of a greenish-yellow colour, but most deliciously fragrant, and well worth growing on that account alone.

M. szovitsianum.—Has large and pretty spikes of a pale blue colour.

MYOSOTIS (BORAGINACEAE)

The "Forget-me-nots" give us some lovely and valuable plants for a moist or shady spot. So long as the ground is damp they do not require shade, in fact they bloom better in the open.

M. alpestris (syn. *M. rupicola*).—Likes a half-shady position between pieces of sandstone, in a light, well-drained, though rather moist soil; is apt to perish in the winter in excessive moisture. It forms close tufts of dark green, rather hairy leaves, and grows only about 2 inches high. The flowers are of a beautiful blue colour, with a yellow eye, which are borne in the greatest profusion during the early summer. Though hardy, it is not easy to keep in health. Easily raised, and comes true from seed. There are considerable differences of opinion as to whether *rupicola* is merely a variety of *alpestris*, or a distinct species. I have taken them as being synonymous, as from a gardener's point of view they are so similar in appearance, and, requiring the same treatment, there is no advantage in separating them. There are several named varieties of *M. alpestris*, the raisers of which claim them to be superior to the type.

M. azorica.—Likes a sheltered, half-shady position in deep, moist, sandy loam. It forms spreading tufts. It has rich purple-blue flowers, borne on arching stems about 6 to 9 inches long. It is not very hardy, but can be easily raised from seed, which should be sown in the autumn, and seedlings kept in frames during the winter and planted out in May. A very choice and lovely plant.

M. dissitiflora.—Likes moist loam in sun and partial shade. It is very similar to *M. sylvatica* in appearance, but blooms earlier in the year, its flowers appearing in January or February. Easily increased by division, and of easy culture. A good plant on account of its early flowering proclivities.

M. palustris.—Grows freely in any wet spot, but so freely does it grow, that it should only be planted where it can have plenty of room to spread without damaging other and choicer plants. " *The Czar* " is a good free-flowering variety of this.

M. sylvatica.—Is of easy culture in almost any soil or position, so long as it does not suffer from drought. It should be treated as a biennial and a stock raised annually from seed. A very pretty plant for massing in waste spots.

M. Reichsteineri.—A tiny creeping species, which will grow in any fairly damp soil. It makes a little matted carpet of smooth, bright green leaves, and in early summer spikes of small turquoise-blue flowers are borne on stems, rising barely 2 inches from the ground. Increased by division. A little top-dressing of sandy leaf-soil should occasionally be applied. A most delightful and choice little plant, and one of the best for making a carpet for bulbous plants. It is a variety of *M. caespitosa*, which is almost identical with *M. palustris*.

NARCISSUS (AMARYLLIDEAE)

Well-known, spring-flowering bulbous plants, of which there are so many new and lovely varieties that it is impossible to keep pace with all the later hybrids, unless one were a specialist in that branch. Many, however, of the commoner kinds should be planted in and about the rock garden, to give colour to it in early spring. In no position do they look better than in grass or coming through a carpet of some creeping rock plant.

NARTHECIUM OSSIFRAGUM (LILIACEAE), Bog Asphodel

A native plant for the bog or marsh garden. Somewhat like an Iris in growth, with spikes of yellow flowers. Pretty plant of easy culture in any wet spot.

NEPETA MUSSINI (LABIATAE), Catmint

A very old garden plant. It forms a dense, prostrate tuft about 10 inches high, with greyish, fragrant leaves, and a great profusion of lavender-blue flowers during the summer. It is a rapid grower in any light soil in full sun. A most valuable and attractive plant both on account of its foliage and flowers, and should be freely used. It can readily be struck from cuttings.

NERTERA DEPRESSA (RUBIACEAE)

A very diminutive, creeping plant for a moist spot. It forms a close, compact mat of bright green leaves about 2 inches high. The flowers are inconspicuous, but the bright orange-red berries which appear in autumn are most attractive. It is not very hardy, and should be protected from snow. Increased by division.

NIEREMBERGIA (SOLANACEAE)

An attractive genus of perennial plants.

N. Frutescens.—A most dainty and attractive plant, like a Linum both in foliage and flower. It likes a rather dry and sheltered position in sandy loam. It forms a half-shrubby plant, about 12 to 18 inches high. The flax-like flowers are blue, shading to white at the edges, and are most lovely. This most attractive plant is unfortunately not very hardy, except in a mild climate. Propagated by seed and cuttings.

N. gracilis.—Light sandy soil in sun. Grows 6 to 12 inches high. Flowers white, streaked with purple, centre yellow. Blooms in the summer, and very freely. Attractive, but not very hardy.

N. Rivularis.—Sunny position in light gritty soil. Dwarf and creeping plant, spreading rapidly by means of underground stems. The ovate leaves rise about 3 inches. The cup-shaped flowers are creamy-white, and rise just above the foliage. A shy bloomer, though of free growth and quite hardy. Easily increased by division.

ŒNOTHERA (ONAGRACEAE), Evening Primrose

Of this large genus the only species suitable for the rock garden are :

Œ. Arendsii.—Light gritty loam on a sunny bank. Of trailing habit. Lovely delicate shell-pink flowers, July to October. Free-growing and very beautiful. It is a hybrid (*speciosa × rosea*).

Œ. caespitosa (syn. *Œ. eximia* and *marginata*).—Requires a light loamy soil. Not particular as to aspect. It is of trailing habit, and grows about 9 inches high. Large white flowers, changing to pale rose colour, and sweet-scented. A handsome plant, of easy culture, and increased by cuttings or division. It is night-flowering.

Œ. eximia (see *Œ. caespitosa*).

Œ. fruticosa Youngii.—Ordinary, well-drained soil. Grows about 18 inches high, and bears a profusion of bright yellow flowers during the summer. A very good species, also night-flowering.

Œ. Fraseri.—Well-drained, light soil. Grows about 12 inches high. Bright yellow flowers in great profusion, from July to October. Of easy culture. This plant is a variety of *Œ. glauca.*

Œ. marginata (see *Œ. caespitosa*).

Œ. missouriensis latifolia (syn. *Œ. Macrocarpa*).—Likes a light, well-drained soil. It grows about 8 inches high, and is of trailing habit. Clear yellow flowers, 4 to 5 inches across, borne in such profusion as to hide the plant. It blooms from June to September. It is night-flowering, and one of the best of the genus. Increased by cuttings made in April, or by careful division.

Œ. rosea.—Grows 12 inches high. Flowers pink, in July. Not very hardy.

Œ. speciosa.—Requires well-drained loam. Forms a neat, almost shrubby plant, 12 to 18 inches high, with quantities of large white flowers, which come out during the day. A lovely plant, and of fairly easy culture, but it does not stand a wet winter well. Increased by division or cuttings.

Œ. taraxacifolia (syn. *Œ. acaulis*).—Does best in a deep, cool, rather rich soil. Grows about 6 to 9 inches high, and is of trailing habit and free growth. Leaves rather greyish and deeply cut. Flowers large white, changing to pale rose as they become older. It is fairly hardy, but is liable to perish in a wet winter or cold soils. Easily raised from seed. Quite one of the best of the genus, and a most desirable plant; also has the advantage of blooming in the daytime, though at its best at night.

OMPHALODES (BORAGINACEAE)

A genus of hardy and attractive plants.

O. Luciliæ.—A rare and rather capricious plant, requiring thoroughly drained and very gritty soil; in fact the compost should be made up of about equal parts of loam, grit, and small stone chips: a little powdered slate is said to be a help. It likes an open, sunny position, and grows 6 to 9 inches high. The leaves are glaucous, grey, and very pretty. Flowers are pale sky-blue, and borne in racemes. It blooms in the summer. A plant, lovely as it is rare.

O. nitida.—Light soil in open position. Leaves glabrous above and downy beneath. Flowers white, borne in long racemes. Fairly rapid grower, spreading by means of strawberry-like runners. A very pretty plant.

O. verna.—Likes a damp soil in half shade. Grows about 4 inches high, and is of spreading and vigorous habit. Flowers deep blue, with a white throat, blooming in early spring. A charming old plant for a shady nook. Is easily increased by division.

ONONIS (LEGUMINOSAE)

The "Rest Harrows" are useful and pretty plants for dry, poor soils, though not of very great interest. They all can be increased by seed or cuttings.

O. arvensis.—A dwarf-growing plant, forming dense, spreading tufts about 6 inches high. Masses of pink flowers in June. Quite a useful plant, and of the easiest culture.

O. fruticosa.—Is a dwarf, shrubby species, growing about 12 inches high. Flowers purple, and borne in racemes during the summer.

O. Natrix.—Also a somewhat shrubby plant, growing about 18 inches high, with yellow flowers veined with red.

O. rotundifolia.—A half-shrubby plant, growing 12 to 18 inches high. Flowers rose-coloured, upper standard veined crimson. A useful and handsome plant for the rougher parts of the rock garden.

ONOSMA (BORAGINACEAE), Golden Drop

A genus of plants, some of much beauty. They all require deep, well-drained, sandy soil in full sun, in such a position that no wet can lie about and rot them. They do well planted between rocks, round which they can get their roots and keep them cool and moist. As some kinds are of but little beauty or value, the following is a selection of the best :—

O. albo-roseum.—Forms a compact tuft about 6 inches high, with hairy, rather silvery leaves. Flowers white, changing to pale rose, borne in racemes during June and July. There is also a form called *alba*, in which the flowers remain white. Both are very pretty, and can be propagated by cuttings in the summer.

O. Bourgaei.—Grows about 6 inches high, forming compact tufts of silvery-white leaves, and bearing deep yellow flowers in June and July.

O. tauricum (syn. *O. echioides*).—Forms compact tufts of rather hairy leaves, about 6 to 8 inches high, with clear yellow, fragrant flowers, borne in drooping clusters on stems about 14 inches high. Can be increased by cuttings. A handsome plant for a dry ledge.

O. Thompsoni.—Forms a tuft of rather hairy leaves. Flowers red, borne in a dense head on an upright stem about 14 inches high.

OPHRYS (ORCHIDEAE)

Small terrestrial orchids, mostly too delicate and difficult to grow to be of much value for the rock garden. There are, however, a few native species which may be tried.

O. apifera (Bee Orchis).—Requires a dry, warm soil of loam and broken limestone, and should have the surface of the ground, in which it grows, covered with cocoa fibre and sand about 1 inch thick to keep it moist. The leaves are glaucous and lie close to the ground. Flowers, borne on stems about 12 inches high, are velvety brown, with yellow markings.

Other varieties worth growing and requiring similar treatment are : *O. muscifera* (Fly Orchis), *O. aranifera* (Spider Orchis), *O. Arachnites*, *O. bombilifera* (Humble Bee Orchis), and *O. Trolli*.

OPUNTIA (CACTACEAE)

Plants of the Cacti order, some of which are hardy in the warmer districts, and many are very beautiful when in flower. They all require a very hot, dry situation in light soil, with plenty of lime rubbish mixed with it. They should be kept dry during the winter. As these can scarcely be considered typically rock plants, but are more generally associated with tropical vegetation, it would be better to group, in a spot reserved for them, when the needed protection during the winter could be more easily given. Most nurserymen keep them, and a selection can be obtained.

ORCHIS (ORCHIDEAE)

Many of the terrestrial Orchids are very beautiful for the bog and rock garden. Orchids, even our own native species, are generally considered difficult to cultivate. This, however, is due not so much to the nature of the plant, as to the time of planting. They should never be moved when in flower or making growth, which so frequently is just the time when they are transplanted, with the result that they die, and thereby get a bad reputation. August and September are the best months for planting them. The following selection will give some of the hardiest and best species :—

O. foliosa.—Rich, rather damp, heavy loam in a sheltered nook. Dense spikes of rosy-purple spotted flowers, rising about 18 inches from the ground. A very handsome species, flowering in May.

O. latifolia (Marsh Orchis).—Damp, rather rich, boggy soil, in partial shade. Purple or red flowers in long, dense spikes, coming into bloom about June. There are several good varieties of this—

O. l. incarnata.—Flesh-coloured.

O. l. sesquipedalis.—Violet-purple colour, in very long spikes.

O. laxiflora.—Moist loam and peat in partial shade. Loose spikes of rich purplish-red flowers in May. Handsome.

O. maculata.—The well-known "Spotted Orchis" will be found an excellent plant for the bog garden. The variety *superba* is very fine.

O. papilionacea (Butterfly Orchis).—Heavy loam and limestone. Flowers reddish-purple.

Other varieties that can be grown are—

O. militaris and *O. purpurea*, in limestone and heavy loam.

O. mascula, O. pyramidalis, O. sambucina, and *O. spectabilis*, in rich, rather heavy, moist loam and peat, with sand added, in a partially shady position.

All Orchids require a considerable depth of soil.

ORIGANUM (LABIATAE)

A genus of shrubby plants of not much value. The following are a selection of the best :—

O. dictamnus.—A sub-shrubby plant for a dry, sunny position in light loam. Grows about 12 inches high. It has mottled, downy foliage, and its heads of small pink flowers are borne from June to August in great profusion. It is rather a tender plant, and will need some protection in a severe winter.

O. pulchrum.—Sunny position in sandy loam. Sub-shrubby plant, with silvery leaves, and rosy-purple flowers in August. A good rock plant.

O. Sipyleum.—A shrubby plant of procumbent habit. Flowers pink.

OTHONNA (COMPOSITAE)

A large genus of glabrous plants only half hardy. The following are the only species suitable :—

O. cheirifolia (syn. *Othonnopsis cheirifolia*).—Dry, sunny position. A vigorous, trailing plant, growing 12 inches high, with greyish, glaucous leaves. The flowers are bright golden-yellow, and are produced during early summer. A useful evergreen plant, which can be easily propagated from cuttings.

O. crassifolia.—Light sandy loam in full sun. A creeping plant of rapid growth, with curious, succulent leaves, like a Sedum, of a bright green colour. Numerous yellow, daisy-like flowers are borne during the summer. A pretty and useful plant. Not hardy, but can so easily be propagated by cuttings that it is quite worth while wintering a few plants in a cold-house.

OURISIA COCCINEA (SCOPHULARIACEAE).

A lovely plant, but of rather uncertain habit in cultivation. The two conditions it requires are half shade and moisture ; given these, it in all probability will thrive. Rather heavy loam seems to suit it best. That, at least, is my experience, but others recommend deep, gritty peat. It is of creeping habit, forming tufts of crinkled leaves about 4 inches high, from which rise stems about 8 inches high, on which bright crimson flowers are borne in racemes during the summer. It is quite hardy, and may be increased by division.

O. macrophylla.—Quite a new introduction from New Zealand, and not yet in general cultivation. It forms tufts of handsome leaves and white flowers in whorls, and rising about 12 inches over the foliage. If it proves hardy, as it appears to be, it should be an acquisition for the rock garden.

Oxalis (Geraniaceae)

A large genus of dwarf-growing plants, few are hardy except our own native species. The following are of proved hardiness :—

O. Acetosella.—The native Wood Sorrel, which, however, grows so freely in woods that it is scarcely worth devoting a place to it in the rock garden.

O. Adenophylla.—Requires cool, sandy loam in partial shade. The foliage and habit resemble *O. enneaphylla*, but the flowers are a lovely, very pale pink, with a blue line down the centre of each petal. A most lovely plant, but as yet very rare in cultivation ; it is, if possible, prettier than its prototype, *O. enneaphylla*.

O. enneaphylla.—Likes a cool, moist, light sandy loam free from lime. It grows more freely in shade, but flowers better if exposed to a certain amount of sunshine. It forms a compact tuft of very pretty, glaucous, grey, crinkled leaves. It has a curious scaly bulbous root. The flowers, which are rather like a Convolvulus, are pearly-white, with a purple stain at the base of each petal, and nestle amongst the leaves. It blooms in June and July, and is quite hardy, and not difficult to grow. There are few more fascinating or dainty plants for the rock garden. There is a very lovely variety, *rosea*, which was collected by Mr C. Elliot in the Falkland Isles.

O. floribunda.—Any soil in partial shade. Forms a compact tuft of pretty leaves growing about 6 inches high, and produces during the whole summer a succession of pretty rose-coloured flowers. It is of the easiest culture, and of rapid growth. There is also a pretty white form equally free-flowering.

Oxytropis (Leguminosae)

A genus of dwarf-growing plants of the Vetch order. They all require a sunny, warm position in well-drained, light sandy loam.

O. baicalensis.—About 4 inches high, flowers blue in July.

O. campestris.—Grows about 6 inches high. Has rather downy foliage. It has erect spikes of yellowish flowers in the summer. Increased by seed or division. Not a very striking plant.

O. pyrenaica.—A dwarf, very prostrate species. The leaves are clothed with a silky down, and only rise a few inches from the ground. Purplish-lilac flowers, borne in rather dense heads. It is of fairly easy culture, and can be increased by seed or division. Blooms in July.

O. montana.—Dwarf-growing, with silky foliage and blue flowers in the summer. Seed and division.

O. Lambertii.—Silky foliage, and rosy-carmine flowers, in August. A rare and beautiful species.

O. Yunnanensis.—Of dwarf tufted habit, with pale blue flowers, rather like a trefoil.

PACHYSANDRA PROCUMBENS (EUPHORBIACEAE)

Dwarf-growing evergreen plant for a shady spot, with small spikes of white flowers in March.

P. terminalis.—A hardy evergreen plant, with dark green, leathery leaves and inconspicuous flowers. There is also a variegated variety. Both like half shade.

PAPAVER (PAPAVERACEAE), Poppy

Only two species of the Poppy family are suitable for the rock garden. Both are of the easiest culture.

P. alpina (syn. *P. pyrenaicum*).—Sunny position in light loam. Very dwarf-growing, forming compact tufts of pretty, finely cut, bluish-grey leaves. The flowers, which rise about 6 to 8 inches over the foliage, are of various colours, there being white, yellow, and scarlet in cultivation. It is difficult to transplant, so it is advisable to raise from seed on the spot assigned to it. A very dainty and attractive plant. The variety, *flaviflorum*, has orange-coloured flowers, and is rather hairy.

P. nudicaule.—The Iceland Poppy is almost too wild a grower for the rock garden, but is so showy and pretty that a place should be found for it in the rougher parts. The original type had yellow flowers, but every shade of orange, yellow, and red are in cultivation, besides a white form. It is practically only a biennial.

PARADISEA LILIASTRUM (LILIACEAE)

The lovely "St Bruno's Lily" should find a place in the rock garden in some shady nook, or planted amongst the shrubs adjoining. It is of the easiest culture, in any ordinary soil in partial shade. Its pure white flowers, about 2 inches long, are borne two to five on each stem, which rises about 18 inches from the ground. There is a larger form, *major*, with longer stems and bigger flowers.

PARNASSIA (SAXIFRAGACEAE)

Plants for a wet spot in the bog garden.

P. caroliniana.—Requires a wet, marshy spot. The stem grows from 18 inches to 2 feet high, and has large white flowers, 1 to $1\frac{1}{2}$ inches across, and large leathery leaves.

P. fimbriata.—Grows freely in any rich, damp soil. Flowers white, and of a good size, with a fringe of white hairs at the base of each petal. Flower-stems rise about 12 to 18 inches from the ground. A handsome plant, of easy culture.

P. palustris.—The native "Grass of Parnassus," which grows freely in damp soil. The white flowers, veined greenish, are borne on stems about 6 to 9 inches high. Easily raised from seed, which should be sown, as soon as gathered, in moist spots assigned to the plants.

PAROCHETUS COMMUNIS (LEGUMINOSAE), Shamrock Pea

A lovely creeping plant for a damp, sheltered spot. Its clover-like leaves rise only some 3 inches from the ground. The flowers, which are pea-shaped, are of a most beautiful azure-blue, and freely borne during the summer. It is rather inclined to go off in extra cold or damp winters. It is a most vigorous grower, quickly covering large spaces, so should not be planted near anything choice. It is a very lovely plant, and should certainly be grown when space will admit.

PARONYCHIA SERPHYLLIFOLIA (ILLECEBRACEAE)

Small, creeping plant of dense, tufty growth, of little value except to clothe some bare, dry bank.

PARRYA MENZIESII (CRUCIFERAE)

A plant nearly allied to the Aubrietias, growing only about 6 inches high, with spikes of soft, rose-coloured flowers.

PASCHKENIA SCHILLOIDES

A bulbous plant for an open situation in light sandy soil. Grows 4 to 8 inches high. Flowers white, striped and tinged with blue, and borne in racemes, on stems about 6 to 8 inches high. Hardy. Increased by division. A very charming little spring-flowering plant.

PELARGONIUM ENDLICHERIANUM (GERANIACEAE)

Requires a sheltered, sunny nook in gritty loam. It grows about 6 inches high, with deep, rose-coloured flowers, borne on stems about 18 inches high. Hardy in most places. An interesting and handsome plant.

PENSTEMON (SCROPHULARIACEAE)

A genus of beautiful plants, many of which, however, are too large and coarse-growing for the rock garden. The following will be found suitable and hardy. They all require a warm spot in light, free loam, and can easily be propagated by seed or cuttings.

P. azureus.—Is of branching habit, bearing numerous violet-blue flowers in whorls during the summer. This plant is quite hardy. *P. Jeffreyanus* is a variety of this, with larger flowers.

P. caeruleus.—Grows about 9 inches high. Has glaucous, grey foliage, and lovely, pale turquoise-blue flowers. It is not very hardy. It comes freely from seed, but, unfortunately, frequently not true, the same batch of seedlings giving many shades of colour, and only a very small percentage of which will be the desired tint.

P. Davidsoni.—Gritty, well-drained soil in a warm position or moraine. Forms a tiny shrub of rather prostrate habit. Small glaucous, leathery leaves. Flowers large and brilliant ruby-red. A really lovely plant.

P. glaber.—Rather dwarf, prostrate habit, with dense heads of a fine shade of blue, tinged with rose. Very variable from seed.

P. glaucus.—Forms a compact plant about 9 inches high, with bluish-grey foliage and dense heads of large, purplish-blue flowers in July. Rather a distinct plant.

P. heterophyllus.—Grows from 12 to 18 inches, forming a graceful, sub-shrubby plant. Flowers pale, violet-blue, with throat of azure-blue. A lovely plant, and hardy, except in a severe winter. It, like many others of the genus, varies considerably from seed.

P. humilis.—Requires a sunny spot in gritty loam and leaf-mould. Forms a compact tuft 8 inches high. Large flowers of a reddish-purple colour in May and June. It should be watered freely.

P. procerus.—Is of creeping habit, forming neat tufts, from which rise 6- to 12-inch stems, bearing dense spikes of amethyst-blue flowers. One of the best of the family and the earliest to bloom. Can be raised easily from seed.

P. Scouleri.—A plant of half-shrubby habit, growing about 12 inches high. Flowers a pretty shade of pale purplish-blue, borne in terminal racemes. A good plant, of easy culture. Propagation by seed or cuttings in spring and struck in a little bottom heat.

PERNETTYA MUCRONATA (ERICACEAE)

Dwarf-growing, evergreen shrub, growing freely in peaty loam, or even in heavy soil with leaf-mould added. Flowers small and pinky-white, followed in the autumn by small purple-black berries. A very useful shrub for the higher slopes of the rock garden. Quite hardy, and will grow readily under trees. Increased by division.

PETROCALLIS PYRENAICA (syn. DRABA PYRENAICA)

A very dwarf-growing little plant for a warm spot in fine, sandy, fibrous loam soil. Pieces of limestone should be buried in the soil for it to get its roots about. It forms dense green tufts, about 3 inches high, from which rise its fragrant, pale lilac-coloured flowers, scarcely half an inch over the foliage. A very dainty little plant for a choice spot, needing careful culture, though quite hardy. A yearly top dressing of lime rubbish is beneficial.

PHILESIA BUXIFOLIA (LILIACEAE)

A lovely dwarf, evergreen shrub. It requires a half-sunny aspect, sheltered from the north, in rather damp, fibrous, sandy peat. The lovely flowers, which are like a Lapageria, are of a carmine-red colour. Not hardy except in the southern counties, and is not easy to cultivate. It may take a year or more before becoming established, or, at least, making any growth. Shoots should be pegged down to encourage them to layer. A most exquisite gem, and worth endless trouble to obtain success.

PHLOX (POLEMONIACEAE)

The taller-growing species of this very large genus are suitable for the border only. But there are many dwarf and creeping kinds which are amongst the most valuable and easiest cultivated plants we have for the rock garden. Any ordinary light soil will suit them, and they are not particular as to aspect, but bloom and grow better in sun. They can be easily increased by cuttings taken in July ; and inserted in sandy soil and placed in a frame shaded from full sun, they root quickly, and should be flowering plants by the following year. Another way is by layers, pegging down some of the prostrate stems in sandy soil : they will soon make roots at that point.

P. amoena.—Of spreading habit, with rosy-coloured flowers in early summer. Very hardy, and of easiest culture.

P. Carolina (syn. *P. ovata*).—Of procumbent habit, with clusters of large rosy flowers, on stems about 12 inches high.

P. divaricata.—Grows about 12 inches high, with flat heads of large, pale lavender-coloured flowers. Very pretty, but not of the prostrate habit of the creeping Phloxes. There are several varieties of this plant, all excellent. They are—

P. d. alba.—White.

P. d. canadensis.—Rather a darker shade of colour from the type, and of looser growth.

P. d. Laphami (Perry's var.).—Finer form of *P. d. canadensis.*

P. d. Douglasii.—Pale lavender-coloured flowers, with an orange eye.

P. pilosa.—Grows about 12 to 14 inches high, and has flat heads of large purple flowers. The true plant is very rare.

P. procumbens.—Of creeping habit, and brownish foliage. Panicles of purple flowers in June from its prostrate growth.

P. reptans.—Creeping habit and rapid growth, covering the ground and rocks with its soft green foliage, about an inch high. The purplish-rose-coloured flowers are borne in clusters on stems 4 to 6 inches high. Easily increased by division.

P. Stellaria.—Forms a fairly compact tuft of narrow leaves, with spikes of bluish-white, star-like flowers. Quite distinct.

P. subulata.—Of dwarf, prostrate habit, forming a compact evergreen mass, about 6 inches high. The leaves are awl-shaped and very numerous. The flowers are rose-coloured, with a dark eye, so freely produced as to hide the plant. It is of rapid growth, and very hardy; the only thing it dislikes is excessive drought. This is the type of the indispensable creeping, mossy Phlox, of which endless varieties are in cultivation, and are amongst the most valuable plants there are for the rock garden, and should be freely grown either to cover a bank or to clothe the face of a rock. They are all lovely, and of the easiest culture. A selection should be made from some catalogue. Mr T. Smith of Newry has a remarkably fine collection, and many of the most beautiful hybrids are of his raising.

PHYSARIA DIDYMOCARPA (CRUCIFERAE)

Hot, dry position in very sandy loam. Curious large, succulent, glaucous leaves, growing about 6 inches high, and yellow flowers. A recent introduction.

PHYTEUMA (CAMPANULACEAE)

Pretty plants for the rock garden, of the Bell-flower order.

P. comosum.—Requires a warm, sunny chink in well-drained, very calcareous, sandy soil. It should have plenty of root room, and should be so placed that water cannot lie about and rot its crown. The leaves are dark green, and only grow about 2 inches high. The flowers are deep purple and of a curious shape, and are borne in flattish heads on very short stems. It is quite hardy, though having the reputation of being difficult to grow; but with plenty of lime rubbish and good drainage there should be no trouble. Slugs are particularly fond of this plant, and if not guarded against will soon destroy it. One of the gems for a choice spot in the rock garden.

P. pauciflorum.—Light sandy, calcareous soil in sun. Forms a compact little tuft of narrow leaves, and has heads of deep blue flowers. Difficult to cultivate, but very attractive.

P. hemisphaericum and *P. orbiculare* are very similar to the last-named, but not quite so choice, though both are good rock plants for a limestone soil.

P. Sieberi.—Requires a sunny aspect in moist, peaty, and loamy soil, with sand added. Forms a compact tuft, with dark blue flower heads on stems about 5 inches high. Blooms in May and June, and can be increased by division.

P. humilis.—Dry, sheltered position in sandy loam. Dark blue flowers on stems 6 inches high, in June. It should be kept dry during the winter, but requires plenty of moisture during the summer. It blooms in June.

P. Scheuchzeri.—Sandy soil in open position. Forms a nice tuft of rather long narrow leaves and round heads of deep-blue flowers, on stems about 8 to 12 inches high. Easily raised from seed.

PIERIS (*see* ANDROMEDA)

PINGUICULA (LENTIBULARIACEAE), Butterwort

Interesting little plants for wet, boggy spots.

P. alpina.—Needs moist peat and gravelly soil, and forms flat rosettes of fleshy leaves. Flowers white, with yellow markings on the tip. Roots firmly by means of woody fibres, and in this is very different to *P. grandiflora.*

P. grandiflora.—Requires moist peat. Forms rosettes of light green, fleshy leaves lying close to the ground, from which rise, on stems about 3 inches high, the deep blue flowers like a violet. It is not easy to cultivate, though a native. This is owing to the roots being very few and only on the surface. Probably the best way would be by sowing seed on the spot assigned to it. *P. vulgaris* is a commoner and smaller form.

P. vallisneriaefolia.—Requires a dripping fissure in limestone rock, with ample drainage. Large, pale yellowish-green leaves. Large, pale lilac flowers, with white centres. Rather a distinct species.

PLATYCODON (*see* CAMPANULA GRANDIFLORA)

PLUMBAGO LARPENTAE (PLUMBAGINACEAE), syn. CERATOSTIGMA PLUMBAGINOIDES

A deciduous plant, with rather woody stems, of a semi-prostrate habit, growing about 12 inches high. It will grow in any soil, but in a light sandy soil it blooms better. The flowers, which are borne in trusses, are of a fine deep blue. It is a valuable plant on account of its late flowers, which last till the November frosts destroy them. Quite hardy, and grows rapidly. Easily increased by division.

POLEMONIUM (POLEMONIACEAE), Jacob's Ladder

Only the dwarfer species of this genus are suitable for the rock garden.

P. confertum.—Requires a warm position in well-drained, deep, loamy soil. It has slender and deeply cut leaves, and clusters of clear blue flowers, borne on stems about 6 inches high. Of easy culture, but dislikes disturbance. Can be raised from seed. *mellitum* is a white form.

P. humile.—Requires a dry, light soil. Forms tufts of pale green leaves and bears numerous pale blue flowers on stems a few inches high. Blooms in June. Hardy in a well-drained position, but a damp subsoil will prove fatal. Propagated by seed or division.

P. reptans.—Is of creeping habit, and has loose panicles of slaty-blue flowers, borne 6 or 8 inches high. Propagated by division or seed. Slugs are very partial to this plant.

POLYGALA (POLYGALACEAE), Milkwort

Interesting little plants, and some most suitable for the rock garden.

P. Chamaebuxus.—Likes a half-shady position in sandy peat and loam, well drained. It is evergreen, and forms compact tufts. Flowers cream-coloured, and borne in profusion. The variety *purpurea* is better, having purple flowers with a yellow centre. Of easy culture, and increased by division. Both are most attractive plants.

P. Rhodoptera and *P. Vayredae* are of the same type, with crimson flowers. They are both of recent introduction.

P. calcarea.—Very similar to the common Milkwort of our hills, and is also a native. It will grow easily in calcareous soil, and is a pretty little plant.

POLYGONATUM (LILIACEAE), Solomon's Seal

Attractive plants for growing amongst shrubs or on the higher parts of the rock garden, where their graceful arching stems will show to advantage. All are of easy culture in any light, well-drained soil in partial shade, and are readily increased by division. They are all deciduous.

P. biflorum.—Grows 1 to 3 feet high, with arching stems, and small greenish-white flowers in pairs.

P. japonicum.—Grows about 2 feet high, and has white flowers tinged with purple.

P. latifolium.—Bright green leaves on arching stems 2 to 3 feet high. Flowers white and of a good size. The variety *commutatum* grows as high as 7 feet, and is glabrous throughout.

P. multiflorum.—The common "Solomon's Seal." Grows 2 to 4 feet high, with bright, glaucous green leaves and white flowers.

P. officinale.—Only grows about 12 to 18 inches high, and is otherwise similar to the last-named.

P. oppositifolium.—Requires rather a sheltered spot. It has arching stems 2 to 3 feet high, with bright, glossy green leaves. Flowers white, marked with reddish lines and dots, and borne in bunches, followed by red berries in the autumn.

P. punctatum.—Angular, arching stems about 2 feet high. Hard, leathery leaves, and white flowers with lilac dots. A handsome plant.

P. roseum.—Arching stems 2 to 3 feet high. Leaves in whorls, and flowers rose-coloured, borne in pairs at the axils of the leaves. Very pretty species.

POLYGONUM (POLYGONACEAE)

A very large genus, of which a few are suitable for planting in the rock garden, and even those, with a couple of exceptions, not of the highest value. They can all be propagated by division.

P. affine.—Likes a moist, though well-drained position in loam. It grows from 6 to 8 inches high, and has spikes of rosy flowers in the autumn. It is a very pretty plant.

P. Brunonis.—Similar to the above, with pale rose-coloured flowers, borne in dense spikes, 12 to 18 inches high.

P. sphaerostachyum.—Dwarf-growing, with spikes of deep crimson flowers. Very handsome, and one of the best.

P. vaccinifolium.—Of neat, trailing habit and rapid growth. Spikes of bright rose-coloured flowers in the summer and autumn. A good plant for covering rocks or banks, and is not particular as to aspect or soil. The best of the genus.

P. viviparum.—Very dwarf habit, with spikes of creamy-white flowers. Quite a pretty little plant, and not so encroaching as many of the genus are.

POTENTILLA (ROSACEAE)

Of this large genus there are only a few that should find a place in the rock garden, but amongst these few are some of the best plants we have. Propagated by seed, cuttings, or division.

P. ambigua.—Well-drained, open position in sandy soil. Dwarf and creeping habit, only about 3 inches high, forming a compact mass. Large, clear yellow flowers. Of moderate, though not rampant growth. Increased by division. A very pretty and charming plant, of the easiest culture, and quite hardy.

P. alba.—Sunny position in ordinary light soil. Of a dwarf habit, only a few inches high. Leaves green, and smooth above, but covered beneath with a white, silky down. Flowers white, with an orange ring at base of petals. Blooms in June. Is of the easiest culture, and not a rampant grower. A good plant.

P. argentea.—Ordinary soil. Creeping and dwarf habit, growing only about 6 inches high. Foliage covered with a silvery down. Flowers yellow. Of easy culture, and useful as a variety, though not otherwise possessing any special charm.

P. aurea.—Sunny position in light soil. Very dwarf habit, only about 2 inches high. Leaves palmate, and fringed with silvery hairs. Large yellow flowers, orange spotted at base. Blooms from May to July. Is of easy culture, and increased by seed or division.

P. calabra.—Sandy soil in sun. Prostrate habit; undersides of leaves silvery. Lemon-yellow flowers, produced during the summer. Is of easy culture and worthy of a place.

P. davurica.—Light sandy soil in sun. A dwarf-growing, compact little bush, about 9 inches high, of almost prostrate habit. Dark green, glossy leaves, and white flowers. Of easy culture. An attractive plant that should be more generally grown. It is generally considered a form of *P. fruticosa.*

P. eriocarpa.—Ordinary soil in open position. Grows about 6 inches high. Large soft yellow flowers with an orange blotch on each petal. Hardy and good grower and well worth a place.

P. fruticosa.—Light sandy soil and sunny aspect. Forms a neat bush, about 2 feet high. Clusters of pretty yellow flowers, freely produced during the summer. A very desirable and useful shrub for massing, and of easy culture. Increased by cuttings.

P. f. humilis.—Is a quite dwarf form of the above, with yellow flowers from spring to autumn.

P. Friedrichseni.—Ordinary soil, open aspect. A shrub of erect habit, growing about 3 to 4 feet high, and covered during the summer with large, sulphur-coloured flowers. Charming, of quite easy culture, and hardy. A hybrid, *P. fruticosa × davurica.*

P. nitida.—Dry, light, poor, sandy soil in a sunny position. Only grows about 2 to 3 inches high. Leaves covered with a silvery down. Flowers delicate rose-coloured, from June to September. Of easy culture, but a shy bloomer, except in poor, light soils. A plant for a choice place. Readily increased by division.

P. nivalis.—Ordinary light soil in an open position. Grows 3 to 6 inches high. Leaves densely covered with a silky down. Flowers white. Blooms in July.

P. nivea.—Light soil and open position. Very dwarf habit.

Leaves grey above, and snow-white beneath. Yellow flowers in the summer.

P. Tonguei.—Ordinary soil in sunny position. Of trailing habit, growing about 2 inches high. Flowers coppery-orange, with a crimson centre. Not a very free bloomer. This plant should be grown so that its branches can hang over some rock or stone. It is of the easiest culture, and one of the best of the genus.

P. verna.—Any aspect in ordinary soil. Forms dwarf tufts, which in summer are covered with bright yellow flowers, about 1 inch across. Quite easy to grow, pretty, and well worth a place. Very closely allied to this plant is *P. alpestris*, which is somewhat coarser in growth, and is also a good plant.

Pratia angulata (Campanulaceae), syn. Lobelia Littoralis

A pretty, creeping plant, indifferent to soil or aspect. It forms a dense carpet, about 3 inches high, covered, in late summer, with white flowers like a Lobelia, and followed by dark blue berries. Of easy culture, and readily increased by division.

P. begonifolia. — Likes rather a sheltered, sunny position in damp, peaty loam. Rather similar to the above, but has larger and rounder leaves, which are downy. White flowers and purple berries. Suitable for the drier parts of the bog garden.

Primula (Primulaceae)

This very large genus of well-known plants, of which there are over two hundred species in cultivation, have botanically been divided into twenty-one sections; but, for our purpose, it will be sufficient to separate them into three groups. The first, the rock-loving kinds, such as *P. auricula* and *P. marginata*, which should be grown wedged between stones, or in rocky crevices. Next, the bog and moisture-loving plants, of which *P. japonica* and *P. sikkimensis* are well-known types; and lastly, those that can be grown in any moist, shady border, which include such species as *P. cashmeriana* and *P. capitata*.

As might be expected in a genus containing so many species of such diversity of habit and requirements, it is not possible to deal with their cultural requirements as a whole, but directions will be given with each as they appear in alphabetical order. The kinds described in the following pages only contain about a quarter of the known species, and are a selection of the most suitable and of easiest culture, it being obviously impossible in a work of this kind to give anything approaching an exhaustive list, nor would it indeed be advisable. Primulas hybridise so easily that new varieties are constantly being put on the market, many of which have but a botanical interest. A selection, which will be found on p. 334, has therefore been made of the best and most distinct kinds not included in the above list. In this country at least, Primulas, though theoretically perennials, are but short-lived; it will therefore be necessary, in order to keep up the stock, to raise plants from seed, which should be sown as soon as ripe; for, if kept over the winter many kinds may take a year, or even longer, to germinate, if they do so at all.

P. algida.—Bog-loving; in peat and loam, in half shade. Obtuse leaves, finely toothed. Rich violet-purple flowers. Rather rare and difficult to keep. Increased by seed, when it can be obtained. Nearly allied to *P. farinosa.*

P. Allionii.—Requires gritty loam and plenty of moisture at its roots. Plant in vertical position, or under ledge of rock, so that no moisture can lie on its leaves, which are very susceptible to damp. Of compact habit, forming cushion-like tufts of rather hairy leaves. Flowers rosy-purple, with a pale centre, on short stems. A very choice plant, but of difficult culture. Increased by seed or division.

P. amoena (syn. *P. cortusoides Sieboldi*). — A half-shady and sheltered position in rich, rather moist loam. Forms tufts of rather rugose leaves, with umbels of violet-coloured flowers on stems about 6 to 7 inches high, in April. Of vigorous growth, increased by seed or division.

P. auricula.—The Auriculas may roughly be divided into two groups. The one self-coloured, with leaves and other parts smooth and not powdery. The other has flowers and stems thickly coated with a white, powdery matter. Of the first group, those known as alpine Auriculas are the hardiest and most suitable for the rock garden. The second group are mainly florists' varieties, and are more delicate. They have again been divided into different sections, according to the colour of the edge of the flower; but I do not propose to deal with these subtleties, and shall take only the alpine section. The other kinds can of course be grown, and a selection should be made of the most distinct and hardiest varieties. The *P. auricula*, the parent of all these numerous varieties, is by no means common. It is a limestone plant, and should be grown wedged in between rocks in a vertical position, in partial shade. A good, rather stiff, loamy soil suits it well. It has glaucous, rather fleshy leaves, and yellow, sweet-scented flowers, borne in dense umbels on stems 4 to 5 inches high.

The variety *P. a. ciliata* (syn. *P. Balbisii*) has its leaves edged with granular hairs, and its yellow flowers are scentless, and not farinose.

P. a. marginata, another variety, has a white margin to its leaves, and yellow flowers. It is very liable to be confused with *P. marginata*, a very distinct plant.

P. Balbisii (see *P. auricula*, var. *ciliata*).

P. Beesiana.—Similar in requirements and habit to *P. Bulleyana.* Flowers rich velvety purple with a yellow eye, borne in whorls. 1½ to 2 feet high. Handsome, free-flowering, and quite hardy.

P. Bulleyana.—Rich, moist loam in half shade. Leaves like the common Primrose. Flowers orange-yellow, shaded on the outside with apricot. Borne in whorls, and rising 9 to 12 inches high. A very handsome new Chinese introduction, and said to be quite hardy.

P. calycina (see *P. glaucescens*).

P. capitata.—Cool, shady position in good soil of peat, loam, leaf-mould, and sand. The flowers, which are of a deep violet-blue, thickly coated with a white powder on outer and lower parts, are borne in dense globular heads on stems 6 to 9 inches high. It blooms in the autumn. It is hardy, but reputed only a biennial, though Mr Farrer says he had a clump for seven years, growing on a well-drained slope, in light soil, which treatment I am trying, but have not had time to fully test its efficacy, though, so far, all is well. It can easily be raised from seed, and is one of the gems of the genus.

P. capitellata.—Shady position in very moist peat and sandy loam. Forms a compact plant, with rather thick leaves and close heads of purplish or deep red flowers, borne about 9 inches high. Hardy and vigorous. A very attractive and uncommon plant.

P. carniolica (syn. *P. Freyeri* and *P. jellenkiana*).—Requires a half-shady spot in gritty loam. It should be grown wedged in between rocks, in a sloping position. Forms rosettes of smooth green leaves. Flowers bluish-purple, with a white centre. Blooms in July, and of vigorous growth. Increased by division and seed.

P. cashmeriana (see *P. denticulata*).

P. ciliatum (syn. *P. auricula ciliata*).

P. clusiana.—Half-shady position in calcareous and gritty loam. Leaves dark green, margined with white. Large handsome violet-carmine flowers, which bloom in April. Vigorous habit, and one of the most beautiful of the genus. It much resembles *P. glaucescens* (which is often sold for it), whose petals are not divided as they are in *P. clusiana.*

P. Cockburniana.—Half-shady position in moist, rich loam and leaf-mould. Forms rosettes of primrose-like leaves. Erect stems rise about 8 to 12 inches, and bear in whorls brilliant orange-scarlet flowers. A unique shade in the genus. Quite hardy, but unfortunately only a biennial; but it can readily be raised from seed, which germinates quickly if sown as soon as ripe. A recent introduction, and a most beautiful and valuable addition.

P. cortusoides.—Requires a sheltered, shady position in rich, sandy loam and leaf mould. Leaves soft and wrinkled, and springing from creeping stems 2 to 4 inches long. The flowers deep rose-coloured, borne in clusters on stems 6 to 8 inches high. Blooms in spring, and foliage dies down early. Of very easy culture, and increased by seed or division. Hardy.

P. c. Sieboldi.—The Japanese variety of this is synonymous with *P. amoena*, which see.

P. deflexa.—Shady position in moist, sandy loam and leaf-mould. Its leaves, which are hairy on both sides, form a rosette. Flowers rose-purple, in a dense head, which are individually deflexed. It is a biennial, and will require same treatment as *P. Cockburniana*.

P. denticulata.—Rich, moist soil in a shady position. Large leaves in rosettes, and globular heads of deep lilac-coloured flowers, on stems about 12 inches high. Blooms in the spring. Quite hardy, and is a very vigorous grower. Easily raised from seed or division. A handsome and valuable plant.

P. d., var. *cashmeriana.*—Differs from the last in having the undersides of its leaves thickly coated with a yellow powder, and having rather lighter-coloured flowers. It is also a charming and useful plant, of robust habit and easy culture. *P. pulcherrima* and *P. Henryi* are also varieties of *P. denticulata*, but neither so good as the above.

P. deorum.—A bog plant, requiring a very wet position in rich loam and leaf-mould. Leaves long and lanceolate. Rich rosy-purple flowers in large umbels, and very freely produced. Division and seed. A rare and lovely plant.

P. erosa (syn. *P. Fortunei*).—Requires an open, sheltered position in light, sandy loam and leaf-mould. Flat heads of light lavender-coloured flowers, with yellow eyes. It is very similar to *P. denticulata*, but may be distinguished from it by its smooth and regularly toothed leaves, which are sometimes quite powdery. Seed and division.

P. farinosa.—A bog plant for a shady position in rich, moist loam, or it can be planted in a moist crevice between rocks. The leaves, which form a rosette, are covered with a silvery-white powder, as is the rest of the plant. Dense umbels of lilac-coloured flowers, with a yellow centre, borne on stems 8 inches high, are freely produced in May and June. Of easy culture, and can be increased by seed or division. A very lovely plant, *P. farinosa*, var. *Scotia*, has deeper-coloured flowers, and is of dwarfer habit.

P. Forresti.—Shady position in moist, sandy loam. The flowers, which are of a rich golden-yellow, shading to deep orange, are borne in umbels, the individual flower slightly deflexed. Flower-stem erect, and about 9 inches high. Both leaves and flowers are fragrant. Quite a new introduction from China, and very handsome. It has been proved to be hardy, and of easy culture.

P. Fortunei.—Open position in gritty loam and leaf soil. Rosy lilac flowers, very like *P. frondosa.* Stems richly powdered with white farina. A very attractive species, but not very hardy. It requires copious moisture at all times.

P. Fosteri.—Half shade in sandy loam. Dwarf habit, forming compact tufts with large carmine-coloured flowers. Vigorous and free-blooming, this hybrid between *P. viscosa* and *P. minima* is one of the best kinds we have.

P. frondosa.—Likes a half-shady position in moist, sandy peat and loam. Similar to *P. farinosa*, except that its leaves are larger. It is of vigorous habit and easy culture. Readily increased by division.

P. glaucescens (syn. *P. calycina*).—Likes a half-shady position in calcareous loam, and does well planted in fissures of rocks. Forms a tuft of bluish-grey, hard leaves. Loose umbels of carmine-lilac flowers in March and April. A good plant, of easy culture.

P. glutinosa.—Requires partial shade in moist, peaty soil mixed with sphagnum. Leaves long and narrow. Flowers purple, borne on stems 4 to 5 inches long. A difficult plant to cultivate. A native of granite soils.

P. grandis.—Partial shade in moist, loamy soil. Foliage large and handsome. Small yellow flowers, of drooping habit, and produced in umbels on stems about 12 inches high. Quite hardy and vigorous. Flowers freely produced in the spring. Increased by seed or division.

P. hirsuta.—Should be grown between rocks or stones in sandy peat or loam plentifully mixed with stones. It forms rosettes of coarse, downy leaves, serrated at the edge. Flowers purplish-crimson, borne on stalks about 4 inches long. It is a granite-loving plant, and not difficult to grow. This plant is rather variable in colour, and of the several forms the best is that known as *P. nivalis*, which has lovely pure white flowers, and is of easiest culture, and increased by division. Other plants known as *P. ciliata*, and its varieties *coccinea* and *purpurea*, are forms of this plant, both of which are well worth growing.

P. integrifolia.—Half-shady position in sandy loam and pieces of limestone. Forms diminutive, dense, crowded tufts of smooth shiny leaves lying close to the ground. Flowers rose-coloured, and borne on very short stems rising scarcely above the leaves. Rather a shy bloomer in cultivation, and not an easy plant to grow.

P. involucrata.—Likes a shady position in very moist, sandy loam. Fragrant flowers, creamy white, with a yellow centre, and borne in umbels on stems 6 inches high. This plant is practically only a biennial, and so should be raised annually from seed, which, if good, germinates quickly.

P. japonica.—Though not very particular as regards soil or aspect, so long as there is a sufficient amount of moisture, it is finer and more effective when grown in half shade in rich, moist loam. The flowers vary considerably in colour, from white to deep crimson, and are borne in whorls on stems from 1 to 2 feet in height. It is of easiest culture, and bold masses of it planted by the side of a stream are very effective. Easily raised from seed, which sows itself freely.

P. kitaibeliana.—Moist soil in partial shade. Downy leaves and rose-coloured flowers. It is a variety of *P. spectabilis.*

P. latifolia (syn. *P. graveolens*).—Likes an open position in sandy peat and loam. Will do well planted between rocks. It requires plenty of moisture during the growing season and perfect drainage. Soft, greyish leaves. Rather broad and large heads of violet-coloured flowers in some profusion during the early summer. A handsome plant, of easy culture. Readily increased by division or seed.

P. Littoniana.—Partial shade in rich, moist loam. Leaves of rather upright habit. The calyx in which the flower-bud is enveloped is bright red. The flower itself varies in colour from rich dark purple to pale lilac. These are borne on stems from 12 to 18 inches high, in pyramidal heads shaped more like an orchid. The effect of the purple flowers and the red calyx is very striking and beautiful. This is quite a new introduction from China. It is reputed quite hardy, and not difficult to cultivate, and should prove a great acquisition.

P. longiflora.—Likes a half-shady position in very moist, sandy loam. Leaves and all its parts covered with a white, mealy powder. Umbels of lilac-coloured flowers, having tubes 1 inch or more in length. A handsome and distinct species, and of easy culture, and increased by seeds.

P. luteola.—Rich, moist loam in partial shade, though this latter is not essential. Forms compact tufts of bright green leaves. Umbels of soft yellow flowers, borne on stems about 6 to 9 inches high. Vigorous, and of easy culture, and should be freely grown, and is one of the best. Increased by division.

P. marginata.—Open situation amongst stones in gritty loam, plentifully mixed with lime rubbish. Forms branching stems, each bearing a rosette of smooth, greyish, powdery leaves, with a silvery edge. Small heads of pale lilac flowers in April and May. One of the best and easiest to cultivate. It is liable to grow leggy, and when this happens it should be taken up and divided.

P. megasaefolia.—Requires a very sheltered position in sandy loam and leaf-mould. Large, round, leathery leaves and rosy-purple or pale lilac-coloured flowers in umbels, on stems about ·12 inches high. It flowers in winter, so will need shelter. It is quite hardy, and is easily increased by division.

P. minima.—Sun or partial shade in a well-drained, sandy soil, with abundant moisture at its roots. Dwarf-growing, and forming tufts of coarsely toothed, prostrate leaves. Flowers rose-coloured, and borne singly or in pairs on short stalks. Not very easy to grow, but is well worth taking trouble about. It may be increased by division.

P. muscarioides.—Shady position in rich loam. A very distinctive species ; the flower spikes of rich purple remind one more of a Grape Hyacinth than a Primula. It is very dwarf in habit. A miniature gem and quite hardy.

P. nivalis (see *P. hirsuta*).

P. obconica.—Sheltered and sunny position in loam and leaf-mould. Umbels of pale lilac flowers freely produced. This species, generally considered a greenhouse plant, will, in favourable climates, grow out of doors, and should find a spot in the rock garden.

P. Parryi.—Partial shade in moist, well-drained, spongy loam, leaf-mould, and peat. Leaves erect, and large umbels of very brilliant crimson-purple flowers. It is difficult to grow, and will not thrive everywhere ; but as it is one of the handsomest of the genus, it is worth taking some trouble about. Readily raised from seed.

P. Palinuri.—North aspect, planted between pieces of sandstone in light loam and leaf-mould. Like an Auricula, but leaves larger and a brighter green. Yellow flowers, rather small. A rather curious and rare species.

P. pedemontana.—Half shade in fissure of rocks in light soil. Forms large rosettes, and bears bright crimson-purple flowers. Very nearly allied to *P. viscosa.*

P. Poissoni.—Rich, moist, loamy soil in partial shade. Rather similar to *P. japonica*, except that its leaves are glaucous. Whorls of lilac-purple-coloured flowers. Easily raised from seed, which should be done annually, for, like others of this family, it is rather liable to die after flowering. It is a handsome plant.

P. pulchelloides.—Rich, deep, moist loam. Rather similar in appearance and habit to *P. sikkimensis.* Flowers pale lilac flushed with rose. The whole plant richly coated with yellow farina. A very handsome plant and quite hardy.

P. pulverulenta.—Rich, moist loam in sun or partial shade. Very similar in foliage and habit to *P. japonica*, except that it has brighter-coloured flowers, and the stems and calyces are coated with a white powder. A very handsome plant, and very effective grown in masses. Easily increased by seed or division.

P. Reidii.—A most lovely plant, but very difficult to grow in this country. Of dwarf habit, it forms rosettes of leaves covered with silky hairs, and bears a few large and lovely ivory-white, drooping flowers. It is best to grow this plant in a frame in light soil. Seed germinates readily.

P. rosea.—Likes a shady position in rich, very moist loam and leaf-mould. It forms good-sized tufts, from which spring stems about 6 inches high, each bearing umbels of lovely rose-coloured flowers, which bloom in early spring. One of the easiest to cultivate and most beautiful of our Primulas. It can easily be increased by seed or division. There is a form known as *P. rosea grandiflora* which has larger and brighter-coloured flowers and is equally robust.

P. scotica.—Is a sturdy, dwarf form of *P. farinosa*, with larger purple flowers, and requires similar treatment.

P. secundiflora.—Requires a damp position, though ample drainage is essential. It appears to do best on a raised mound, where the roots can descend into moisture below. Habit much the same as *P. sikkimensis*. Flowers a rich purple, very freely produced and sweet-scented. One of the many recent introductions from China, and well worth growing.

P. sikkimensis.—Rich, deep, very moist soil in shady position. It forms nice tufts, which die down completely in the winter. The lovely, drooping flowers are bell-shaped and sweetly scented, and are borne in umbels on the top of tall, slender stems, which sometimes are nearly 3 feet high. It blooms in May and continues in flower for a long time. It is one of the easiest to cultivate, and quite one of the loveliest. It can readily be raised from seed or division.

P. spectabilis. — Likes loamy, calcareous soil, and should be planted in well-drained fissures of rocks. It has bright green viscous leaves margined with white. Flowers large, and of a violet-carmine colour. It is rather difficult to grow successfully. It is very nearly allied to *P. glaucescens*.

P. Stuartii.—Shady position in rich, moist, sandy loam. Very large leaves, green on top and powdery underneath. Bright golden-yellow flowers are borne in umbels. There is also a variety, *purpurea*, with rich purple-coloured flowers. Both are very difficult to maintain in health, and seedlings are very liable to damp off. They are very lovely, and considered by some varieties of *P. sikkimensis*, but unfortunately do not possess its constitution.

22

P. suffruticosa.—A shrub-like species, and very distinct. It likes a warm, sheltered spot in light stony soil. Leaves narrow and spatulate. Flowers rosy-purple, and borne on stems 4 to 5 inches high. It blooms in May. It is rather tender, and in most places requires some protection during the winter. Can be readily increased by cuttings.

P. tyrolensis.—Open position in loamy soil. This species is very similar to *P. Allionii*, but leaves are of a brighter shade of green, there are fewer flowers borne on each umbel, and it is not so impatient of exposure to sun and rain.

P. Veitchii.—Good, loamy soil in sheltered position. In foliage and habit rather like *P. cortusoides.* Rose-coloured flowers, with an orange ring at the throat. It is quite hardy and vigorous. It dies down completely during the winter. Increased by division.

P. viscosa.—Light, gritty, sandy, peaty loam in any aspect, wedged between rocks or stones. Rosy-purple flowers, with a white eye, blooming in summer. It is of the easiest culture, so long as the soil is free from lime, which it dislikes. Readily increased by seed or division. The flowers vary considerably in colour.

P. winteri.—Good, loamy soil in shady position. Forms tufts of broad, leathery leaves. Flowers delicate soft lilac with fringed petals. Whole plant heavily powdered. A new introduction from the Himalayas.

P. wulfeniana.—Half-shady position between stones in well-drained, calcareous soil. Forms tufts of rather shiny leaves. Flowers deep purple, and borne in loose heads. Blooms in April. Of the easiest culture, and quite hardy. It is an excellent rock plant. Increased by division. The following are some hybrids :—

P. assimilis (superhirsuta × integrifolia).—Large downy leaves and purple flowers.

P. biflora (glutinosa × minima).—Flowers lilac-mauve.

P. Facchinii (minima × spectabilis).—A strong-growing form of *minima.*

P. Heerii (integrifolia × viscosa). — Free habit and crimson flowers.

P. kewensis (floribunda × verticilata).—Yellow flowers in whorls. Hardy only in southern counties.

P. Sturii (minima × villosa).—Rose-lilac flowers.

P. unique (Cockburniana × pulverulenta).—One of the most beautiful hybrids. Striking cinnabar-red flowers. Quite hardy, and a good perennial.

P. Venzoi, a hybrid (*wulfeniana × tyrolensis*).—Flowers rosy-purple, freely produced. Hardy and free flowering.

PRUNELLA (LABIATAE), Self-Heal

A genus of plants suitable for the rougher parts of rock garden.

P. grandiflora.—Fairly light rather damp soil in partial shade. Of compact habit, growing about 6 to 12 inches high. Flower violet-purple, produced in August. Fairly hardy. Readily increased by division, but has not any special merit for the rock garden.

P. laciniata.—Same habit as above, requiring similar treatment. Flowers white, freely produced in summer.

P. Webbiana.—Of dwarf and compact habit, growing about 9 inches high. Reddish-crimson flowers with darkish-coloured bracts. The best of the genus.

PRUNUS (ROSACEAE)

A genus of hardy trees and shrubs, of which few are at all suitable for the rock garden.

P. prostrata.—Ordinary soil in open situation. Of semi-prostrate habit. Profusion of rose-coloured flowers in spring. Hardy, deciduous shrub, and increased by cuttings.

P. pumila (syn. *Cerasus adepressa*).—Open position in ordinary light soil. Prostrate habit. White flowers, borne in umbels during May. Very pretty, and quite hardy and easily cultivated.

PULMONARIA (BORAGINACEAE), Lungwort

A genus of plants more suitable for borders, though a few varieties may find a place in the less choice parts of the rock gardens. Propagated by seed or division.

P. arvenense.—Ordinary soil in open position. Compact habit, growing about 6 inches high. Flowers purple, borne in early summer. Quite hardy. Increased by division.

P. angustifolia.—Pretty blue flowers. There is also a variety *alba*, with white flowers. Both quite hardy.

P. a. azurea.—Azure-blue flowers of a brilliant shade.

P. rubra.—Beautiful clear rose-coloured flowers freely produced. The most attractive of the genus. Also quite hardy and of easy culture.

PYRETHRUM (COMPOSITAE)

A genus of herbaceous plants, mostly too coarse-growing for the rock garden ; but the following are of dwarf habit. They are of easy culture in ordinary soil and open position. Propagated by division or seed.

P. argenteum.—Shrubby habit, growing only a few inches high. Silvery foliage. Flowers yellow.

P. densum.—Dwarf, shrubby plant, with silvery, fern-like foliage. Flowers dull yellow.

P. Hausknechi.—Silvery foliage and yellow flowers. Would grow in the wall garden.

PYROLA (ERICACEAE), Wintergreen

A genus of dwarf evergreen, hardy plants of much beauty, but some rather difficult to cultivate.

P. elliptica.—Half-shady position in moist, sandy, and peaty soil. Grows about 6 inches. White campanulate flowers in racemes during June and July. Increased by division. Pretty, and not specially difficult to cultivate.

P. incarnata. — Half shade in moist, sandy vegetable soil. Rosettes of roundish leaves. Grows about 6 to 8 inches high. Flowers rosy-red colour. Hardy, but difficult to grow with any success. It is very attractive, and about the prettiest of the genus. Propagated by division.

P. rotundifolia.—Half shade in moist, peaty, and sandy soil. White fragrant flowers, borne in drooping racemes on erect stems about 6 to 12 inches high. Leaves roundish, forming rosettes. Blooms in the summer. Increased by division. Not at all difficult to grow, and a very charming little plant.

P. uniflora (see *Moneses uniflora*).

PYRUS (ROSACEAE)

This large genus gives some very beautiful and suitable species.

P. Maulei (syn. *Cydonia Maulei*).—Ordinary soil and open position. Dwarf habit. Flowers bright red, followed by golden-yellow fruit. A very beautiful spring-flowering shrub.

P. prostrata (syn. *Cydonia prostrata*).—Ordinary soil; open situation. Prostrate habit. Rich crimson-coloured flowers in spring. Also a very lovely shrub, of easy culture.

PYXIDANTHERA BARBULATA (syn. DIAPENSIA BARBULATA)

A very dwarf little evergreen shrub, only growing about 2 inches high. Requires a sunny position in nearly pure sand, with a very little vegetable loam mixed with it. The solitary white or rose-coloured flowers are stalkless, and borne on the branches in profusion during early summer. A very lovely little plant. Hardy, but not easy to cultivate. Increased by division.

RAMONDIA (GESNERIACEAE)

A small genus of attractive plants, of easy culture in a shady spot, in light, well-drained, damp, peaty soil. They are excellent for planting in vertical fissures, as they like such positions, where no moisture can lie on their large, flat rosettes of leaves. They will quickly shrivel and die if exposed for long to the direct rays of the sun, so an aspect either north or east should suit them. They are all lovely, of easy culture, and quite hardy. Propagated by seed, or by one of the leaves. These should be broken off close to the plant, and the footstalk inserted in moist, sandy peat, and kept close.

R. pyrenaica.—Forms large, flat rosettes of dark green, crinkly, rather hairy leaves. Flowers violet-purple colour, with an orange eye, borne on stems about 4 inches high. Blooms in June.

R. p. alba is a pure white form, even more lovely than the type.

R. p. rosea is a rose-coloured form, also extremely beautiful. Between these two last there are a variety of intermediate shades.

R. Serbica.—Has rather brighter-coloured leaves, and the flowers are a very pleasing shade of mauve. It requires similar cultivation to the last.

R. S., var. *Nathaliae.*—Is a variety of the last, with rather deeper-coloured flowers.

R. Heldreichii (see *Jankea Heldreichii*).

RANUNCULUS

A very large genus, giving many lovely plants, of which the following are a selection of the most suitable :—

R. aconitifolius.—Half-shady position in rich, moist loam. A much-branched plant, growing 8 to 12 inches high, bearing a profusion of small pure white flowers in May and June. Propagated by division. Quite hardy, and a very pretty and excellent plant for the bog garden.

R. alpestris.—Sunny position in moist, gritty loam. Forms compact tufts about 4 inches high. Leaves three-lobed, and of a dark glossy green colour. Flowers pure white, with a yellow eye, borne two or three on each stem. Flowers very freely produced during the whole summer. Quite hardy, and of easy culture. Propagated by seed or division.

R. amplexicaulis.—Cool, light loam, in open position. Leaves glaucous, and stem-clasping. Flowers pure white, with a yellow centre, and very freely produced. Grows 7 to 10 inches high. Blooms in April and May. A very lovely plant, of easy cultivation, and should be freely grown. Propagated by seed and division.

R. anemonoides.—Cool, moist position, in light loam. Leaves glaucous green, and divided. Large white, pink-tinted flowers, on stems 4 to 6 inches high, in April and May. Hardy, and easily cultivated. A very charming little plant. Increased by seed or division.

R. bulbosus fl. pl.—This is a double variety of the common Buttercup.

R. bulbosus F. M. Burton.—Is a pale, sulphur-coloured variety of the common Buttercup.

R. crenatus.—Gritty soil in open position. Very similar to *R. alpestris* in habit and appearance.

R. glacialis.—Open position in very gritty, rather heavy, moist loam. Forms good tufts 6 to 8 inches high. Of spreading habit. Leaves palmate, dark green, and usually smooth, but some are downy. Flowers white or reddish, suffused with purple, with a hairy calyx, borne in profusion from June to August. It is of easy culture, and readily increased by division. This species is found growing at a higher elevation than any other European plant.

R. gramineus.—Open position in cool, light loam. Grows 6 to 12 inches high. Grass-like, bluey-green leaves. Flowers yellow, borne three or four on each erect stem. Blooms in May and June, and very floriferous. Of easy culture, and a very charming plant of moderate growth. Division or seed.

R. Lyallii.—Peaty soil in open position. Very large, peltate, glossy leaves. Pure white, waxy flowers, 3 to 4 inches across. Grows 2 to 3 feet high. A very difficult plant to cultivate, and as handsome as difficult.

R. montanus.—Open position in light, sandy loam. Dwarf and compact-growing, and of spreading habit. Flowers yellow, and freely produced from May to July. Of easy culture and vigorous growth. Increased by seed and division.

R. nyssanus.—A large edition of the common Buttercup, with citron-yellow flowers in May. A free-growing species.

R. parnassifolius.—Open position in light, calcareous soil. Leaves dark brownish-green, rather heart-shaped. Flowers pure white, one to a dozen borne on each many-branched stem, about 5 inches high. A most lovely and attractive plant, of easy culture. Propagated by division or seed.

R. pyrenaeus.—Rather moist, open position in light loam. Grass-like leaves, 6 to 10 inches high. Flowers white, produced from June to August. Of easy culture, and a very attractive plant, especially when grown in fairly large masses. Very similar to this is *R. plantagineus*, in fact by some considered only a variety.

R. rutaefolius.—Open situation in sandy loam. Leaves pinnate and glaucous, and of a bluey-grey colour. Flowers white, with an orange centre, which are borne in some profusion from May to July. Of easy culture, and increased by division or seed.

R. Seguieri.—Almost similar to *R. glacilis.*

R. Thora.—Open position in gritty loam. Leaves smooth, growing about 6 inches high. Flowers yellow, and borne in some profusion in May. Of easy culture. The tuberous root is said to be poisonous.

RHEXIA VIRGINICA (MELASTOMACEAE)

A half-shrubby plant for the bog garden in deep, moist, sandy peat. Forms a compact little bush 6 to 12 inches high. Flowers rosy-purple, on square stems, borne during the summer. Hardy, but rather difficult to cultivate. Division. Other species of this genus are not sufficiently hardy.

RHODODENDRON (ERICACEAE)

Of this large genus of beautiful evergreen shrubs I shall only deal with those of dwarf habit suitable for using amongst the larger-growing rock plants ; but for massing on heights to form a background there are no better shrubs, and few as good.

R. ciliatum.—Peaty soil in sheltered position. Hairy leaves, and flowers reddish-pink, and of good size. Compact and dwarf habit, only growing about 2 feet high. A very good shrub.

R. ferrugineum (Alpine Rose).—Has scarlet-coloured flowers.

R. hirsutum.—Red flowers.

R. myrtifolium.—Pink flowers.

R. ovatum.—Rosy-purple, spotted darker purple.

R. parviflorum.—Sulphur-coloured flowers.

R. racemosum.—Pale pink flowers.

The above are a few of the dwarfer species, but there are others equally good. They all like a sheltered and cool position in a fibrous, peaty soil devoid of lime, except *R. hirsutum,* which will grow in a limestone soil.

RHODORA CANADENSIS (ERICACEAE)

A deciduous shrub nearly allied to the Rhododendron. Likes a moist, peaty soil. Leaves oblong, and downy beneath. Rosy-purple flowers in clusters before the leaves. Grows 2 to 4 feet high.

RHODOTHAMNUS CHAMAECISTUS (ERICACEAE)

A shrub also nearly allied to the Rhododendron genus. Peaty soil in limestone fissures of rocks. Dwarf habit, only growing about 6 inches high. Leaves ciliated, small, and fleshy. Flowers purplish-pink, solitary, at end of branches. A difficult plant to cultivate, but very pretty.

RODGERSIA PODOPHYLLA (SAXIFRAGACEAE)

Requires shady position in a rich loam and peaty soil. Large, erect, palmate leaves, five-sected, of a bronzy-green colour, growing from 2 to 4 feet high. The flowers yellowish, borne in spikes, are inconspicuous. Propagated by division of its stoloniferous rootstock. A good plant for bog garden. Deciduous.

ROMANZOFFIA SITCHENSIS (HYDROPHYLLACEAE)

Gritty soil in sun. Grows only 4 inches high, and has white flowers in May. Is very like some of the Rockfoils.

ROMNEYA COULTERI (PAPAVERACEAE)

This shrubby perennial is better known as the Californian Tree Poppy. Likes open, though sheltered position, in rich, sandy loam. Grows 4 to 6 feet high. Glaucous leaves. Flowers pure white, with yellow stamens. The petals are most beautifully crinkled like tissue paper. It is not reputed very hardy, but will stand a good deal of frost. Increased by division, but it should be carefully done, as it rather resents disturbance. One of the most beautiful half-shrubby plants that can be found for associating with the taller-growing shrubs in the rock garden.

ROSA (ROSACEAE)

Description of the Rose, the fairest of flowers, is unnecessary. Besides the following dwarf-growing varieties, many of the new *Wichuriana* hybrids, such as "*Dorothy Perkins*," "*Crimson Rambler*," "*Lady Gay*," etc., will, if space permit, look lovely growing over some large rock or bank, while for the wild garden such species as *acicularis, polyantha, gd. fl., rugosa* hybrids, etc., would look lovely falling over some craggy height. Of the dwarf kinds the following are the best :—

R. alpina.—Flowers single, pink or red colour. Grows about 2 feet high.

R. al. pyrenaica.—Is a variety, but quite distinct. Of dwarfer habit, and stems spiny. Flowers rosy-red.

R. nitida.—Is also very charming, only growing 12 to 18 inches high, with rosy-crimson flowers.

Also the native Burnet Roses give every shade from creamy-white to bright rose, and should find a home in some sunny spot.

ROSMARINUS PROSTRATA

A prostrate form of the well-known shrub. It only grows about 6 to 8 inches high. It likes a dry, sunny, sheltered position. A most charming little shrub for growing over some rock. It is of vigorous habit, but not hardy everywhere, or, at least, is likely to suffer in severe frost.

RUBUS (ROSACEAE), Bramble

Of this large genus there are a few species suitable :—

R. arcticus.—Peaty soil in a sheltered nook. Grows only about 6 inches high. Flowers bright carmine-pink. Hardy, and a very charming little plant.

R. Chamaemorus (Cloudberry).—Likes rather a damp soil. Of erect habit, but only growing some 4 to 8 inches high. Large white flowers in July. Hardy, and very pretty.

R. pedatus.—Sheltered position in peaty soil. Of rather trailing habit. Leaves palmate. Flowers white and large. A charming plant.

R. fruticosa Caesius (Dewberry).—Damp, peaty soil. Prostrate habit. Flowers white.

RUSCUS (LILIACEAE)

Half-shrubby plants, useful for shady places in or near the rock garden. They are not particular about soil, but prefer that of rather a free and leafy nature. Propagated by division of the roots.

R. aculeatus (Butcher's Broom).—Insignificant flowers. Berries bright red.

R. Hypophyllum.—Flowers insignificant. Berries red.

R. racemosus (Alexandrian Laurel).—A pretty foliage plant with dark, glossy green leaves.

SALIX (SALICINEAE), Willow

There are some dwarf species of the Willows which are pretty, and might find a place in the rock garden in the less choicer parts. All are of the easiest culture. The best for this purpose are *S. lanata, S. reticulata,* and *S. herbacea.*

SANGUINARIA CANADENSIS (PAPAVERACEAE), Blood Root

Likes a shady position in rather moist, peaty soil. Leaves large and greyish, springing from the prostrate rootstock, and about 6 inches high.   Handsome white flowers, borne singly on stems about 8 inches high.   Propagated by division, and of fairly easy culture. It derives its name from the red juice that is in the leaves and stems.

SANTOLINA (COMPOSITAE), Lavender Cotton

A genus of shrubs which mostly have yellow flowers and silvery foliage.   They grow about 2 feet high, and are of easy culture. Propagated by cuttings.   They are useful for parts of the rock garden, but should not be associated with any of the choicer plants. The following are suitable:—*S. Chamaecyparissus, S. c. incana, S. c. Squarrosa, S. c. tomentosa,* and *S. rosmarinifolia.*

SAPONARIA (CARYOPHYLLEAE), Soapwort

A genus of plants nearly allied to the Pinks.   Easily propagated by division or seed.

S. Boissieri.—Sunny position in light sandy loam.   Of vigorous and spreading habit.   Flowers bright pink.   Of easy culture.

S. caespitosa.—Sunny position in light sandy soil.   Forms rosettes 3 to 6 inches high of glabrous leaves.   Flowers rose-coloured, on short stalks, in July.   Hardy, and a pretty little plant.

S. lutea.—Sunny aspect in sandy soil.   Compact habit, and only grows from 3 to 6 inches high.   Leaves narrow.   Yellow flowers with a woolly calyx.   Not very hardy.

S. ocymoides.—Sunny position in deep loamy soil.   Prostrate, trailing habit.   Flowers rose-coloured and very numerous, and produced from May to August.   Of very easy culture, and quite hardy.   Should be planted so that its trailing stems can fall over a rock.   A very pretty and valuable species.   There is a variety, *splendidissima,* even better than the type.

S. wienmanniana.—Loam in sunny position.   Bears pink flowers.

SARRACENIA (SARRACENIACEAE), Pitcher Plant

A few species of this orchid are fairly hardy in favoured localities and may be grown in the bog garden in moist peat and sphagnum, in a sheltered position.   The following are the best species to try: —*S. Drummondi, S. purpurea,* and *S. flava.*

SAXIFRAGA (SAXIFRAGACEAE)

This very large genus of dwarf-growing plants is of the greatest possible value for the rock garden.   There are over three hundred species, so it is not surprising that considerable confusion exists as to classification and names. They have botanically been divided into fifteen sections, but for our purpose it will be simpler to arrange them in groups, more or less according to their cultural needs. The species, for convenience sake, will he arranged alphabetically, and after each will be found the number of the group to which it belongs. If it needs any special treatment, this will be given; otherwise it may be understood that it will require the same cultivation as was given for the group. The Saxifrages are all readily increased by division or seed. It may generally be taken that any species showing silvery encrusted markings on their leaves require a limestone soil, or lime in some form.

Group I. The Mossy

These make compact, mossy tufts, and are of the easiest culture. They are about the most valuable species for the rock garden, not only on account of the wealth of their bloom in summer, but also because of their evergreen foliage, which is beautiful even in the depth of winter. These species do best in well-drained, gritty soil, in an open, sunny position. Some, however, of the red-flowered kinds, such as S. "*Guildford Seedling*," keep their colour better if planted in partial shade. Examples of this group are *S. muscoides*, *S. trifurcata*, and *S. Wallacei*.

Group II. The Encrusted or Silver Saxifrages

These form flat rosettes of stiff, leathery leaves, more or less encrusted with a silvery deposit, chiefly on the edges. From the centres of these rosettes rise tall, loose spikes of flower. These species require a sunny position, and look best when planted in some crevice or chink of a rock, where they can have a deep root-run in well-drained, gritty loam, plentifully mixed with lime rubbish. They are mostly of easy culture. Examples of this group are *S. Aizoon* and its varieties, *S. longifolia*, and *S. Cotyledon*.

Group III. The Cushion

These are so called because they make dense, hard little cushions, somewhat variable in appearance, being in some cases formed of erect, spiny leaves, while in others of small flat rosettes. They include some of the most difficult of the genus to cultivate. As a general rule they require an open, sunny position, yet one not too sunburnt, in well-drained, light gritty loam, plentifully mixed with lime rubbish. Stone chips in the soil and around the plants will be found beneficial. Examples of this group are *S. burseriana* and its varieties, *S. diapensioides*, and *S. apiculata*.

Group IV. The Creeping

S. oppositifolia and its varieties are typical of this group, which contains but few species. They require a sunny position in well-drained, gritty loam.

Group V. Umbrosa "London Pride"

The species included in this group are mostly of easy culture, and not particular as to position, doing equally well in sun or partial shade. All they require is good, well-drained, gritty soil. *S. Geum* and *S. umbrosa* are typical.

Group VI. Megasea

These plants are of quite a distinct type, and do not form the compact cushions or tufts so typical of the other species. They have large fleshy leaves, sometimes as much as 15 inches across, which often in winter and early spring take a fine dark crimson colour. The flowers are borne in bold spikes. They will do well in partial shade, and are not very particular as to soil ; any good gritty loam seems to suit them. They are useful for associating with the stronger-growing plants. *S. cordifolia* is an example of the type.

Other species not included in any of the above groups will be dealt with as they occur in the alphabetical list. Provided the soil is light and well drained, but little difficulty should be experienced in growing any of the Saxifrages.

S. aegilops (Group I., Mossy).—Rather blunt-looking leaves and numerous pink flowers in June and July. Grows about 6 inches high.

S. afghanica (see S. Stracheyi).

S. aizoides (Group II., Encrusted).—Though belonging to this group, it is very different to the type, having rather succulent-looking leaves with no trace of silver on them. It has yellow flowers, dotted with yellow, and blooms in June and July. It is a native, and is found growing in wet bogs, so will be found useful for a moist spot in the bog garden.

S. Aizoon (Group II., Encrusted).—This species is one of the most typical of the group. It has yellowish-white flowers, borne in panicles on erect stems about 6 inches high, in June. A very variable species, and some doubt exists as to what the true plant is. The following are the best varieties :—

S. A. balcana.—Flowers large, white spotted pink.

S. A. flavescens.—Flowers pale yellow. Distinct, and good variety, and free-blooming.

S. A. lutea.—Flowers yellow ; also a good plant.

S. A. minor.—A small form with speckled flowers.

S. A. paradoxa.—Flowers yellowish-green, not very attractive; but foliage is very pretty. Rosettes of narrow blue-grey leaves heavily margined with silver, and is worth a place for the foliage alone.

S. A. rosea.—Flowers clear, pure pink, and unspotted, and quite one of the best.

S. A. rosularis.—Flowers white, spotted crimson. Strong and vigorous-growing, forming large rosettes, curving slightly inwards.

S. A. sturmiana.—Rosettes not quite as large as the last, and quite flat, otherwise similar. There are other varieties of *S. Aizoon*, but they are only of botanical interest.

S. Allioni (Group I., Mossy).—A very dwarf-growing mossy, with white flowers.

S. ambigua (Group III., Cushion).—Spikes of pale flesh-coloured flowers. A pretty and rather rare plant.

S. Andrewsii (Group V., Umbrosa).—Supposed to be a hybrid between *S. Geum* and *S. Aizoon*. White, pink-spotted flowers in loose panicles. The leaves are long and narrow, and more of the encrusted type, while the flowers are typical of the *" London Pride "* species. A very good plant, and of easiest culture.

S. apiculata (Group III., Cushion).—Forms dense tufts of bright green spiny leaves. Flowers pale primrose-yellow, in panicles about 4 to 6 inches high. Blooms in March, and is one of the best and freest-flowering species, of very easy culture. There is a white form of this, of recent introduction, which is quite as robust, and a great acquisition.

S. a. Maylii.—Is a late-flowering form.

S. aquatica (Group I., Mossy). — Rather coarse, fleshy-looking foliage. Requires a very moist position in sandy peat and loam. Large white flowers in rather dense heads. A difficult plant to obtain true to name.

S. aretioides (Group III., Cushion).—Forms dense, hard, tiny rosettes of ligulate, silvery-grey, spiny leaves. Flowers golden-yellow, on short, few-flowered stems. A rare plant, and rather difficult to cultivate. There is a very lovely form, with pale primrose-coloured flowers, named *S. primulina*, and even more difficult to grow.

S. aspera (Group IV., Creeping).—Rather large flowers, yellowish-white, in very loose panicles. Blooms in May and June. Rather a distinct, but not a very attractive species.

S. biflora (Group IV., Creeping).—Likes very gritty, well-drained soil. Rather loose habit, and its leaves are not so closely packed as in the native *S. oppositifolia*, to which it is nearly allied. The flowers large, and of a pale pink to deep red colour, and are borne two to three on a stem, and not singly, as in others of the type. It is not of particularly easy culture, but a handsome plant.

S. bryoides.—Is a glabrous form of above, distinct and stronger.

S. Boryi (Group III., Cushion).—Forms a very compact little tuft of very small rosettes. It has white flowers very like *S. Boydii alba.* A rare plant, but not difficult to grow.

S. Boydii (Group III., Cushion).—A hybrid, *S. aretioides* and *burseriana.* Forms dense, spiny tufts of greyish-coloured leaves. Large yellow flowers. A very slow-growing species, and not easy to cultivate. *S. B. alba* is a white form. Very handsome and vigorous, quite one of the best, and of very easy culture.

S. bronchialis (Group IV., Creeping).—Creamy-white flowers in panicles, and spiny leaves.

S. Bucklandi (Group V., Umbrosa).—Rather like a small version of *S. Geum,* and of easy culture, and quite pretty.

S. burseriana (Group III., Cushion). — Forms dense little cushions of grey spiny leaves. Flowers large and solitary. Buds and stems ruby-red. Blooms in March. One of the most beautiful of the genus. Though not difficult to cultivate, it is liable to " go off." An annual top-dressing of grit and loam, worked into the crown of the plant, will be found beneficial. Rather a shy bloomer. There are several forms of this.

S. brunoniana. — Allied to *S. sarmentosa.* Flowers yellow. Hardy. A recent introduction which should prove popular.

S. b. elegans.—Compact. Somewhat smaller than the type. White flowers flushed with lilac. Easy to grow, and a gem.

S. b. Gloria.—Of free habit; and has enormous pure white flowers, sometimes 1¼ inches across, on stems 4 to 5 inches high. A glorious plant, the gem of this species, if not of the group.

S. b. major.—Has larger flowers, and more freely produced than the type, and is of more vigorous habit. It is also a very desirable plant.

S. b. speciosa.—Is freer-flowering, and of more generous habit than the type. The flowers are borne on very short stems.

S. caesia (Group III., Cushion).—Forms very minute rosettes, each leaf spotted with silvery dots. Large milk-white flowers, one or two on each slender stem. A rare plant, and difficult to get true to name. *S. crustata* is sometimes sold for this plant.

S. caespitosa (Group I., Mossy).—A pretty, free-growing species, with numerous white flowers.

S. c. purpurea is a red variety of the above.

S. Camposii, syn. S. Wallacei (Group I., Mossy).—Very free and vigorous habit. Large white flowers, borne in the greatest profusion in May. The best of the white-flowered mossy Saxifrages.

S. cartilaginea (Group II., Encrusted).—Drooping panicles of white flowers in early summer, with rosettes of silvery-grey leaves. One of the best of this group. Very similar to it are *S. catalaunica*, *S. carinthiaca*, and *S. carniolica*, which latter is the most distinct.

S. ceratophylla (see *S. trifurcata*).

S. Churchilli (Group II., Encrusted).—Forms fine rosettes of acutely pointed grey leaves, and panicles of white flowers.

S. "Cherry Trees" (Group III., Cushion).—A hybrid, *S. aretoides* × *burseriana*, the same parentage as *S. Boydii* has, but is more robust. The flowers are a pale lemon-yellow, large, and very handsome. A most desirable plant.

S. ciliata (Group VI., Megasea).—The fleshy leaves are slightly hairy. Flowers white. It is an early-flowering species, and should have a sheltered position.

S. cochlearis (Group II., Encrusted).—Forms rosettes of blue-grey, silvery spatulate leaves. Slender panicles of white flowers, in June. A good plant. There are two recognised varieties : a larger form, *major*, and a smaller, *minor*.

S. cordifolia (Group VI., Megasea).—Has roundish, heart-shaped, rather fleshy leaves on rather serrated stalks. Heads of large, clear rose-coloured flowers. Blooms from March to May, and grows about 12 inches high. There are several varieties.

S. c. purpurea.—Has rich crimson flowers and handsome foliage.

Of the garden hybrids, "*Brilliant*" has rosy-purple foliage and richly coloured foliage ; "*Coralie*" has rich rose-coloured flowers and red stems ; "*Giant*" has bright rose-coloured flowers and large bronzy leaves ; "*Progress*" has rosy-purple flowers.

S. Cotyledon (Group II., Encrusted).—Bears erect stems 1 to 2 feet high, much-branched, and pyramidal in form and many-flowered. The flowers are white and free from dots. A very handsome and indispensable species, typical of the encrusted group. There are several forms, but the differences are very slight.

S. C. icelandica.—Flowering spike about 3 feet high. Blooms in July.

S. C. pyramidalis.—Has somewhat larger flowers, dotted with crimson, and slightly narrower leaves.

S. C. gracilis and *minor*.—Are rather smaller forms.

S. C. Nepalensis.—Has red stems.

S. C. montavoniensis.—Is of dwarfer habit. A handsome plant, and is reported to dislike lime. This species is considered by some to be distinct, and not a variety of *S. Cotyledon*.

S. crassifolia (Group VI., Megasea). — Large, fleshy leaves. Flowers red, borne in thyrsoid panicles on stems about 12 inches high. Handsome. There is a white form, *alba*, and a dwarfer, *nana*. Also a variegated form, *aureo-marginata*, with a gold edge to the leaves.

S. C. cristata (see *S. crustata*).

S. crustata (*Group II., Encrusted*).—Compact silvery rosettes from which rise erect panicles of white flowers. *S. crustata* and *S. pectinata* are so nearly allied as to be almost indistinguishable.

S. cuneifolia (*Group V., Umbrosa*).—Like a small version of "*London Pride*," with a yellow mark at the base of each white petal. *S. apennina* is a variety of this species.

S. Cymbalaria.—A very pretty little annual, with bright green, rather fleshy-looking leaves and citron-yellow flowers. Attractive, but only an annual. It sows itself freely, but never encroaches.

S. decipiens (*Group I., Mossy*).—Very similar to *S. hypnoides*, but the foliage is rather hairy. There is a very fine form of quite recent introduction, named *S. decipiens hybrida grandiflora*, with foliage larger than the type, and of a brilliant pink colour. Other forms are *S. hirta*, *S. Sternbergii*, and a red form, *S. atropurpurea*.

S. diapensioides (*Group III., Cushion*).—Forms very hard, dense tufts of very small, tight rosettes, of a blue-grey colour, picked out with silver. Flowers large and white, three to four in terminal heads on short stems, about 3 inches high. Blooms in March and April. This species likes plenty of lime. One of the very best and most beautiful of Saxifrages, and not difficult to cultivate.

S. diversifolia.—Very similar to *S. Hirculus*, and likes a moist spot. Flowers yellow, obscurely spotted, borne in branched, flat heads. Of moderately easy culture, but a rare species.

S. "Dr Ramsey" (*Group II., Encrusted*).—Is a hybrid, *S. macnabiana* × *S. lantoscana superba.*—It has pure white flowers, with a few red spots, and is handsome.

S. Elizabethae (*Group III., Cushion*).—Forms dense tufts of dark green spiny leaves. Flowers large canary-yellow, three or four to each head. Of the easiest culture, and one of the best of the genus.

S. Engleri (*Group II., Encrusted*).—A hybrid, *S. Aizoon* × *S. cuneifolia*. Narrow, dark green leaves, changing to golden-yellow in the winter. Margins slightly crustaceous. Flowers white and small. Rather a shy bloomer.

S. exarata (*Group I., Mossy*).—Leaves wedge-shaped, sessile, and three-lobed. Flowers white, four to six in a panicle. Grows about 6 inches high, and blooms in June and July.

S. Faldonside (*Group III., Cushion*).—A hybrid of *S. Boydii*. Compact tufts of blue-grey, spiny leaves. Flowers round and very large and of a lovely yellow colour. A most exquisite plant, though reputed not very robust. It blooms in March, but not very freely.

S. Ferdinandi Coburgi (*Group III., Cushion*).—Forms a close tuft of spiny, blue-grey leaves, and heads of small, deep yellow flowers. A new species, pretty, easy to cultivate in limestone chips. It blooms in March, and only grows a couple of inches high.

S. Fergusoni (Group I., Mossy).—Practically a variety of *S. Rhei.* A good red "mossy," and about the earliest of that group to flower. Blooms in March.

S. florulenta (Group II., Encrusted).—Requires a shady position in a well-drained crevice in vegetable soil. Forms large rosettes, 5 to 7 inches across, of dark green spiny leaves, without a trace of the silver encrustation. Flowers pale lilac, in thrysoid panicles. A very slow-growing species, taking several years to mature the rosettes, from which the flower-spike rises. After flowering the plant dies. A very difficult plant to grow.

S. Fortunei.—Likes a partial shady position in gritty, well-drained loam. Leaves reniform, cordate, dark green, and glossy. White flowers in erect, many-flowered panicles. Blooms in October. A pretty and useful plant on account of its late-flowering character.

S. Frederici-Augusti (Group III., Cushion).—Forms bluish, rounded rosettes. Flowers small and pink, with purple-red calyces borne in spicate heads ; the whole flower-spike covered with a dense purplish-rose-coloured fur. A rare plant, rather like *S. Griesbachi.*

S. Geum (Group V., Umbrosa).—A species very near to *S. umbrosa,* and a native, growing freely in Killarney.

S. G. cochlearis.—Is a dwarf variety.

S. granulata.—Rather a distinct deciduous species, forming little bulbs. Of vigorous growth, and spreading fairly quickly. It likes a partially shaded position in gritty soil. Leaves reniform. Flowers large and pure white, borne in heads on branching stems about 12 inches high. A pretty and easily grown plant. There is also a double form which is very attractive.

S. Griesbachi (Group III., Cushion).—Forms compact rosettes, glaucous blue leaves, with a silvery margin, from which rise in February spikes of inconspicuous flowers, with crimson bracts. The rosette from which the spike rises dies after flowering, but side rosettes are formed. A distinctive plant, rather like *S. Frederici-Augusti.* It is not difficult to cultivate.

S. gutheriana (Group V., Umbrosa).—Very nearly allied to *S. Geum,* and has heads of white flowers. The variety *S. g. variegata* has soft pink flowers, with a broad stripe of yellow on its glaucous leaves.

S. Hirculus.—Requires a damp position in peaty soil. It is of stoloniferous habit, with dark green leaves. Very beautiful, large, bright yellow flowers in July. It is not an easy plant to grow, and a shy bloomer. There is a form, *S. H. major,* which is finer, more vigorous, and blooms more freely.

S. Hostii (Group II., Encrusted).—Rosettes of narrow, dark grey-green leaves, and numerous spikes of white flowers, spotted purple. There are two varieties, *S. H. altissima* and *S. H. elatior,* both good.

23

S. hypnoides (Group I., Mossy).—The common native Saxifrage, with white flowers, known as Dovedale Moss, and of the easiest culture. It is typical of this group. There is a more compact form, *S. h. densa*, and a variegated form, *S. h. variegata*, and another variety known as *S. Whitlavii*.

S. juniperina (Group III., Cushion).—Forms compact tufts of dark green, spiny leaves. Yellow flowers, rather like *S. sancta*, but produced rather earlier. A vigorous plant, but a very shy bloomer.

S. Kestonii (see *S. Sardica*).

S. kolenatiana (Group II., Encrusted).—Rather like *S. Aizoon*, but with pink flowers. A very attractive species, nearly allied to *S. cartilaginea*. There is a larger form, *major*.

S. Kotschyi (Group III., Cushion).—Forms bluish-green, densely tufted rosettes, with bright yellow flowers. A pretty and good plant.

S. la graveana (Group II., Encrusted).—A very compact species of *S. Aizoon*, for a hot crevice. This species appears in catalogues under the name *S. La Gave Dauphne*.

S. latina (Group IV., Creeping).—Very similar to *S. oppositifolia*. Flowers the same, but the creeping stems are more erect. A new introduction. Early flowering and very desirable.

S. Leichtlini (Group VI., Megasea).—Grows about 12 inches high. Leaves large and crimson-coloured. Flowers rose-coloured. A good species on account of its handsome foliage.

S. lilacina (Group III., Cushion).—Makes tufts of very small, hard, dense rosettes. Large, rich lilac-blue, solitary flowers on stems about 1 inch high. It likes a partially shaded position. Of easy culture and vigorous habit, this new species is likely to prove a great acquisition to this large genus.

S. lingulata (Group II., Encrusted).—Makes rather heaped-up tufts of blue-grey leaves, of unequal length. White flowers, in large, very branching panicles. A very variable species. A most attractive and very beautiful plant, somewhat like a small *S. Cotyledon*.

S. l. lantoscana.—A beautiful variety of *S. lingulata*, with heads of white flowers in arching panicles. There is even a better form, *S. l. l. superba*.

S. longifolia (Group II., Encrusted).—The finest of all the silver Saxifrages, making enormous rosettes, several inches across, of blue-grey leaves edged with silver. White flowers in large, dense, pyramidal panicles. The true *S. Longifolia* may be known by its never making side rosettes. It takes a couple of years to come to maturity, and when it flowers the plant dies, but produces seed very freely. Flowers in June and July.

S. macnabiana (Group II., Encrusted).—Forms large, rounded rosettes of narrow, rather erect leaves. Flowers creamy-white, lightly spotted. It is a vigorous and rapid grower, and a very beautiful and desirable plant. It is a hybrid, *S. Cotyledon* and *S. Hostii.* The true plant is not easy to obtain.

S. marginata (*Group III., Cushion*). — Forms small, dense rosettes of oblong leaves, with the margins dotted with lime encrustations. White flowers, borne in rather compact heads.

S. maweana (*Group I., Mossy*). —Very similar to *S. Camposii*, but of more compact habit. It requires a hot, sunny position. It is a good plant, but not as fine as its prototype.

S. media (*Group III., Cushion*). — Rather similar to *S. Griesbachi*, but the flowers are borne in racemes instead of spikes ; the small flowers are enclosed in purplish calyces. Of vigorous habit and easy cultivation.

S. minima (*Group II., Encrusted*).—A small and attractive silver Saxifrage of the *Aizoon* type.

S. montavoniensis (see *S. Cotyledon*).

S. muscoides (*Group I., Mossy*).—The type of the red-flowered mossy Saxifrages, from which endless varieties have been raised. They are amongst the most desirable species of Saxifrage. As the colour of the flowers quickly fades in sun, a partially shaded position is best. The following are some of the best varieties :—

S. m. " Bakeri."—Dwarf habit and red flowers.

S. m. atro-purpurea.—Bright rose-coloured flowers, deeper than the type.

S. m. " Bickham's Glory."—Similar to *Guildford Seedling*, but rather earlier flowering.

S. m. Clibrani.—Bright crimson flowers, very handsome.

S. m. Gloria.—Similar to *S. decipens hybrida, gd. fl.* Vigorous habit, with very fine, large crimson flowers. Quite new, and likely to prove a great acquisition.

S. m. Guildford Seedling.—Deep crimson flowers. One of the best.

S. m. " Miss Willmot."—Very fine creamy-white flowers.

S. m. Rhei.—Fine rose-coloured flowers. Of larger habit than the type.

S. m. R. superba.—A deeper-coloured and larger form of the above.

S. m. " R. W. Hosier."—Deep crimson flowers, changing to plum colour. A very handsome and fine variety.

S. m. sanguinea superba.—Very handsome new crimson variety, quite one of the best.

S. nepalensis (see *S. Cotyledon*).

S. odontophylla (*Group VI., Megasea*).—Has handsome, rather heart-shaped leaves, and panicles of pink flowers.

S. oppositifolia (*Group IV., Creeping*).—Very small, dark green, opposite leaves on trailing stems. Flowers very large and of a purplish-crimson colour, and borne in the greatest profusion in the beginning of March. If planted in anything of rich soil, it will be liable to run to leaf too much and not flower well. It is a very handsome plant, of which there are several forms, which, except in name, differ but slightly. They are *coccinea, splendens, major, W. A. Clark*, and *latina*, which has more compact-shaped flowers of a rosy-purple colour. There is also a white form which has flowers smaller than the type.

S. Paulinae (*Group III., Cushion*).—Rather similar to *S. Boydii*, but far more vigorous, and has larger flowers, of a lovely pure lemon-yellow, freely borne. One of the gems of the genus.

S. pectinata (see *S. crustata*).

S. peltata (*Group VI., Megasea*).—To see this handsome Saxifrage at its best, it should be planted in rich, very moist soil, such as the edge of a stream. It has large fleshy leaves, sometimes 15 to 18 inches across, and heads of pale pink flowers on stems 2 to 3 feet high. A very fine plant for a marshy spot.

S. "Primrose Bee" (*Group III., Cushion*).—This hybrid, raised by Bees, Limited, may be described as a soft, primrose-coloured form of *P. marginata*.

S. primuloides (*Group V., Umbrosa*). — Forms dark green rosettes, and loose racemes of bright carmine-rose-coloured flowers. Very pretty, and of easiest culture.

S. purpurascens (*Group VI., Megasea*). — Large, handsome, glabrous, obovate leaves. Flowers purple, in June.

S. pyramidalis (see *Cotyledon*).

S. retusa (*Group IV., Creeping*).—Like a very small, smooth-leaved *S. oppositifolia*. It has lovely ruby-red flowers, in May. A shy bloomer, and of slow growth. A very attractive plant.

S. rivularis.—Requires a very moist position. It has large white flowers, one or two on each stalk. Stems decumbent and rooting. A native. An attractive plant for a wet spot.

S. rocheliana (*Group III., Cushion*).—Forms a compact tuft of small rosettes of leaves, white at the edges, with distinct impressed dots. Rather flat heads of white flowers in April. A very good plant, and of easy culture, and blooms freely.

S. rotundifolia (*Group VI., Megasea*).—Rich soil in a half-shady position. Large, roundish, fleshy leaves. Flowers white, spotted with pink, in May and June. A deciduous plant for the bog garden.

S. rudolphiana (*Group IV., Creeping*).—Very like *S. retusa*, but of more compact habit. It is a rare species and difficult to cultivate.

S. Salomoni (*Group III., Cushion*).—Makes tufts of spiny grey leaves. Pure white flowers, one to three on each stem. Blooms in early spring. It is a garden hybrid, *S. burseriana* × *S. rocheliana*, and is of much beauty and value, and of easy culture.

S. sarmentosa ("*Mother of Thousands*").—This species, though only considered half hardy, can in favoured climates be grown out of doors, provided it is planted in a sheltered position, in full sun, fairly protected from the winter rains. It spreads by means of creeping runners. It has hairy, heart-shaped leaves, which are red beneath. Flowers white, the two inner petals having a yellow spot, and the central one scarlet spots at the base. Of easy cultivation.

· *S. sancta* (*Group III., Cushion*).—Forms large, dense cushions of bright green spiny leaves. Small yellow flowers, borne in rather dense heads, on stems about 2 inches long. Blooms in early spring. One of the best known Saxifrages, and very like *S. Juniperina*. It is of the easiest culture, but is not a profuse flowerer.

S. scardica (*Group III., Cushion*).—Rather pointed, silvery-grey leaves in hard rosettes. Flowers white, and borne four to six in flattish heads, on stems about 2 inches high. Blooms in March. Not difficult to cultivate, and fairly vigorous. A very desirable plant, but difficult to get true. *S. Kestonii* is very nearly allied, but blooms somewhat earlier.

S. serratifolia (*Group V., Umbrosa*).—Very similar to *S. Geum*, but with long and very serrated leaves.

S. speciosa (*Group II., Encrusted*).—A hybrid of *S. longifolia*. It forms very compact tufts of handsome dark green silvery leaves. Flowers white, and borne in rather dense heads on short stems. A pretty and attractive plant.

S. splendens.—Is also another hybrid, *S. longifolia* × *Cotyledon*. It has handsome rosettes of silver-margined leaves, but the flowers are of rather an ugly shade, of a greenish-white colour.

S. squarrosa (*Group III., Cushion*).—Rather similar to *S. caesia*. It forms tiny tufts of rosettes of stiff little green leaves very minutely marked with silvery dots. Flowers pure white, and larger than *S. caesia*, and borne two to three on slender stems. Blooms in June.

S. Stracheyi (*Group VI., Megasea*).—Only grows about 6 inches high, with pretty bluish-pink-coloured flowers. There is also a pretty white variety.

S. stellaris.—A small-habited native species, for a very wet spot in peat, sand, and sphagnum moss. Its flowers are white, spotted crimson, and borne in feathery heads like a small "*London Pride.*"

S. Stribnryi (*Group III., Cushion*).—Very similar to *S. Frederici-Augusti*, but flowers borne in a flat head instead of a loose spike. A vigorous and attractive plant of quite recent introduction.

S. taygetea (*Group VI., Umbrosa*).—Very similar to *S. rotundi-folia*, of which it was at one time considered only a variety.

S. thessalica (*Group III., Cushion*). — Forms flat rosettes of narrow, pale blue-grey leaves, rather thorny in appearance. Flowers and bracts deep crimson, and spike red. A very distinct plant, more like *S. Frederici-Augusti* than any other, but there is some confusion about it. It is a rare species. Of vigorous habit.

S. tombeanensis (Group III., Cushion).—Very like *S. diapensioides*, but not as good. Its rosettes are rather more spiny, and leaves devoid of silver markings. Flowers white.

S. trifurcata (Group I., Mossy).—Has rather distinctive foliage, its leaves being rather like stags' horns. It is of vigorous growth, and quickly makes large tufts. The panicles of flowers, which are white and of a good size, are borne on slender stems about 6 inches high, and in such profusion as to hide the plant. Of the easiest culture, and quite one of the best of the mossy Saxifrages. *S. ceratophylla* is a variety of this species.

S. triternata (Group II., Encrusted).—Of the *Aizoon* type, forming small rosettes, and bearing heads of lovely rose-pink flowers.

S. umbrosa, "London Pride."—This well-known Saxifrage needs no description. It is quite indifferent to position, growing well under trees, and making a fine show in summer, with its airy spikes of white flowers dotted with crimson.

S. valdensis (Group II., Encrusted).—So very closely allied to *S. cochlearis* that it may be considered but a small variety of it. A very attractive plant, of easy culture, and will do in a position not fully exposed to the sun.

S. Vandellii (Group III., Cushion).—Forms very hard, dense tufts of spiny grey leaves, quite devoid of any trace of silvery markings. The flowers are pure white, and borne several on a head on stems 3 to 4 inches high. It is doubtful if this species likes lime.

S. Wallacei (see *S. Camposii*).

S. Wulfeniana (Group IV., Creeping).—Very akin to, if not a variety of, *S. retusa*.

S. Zimmeteri.—A hybrid between *S. Aizoon* and *S. cuneifolia.* Small rosettes of dark glossy green leaves, and white flowers in loose clusters.

The above fairly represent the best species.

SCABIOSA (DIPSACEAE), Scabious

A genus of the Compositae order, of little value for the rock garden, being mostly too coarse-growing. The following are the best species :—

S. alpina (see *Cephalaria alpina*).

S. caucasica.—Grows about 12 inches high, and has flower-heads of a pale blue colour. Blooms from June to August. It is of the easiest culture in any soil.

S. pterocephala.—Forms mounds, 4 to 6 inches high, of grey-green foliage. Flowers pale purple, freely produced. A very pretty species, of easy culture in any light soil.

S. Webbiana.—Rather hoary foliage, and creamy-white heads of flowers in July. Grows about 6 inches high. Division and seed.

SCHIZOCODON SOLDANELLOIDES (DIAPENSIACEAE)

Half-sunny position in well-drained, rather moist peat, loam, and sand. Forms rosettes of leathery-looking leaves, very similar to *Galax aphylla*. The flowers are bell-shaped, fringed, and of a deep rose colour in the centre, shading to white; they are pendulous, and borne in heads of six to eight. Blooms in April. A species from Japan, but of difficult cultivation, and as yet a rare plant. It is very nearly allied to the *Shortias*.

SCILLA (LILIACEAE), Squill Bluebell

A genus of pretty bulbous plants, early-flowering, and suitable for growing through dwarf rock plants. They are of easy culture in ordinary light soil. They should be planted in the autumn. They die down after flowering. Increased by division. The following is a selection of the most suitable :—

S. amoena.—Leaves about 9 inches long. Flowers rich indigo-blue, with conspicuous yellow ovaries. Blooms in March.

S. bifolia. — Dark blue flowers, freely produced as early as February. And its varieties.

S. itálica.—Small pale blue flowers, in spreading racemes. Flowers in May. Should have a sheltered spot. Not quite so hardy as some of the other species.

S. sibirica. — Deep blue flowers, very freely produced. A vigorous plant of much beauty, blooming in April. A well-known plant. Amongst other species is *alba*, very attractive. A selection should be made from some bulb list.

SCUTELLARIA (LABIATAE), Skull Cap

Of this numerous genus, the following are suitable species for the rock garden. They are all of easy culture, in ordinary soil in a sunny position. They are readily increased by cuttings or division.

S. alpina.—Of procumbent and spreading habit, growing 9 to 12 inches high. Flowers purple, with the lower lip yellow. Very freely produced in August. A pretty plant, vigorous, but not too rampant.

S. macrantha.—Procumbent habit. Grows 12 to 18 inches high. Flowers purplish-blue, and very freely produced in August. A useful plant for associating with the bolder-growing species.

S. indica.—Procumbent habit. Blue flowers, very freely produced. Dwarf-growing and pretty.

Sedum (Crassulaceae), Stonecrop

Dwarf, spreading, succulent-looking plants, often confused with Saxifrages, though bearing no resemblance to them. They are all of the easiest culture, some species, in fact, becoming almost a weed. They are useful for covering waste spots, and are typical rock plants, but must be kept within bounds. They are all very readily increased by division. The following are some of the best kinds :—

S. acre.—The common British species, which will grow anywhere, and in summer looks pretty, covered with its bright yellow flowers. There are several varieties of it : *S. a. aurea* and *variegatum.*

S. anglicum.—A native species, very like the last, but bearing rosy-coloured flowers in June. Very floriferous.

S. brevifolium.—The leaves are covered with a silvery-rose powder. Flowers pinky-white. Not very hardy, so requires rather a sheltered position. Very pretty.

S. dasyphyllum.—Very similar to the last, and is in summer a sheet of soft, pink-coloured flowers. One of the best. Not supposed to be very hardy, though with me it grows like a weed, in any position, and receives no attention.

S. Ewersii.—Of somewhat trailing habit, with glaucous leaves, evergreen. Flowers pink or pale violet. A very good species, and quite hardy. Its variety, *turkestanicum,* has rose-coloured flowers, and is even better.

S. kamtschaticum.—Rather distinct, of more erect habit, with broader leaves than most of the type. Flowers a deep orange colour. Quite hardy, and of easy culture. It is quite one of the handsomest of the genus. There is a variety which has very pretty leaves, variegated, with orange-coloured markings.

S. primuloides.—A distinct and attractive new species from China. White flowers rather like Lily-of-the-valley.

S. pulchellum.—Of trailing, dwarf habit. Flowers bright red or purplish, arranged in branching cymes. A very handsome evergreen species. Quite hardy.

S. roseum (syn. *S. Rhodiola*).—A taller-growing species, with erect stems 8 to 12 inches high. Reddish-purple flowers in flat terminal heads. Handsome.

S. spathulifolium.—Is of creeping habit. Makes rather dense rosettes of fleshy, glaucous leaves ; terminal, many-branch heads of bright yellow flowers in profusion in July. One of the best.

S. spectabile.—This well-known species grows about 18 inches high, with large, fleshy, yellowish-green leaves, and flat, terminal heads of rosy-pink flowers in August and September. There is also a white form.

S. spurium.—Trailing species, with flat heads of handsome pink or white flowers. There is an even better form, *atrosanguineum,* which has deep rosy-red flowers. Both are very free-flowering and handsome.

S. testaceum.—Has rather waxy-looking white flowers, borne in flattish heads. One of the best.

The above are a few of the best and most distinctive.

SEMPERVIVUM (CRASSULACEAE), House Leek

A genus belonging to the same order as the last. There are over a hundred species, but many of them are either unsuitable or not hardy. All of the easiest culture in any hot spot and in light soil. They are most useful for walls, growing readily in any odd crevice. They are readily increased by division of the offshoots.

S. arachnoideum (Cobweb House Leek).—A most distinctive species, the top of the rosettes being covered with innumerable fine threads, stretching from point to point, looking exactly like a spider's web, from which it gets its popular name of "Cobweb House Leek." Spikes of handsome rose-coloured flowers appear in the summer. It is a most charming and attractive plant, and should be grown in large patches in some dry and hot spot.

S. a. Laggeri.—Is a larger form of the above.

S. ciliatum.—The margins of the leaves are fringed with transparent, hair-like bodies. Flowers, in close, flat heads, are a good yellow colour. A hot and dry spot.

S. doellianum.—Rosettes rather hairy, with tips connected by a few cobwebby threads. Flat heads of bright red flowers, in dense panicles 4 to 6 inches high.

S. rubicundum.—The leaves are bright orange, tipped with green; very distinct.

S. trista.—Red-brown rosettes and bright red flowers. Pretty.

Other varieties are: *S. arvernense, S. Tectorum, S. calcareum, S. globiferum, S. piliferum,* and many others.

SENECIO (COMPOSITAE), Grounsel, Ragweed

A large genus of over one thousand species, but only a few are suitable, being mostly too coarse-growing. They are all of easy culture in any loamy soil, and readily increased by seed, division, or cuttings. The following are a selection of the best:—

S. aurantiacus (syn. *Cineraria aurantiacus*).—Sunny, sheltered position in light sandy soil. Handsome silvery foliage, and flat heads of orange-coloured flowers. A handsome plant, and not of too vigorous a habit, and worthy of a choice spot.

S. clivorum.—A large-growing, handsome plant for the bog or wild garden, in deep, rich soil. It grows as high as 6 feet, but does not spread too much. The flowers are large and of a deep orange colour, and borne in many-flowered heads.

S. Doronicum.—Has blue-grey leaves, white beneath. Flowers deep orange-coloured, and produced in May. A handsome plant.

S. incanus.—Bright silvery-coloured leaves and large, flat heads of yellow flowers. Dwarf-habited plant, only growing from 3 to 6 inches high. Pretty.

S. japonicus (syn. *Ligularia japonica*). — Leaves round and deeply incised. Heads of yellow flowers on stems 3 feet high. A good plant for the bog.

S. pulcher.—Glaucous, blue-grey leaves. Flowers purple, with a yellow disc, borne on branched stems about 18 inches high. A handsome plant, blooming in the late autumn.

SHORTIA (DIAPENSIACEAE)

Very attractive plants for a moist, peaty spot.

S. galacifolia.—Partially shaded position in some cool, rather damp spot, in peat, loam, and leaf-mould, with sand added. The best sort of leaf-mould to use is that got in oak plantations. The soil must be free from lime. Of compact habit, making a low mound of leathery leaves, which assume a brilliant tint in autumn. The flowers are ivory-white and crimped at the edges, anthers lemon-coloured, buds and stems ruby-red. The flowers are solitary and bloom in April. Of fairly easy cultivation, and quite hardy. A most lovely plant, and worthy of no little attention.

S. uniflora. — The cultivation and position the same as for *S. galacifolia.* It forms a nearly prostrate tuft of leathery leaves of a crimson colour. The flowers, borne on 3-inch stems, are rather similar in form to *S. galacifolia*, but somewhat larger, and of a pink tinge. Not easy to cultivate, it being difficult to establish. An exquisite plant.

SILENE (CARYOPHYLLACEAE), Catchfly

A genus giving some very attractive plants for the rock garden, and mostly of fairly easy culture.

S. acaulis (Cushion Pink).—Open, sunny position in light, gritty, sandy soil. It forms very compact little mats, about 1 inch high, of small, rather spiny little leaves   Bright rosy-pink flowers in summer. Easy to cultivate, but rather a shy bloomer. It is an attractive and indispensable plant. There are several varieties: "*Bernarti*," which has flowers much larger than the type and more freely borne ; *fl. pl.*, a double form ; and *alba*, a white.

S. alpestris.—A position in full sun, but where its roots can get into cool, rather moist soil. It is of dwarf, compact habit, growing only 4 to 6 inches high. Lovely little pure white flowers, delicately notched at the edges. It blooms freely in the summer. It is of easy culture and quite hardy. A most lovely and altogether indispensable plant. Increased by seed or division.

S. californica.—Sunny position in light gritty soil. Of rather prostrate habit. Deeply cut brilliant orange-scarlet flowers.

S. Elizabethae.—An open, sunny position in very well-drained, sandy soil. Rather narrow leaves, slightly viscid. Flowers like a diminutive *Clarkia*, and of a bright rosy colour, which are quite freely produced in July. Increased by seed or division.

S. Hookeri.—Sunny position in light gritty loam. Large salmon-pink flowers.

S. maritima (Sea Campion).—A native plant growing in shingle on the seashore. It forms trailing mats of glaucous foliage, and solitary white flowers with purple, inflated calyces. Blooms in June. Useful for draping over some rock. It is of easiest culture, but of not very great attraction. There is a double form rather better than the type, and worthy of a place in the less choice parts.

S. pumilo.—Light gritty soil in a sunny position. Very dwarf-growing, making dense little tufts of shining green leaves about 1½ inches high. Bright rose-coloured flowers in the summer. A pretty plant, rather uncertain in cultivation.

S. pusilla.—Light sandy soil in sun. Forms close tufts of bright green foliage. White starry flowers in spring.

S. Schafta.—Any position in light sandy soil. Forms neat tufts 4 to 6 inches high. Flowers purplish-rose, in the greatest profusion from July to September. Of the easiest culture, and quite a useful plant on account of its late flowering, though the colour of the flowers is not of a particularly pleasing shade. Readily increased by seed or division.

S. virginica (Fire Pink).—Sunny position in light loam. Grows from 1 to 2 feet high, and of rather straggling habit. Flowers large, nearly 2 inches across, and of a brilliant scarlet colour. A very handsome plant for association with the taller-growing plants. Readily increased by seed or division.

SKIMMIA (RUTACEAE)

Dwarf-growing evergreen shrubs, of which *S. japonica* and *S. Fortunei* are the most suitable.

SOLDANELLA (PRIMULACEAE)

Charming little true alpine plants, found on the snowline. There are several species in cultivation. They have rather a bad reputation as to culture, but are not really difficult if a few points are observed. They like moisture in summer, but require to be kept dry during the winter. A partially shady position, or, in a dry climate, the edge of the bog garden, suits them. The soil should be composed of peat, leaf-mould, loam, and a little sand. Stones should be placed about the plant to prevent evaporation, and during dry weather, occasional copious waterings. A pane of glass should be placed over the plants in October till the flowering season, which is very beneficial in producing flowers. They can be increased by seed or division.

S. alpina.—Roundish leathery leaves, and beautiful fimbriated, pendulous, bell-shaped flowers, of a lovely shade of blue. These are borne two to four on each stem, which rises about 3 inches high. Blooms in April. This is quite one of the best of the genus. There are several varieties, but differing little from the type. *S. al. alba* is a white form. *S. al. pyrolaefolia* is a good form of *S. alpina*.

S. minima.—Dwarfer form, with solitary flowers of a lovely suffused lilac colour, and the interior striped with purple, which are borne on 2-inch stems. A lovely little plant.

S. montana.—Leaves almost round. Two to four purple, deeply cut, and pendulous flowers are borne on each stem, about 4 inches high. A very lovely plant, blooming in April.

S. pusilla.—Flowers blue, with margins notched. One or two flowers borne on each stem, 2 to 3 inches high. There is also a white form of this. It is an easy plant to cultivate, and very attractive. There is some confusion as to the name of this species. There are also several hybrids, but not in general cultivation.

SPHAERALCEA MUNROANUM (*see* MALVASTRUM MUNROANUM

SPIGELIA MARILANDICA (LOGANIACEAE)

Deep, moist, sandy peat in partial shade. Of erect habit, with acute sessile leaves. Flowers 1½ inches long, red outside, and yellow within, and borne six to twelve in a terminal spike on stems about 12 to 15 inches high. A very desirable plant for the bog garden, and not of difficult culture.

SPIRAEA (ROSACEAE)

A large genus of handsome shrubs, of which a few of the dwarfer kinds are very suitable for associating with other shrubs in the rock garden. The following are a selection, blooming in summer :—

S. Bumalda.—Has heads of pink flowers.

S. bullata.—A dwarf shrub, only growing 12 to 18 inches high, with deep pink flowers.

S. decumbens.—A dwarf, trailing shrub, with flat terminal heads of white flowers. One of the best.

S. caespitosa.—Grows only 6 inches high, and produces white flowers in dense heads.

S. pectinata.—Of trailing habit. Flowers creamy-white, in woolly racemes. Grows about 6 inches high, and is very pretty.

For the bog garden the following will be found very desirable :—

S. Aruncus.—With creamy-white plumes from 4 to 6 feet high.

S. astilboides.—Like *S. Aruncus*, but only growing about 2 feet high.

S. gigantea (syn. *S. camtschatica*).—Large, flat heads of white, sweetly scented flowers, on stems from 4 to 10 feet high.

S. palmata.—Plumes of soft, bright rose-coloured flowers. Grows about 2 to 3 feet high. Blooms from June to August.

S. venusta (syn. *S. lobata*).—Feathery heads of rosy-pink flowers, growing from 3 to 8 feet high, and blooming in August.

STATICE (PLUMBAGINACEAE), Sea Lavender

Pretty and useful plants for a sunny position in sandy soil. They are all of easy culture. The dwarfer and best kinds are :—

S. bellidifolia (syn. *S. caspia*).—Lavender-coloured flowers on branching stems. Blooms from August to September.

S. tartarica.—Tufted habit and glabrous leaves. Grows about 12 inches high. Flowers ruby-red, in many-branched heads. Blooms in June and July.

S. t. angustifolia (syn. *S. incana*).—Has narrow leaves, and grows about the same height.

Other species suitable for the rock garden are—*S. minuta*, *S. eximia*, *S. sinuata*.

STERNBERGIA (AMARYLLIDACEAE), Winter Daffodil

A genus of bulbous plants of value because of their flowering in autumn. They require a sunny position in light sandy soil.

S. colchiciflora.—Flowers erect and nearly 1½ inches long, and of a pale sulphur yellow. Very fragrant.

S. fischeriana.—Similar to *S. lutea*, but flowering in the spring.

S. lutea.—Has leaves about 12 inches long and ½ inch broad. Flowers yellow.

S. macrantha.—Bright yellow flowers. Leaves blunt and rather glaucous.

Stylophorum diphyllum (Papaveraceae)

Greyish foliage and large yellow flowers. Blooms in June. Is of easy culture, and grows about 12 to 18 inches high.

Symphyandra (Campanulaceae)

A small genus belonging to the Campanula order. They require well-drained, rich, sandy loam and leaf-mould.

S. pendula.—Is of trailing, pendulous habit. Flowers large and funnel-shaped, and of a transparent creamy-white. Blooms in August. Hardy, and of easy culture. A very choice plant for a shady position to hang over some rock. Slugs are very fond of it. Division or seed.

S. Wanneri.—Of erect habit, growing about 12 inches high. Blue funnel-shaped flowers, freely produced, on branching racemes. Blooms in the summer. Of easy culture, and likes a half-shady position.

Tanakaea radicans

Likes a north aspect in peaty soil. It has rosettes of leathery, lanceolate leaves. Flowers white and small, in feathery spikes, rather like a Spiraea. Blooms in early spring. A recent introduction from Japan.

Teucrium (Labiatae), Germander

Few species of this genus are worth growing. They are all of easy culture in any light soil. Increased by seed or division.

T. Chamaedrys.—A good wall plant. Rosy-purple flowers in whorls.

T. Marum (Cat Thyme).—Rosy-lilac flowers in pairs at axils of upper leaves.

T. pyrenaicum.—Purple and white flowers in whorls. Prostrate habit, growing only about 4 inches high. Quite a pretty little plant for an odd corner, and the best of the genus.

T. Polium.—Silvery foliage. Flowers white, yellowish, or purple, in whorls.

Thalictrum (Ranunculaceae) Meadow Rue

Of this genus the following are the most suitable for the rock garden. They can be increased by seed or division.

T. alpinum.—Cool, peaty corner. Grows 8 to 10 inches high. Flowers purplish, in drooping racemes.

T. anemonoides.—Light, well-drained soil in a sheltered corner. Grows 6 inches high. Foliage like a maiden-hair fern. Flowers white, nearly an inch across, like an Anemone. Hardy, and of fairly easy culture. A very choice plant for a cool, moist corner. There is a double form with flowers smaller than the type.

T. aquilegifolium.—A very good plant for the bog garden. Handsome, fern-like foliage. Flowers white, and borne in corymbose panicles on stems about 3 feet high. Blooms from May to July.

T. minus.—Any soil and in any position. Very pretty, finely cut leaves. Loose panicles of yellowish flowers. A native, and of the easiest culture. There are a number of varieties.

T. tuberosum.—Deep, peaty soil. Fern-like foliage, and cream-coloured flowers in profusion in June. Quite hardy, and of easy culture. A pretty plant.

THYMUS (LABIATAE), Thyme

Of this genus there are some very attractive species, mostly of creeping habit. They are all of easy culture in any light, well-drained soil. Propagated by seed or division.

T. azoricus.—A small shrubby plant, with purple flowers in July. Grows about 6 inches high.

T. Serpyllum ("Wild Thyme").—The native species, making a dense carpet of its fragrant, small, dark green leaves, and covered in summer with rosy-crimson flowers. From this plant several garden hybrids have been raised, which are pretty and very choice for the rock garden, to carpet a bank or fall over a stone.

T. S. alba.—Is a lovely, pure white form.

T. S. atropurpureus.—Dark purple flowers in the greatest profusion. A most attractive plant.

T. S. lanuginosus.—A woolly-leaved form, with rosy-purple flowers.

Other forms are *T. S. coccineus*; and *T. S. rotundifolius*, which has rounded leaves and is more floriferous than the type.

TIARELLA (SAXIFRAGACEAE)

Attractive plants for shady position.

T. cordifolia ("Foam Flower").—Forms a compact tuft, from which are sent out numerous runners which root easily. Leaves rather like a Heuchera. These turn a pretty russet-red in the autumn. Long heads of starry white flowers in the spring. Of easy culture, and a very delightful plant, growing about 6 to 8 inches high. It does better if occasionally divided.

T. unifoliate.—Like a large edition of *T. cordifolia*, but emitting no runners. Long heads of creamy-white flowers on stems about 2 feet high, and very freely produced. Of easy culture in good, deep, rich soil. A rare and very handsome plant.

TRIENTALIS EUROPEA

Half-shady position in peaty soil. Slender, erect stems, bearing whorls of leaves and starry, white, pink-tipped flowers. Is not difficult to cultivate if good, well-rooted plants are obtained. It is a native plant, found growing in woody and mossy places. Increased by division. Quite a good plant.

TRIFOLIUM ALPINUM, Clover

Of trailing habit, with large rosy-crimson flowers in June. A handsome plant, and the only one worth cultivating out of this large genus.

TRILLIUM (LILIACEAE), Wood Lily

Very pretty deciduous plants for a shady position. They thrive in deep, rich loam and leaf-mould soil, so long as it is devoid of lime. They can be propagated by careful division of the roots or by seed.

T. grandiflorum.—On stems from 1 to 2 feet high. The three large leaves are borne surmounted by the big, lovely, white, three-petalled flowers. A very beautiful plant, and of easy culture.

T. erythrocarpum ("Painted Wood Lily").—A very lovely plant. The pure white flowers, like a small *T. grandiflorum*, have purple streaks at the base of each segment. Rather difficult to grow, and a shy bloomer.

Other species worth growing are the rose-coloured form of *T. grandiflorum, T. sessile, T. californicum,* and *T. nivale.*

TROLLIUS (RANUNCULACEAE), Globe Flower

Very handsome plants for a moist position in deep, rich soil. Easily propagated by division or seed. They mostly grow about 2 to 3 feet high, and are amongst the best and finest plants for the bog garden, and are all of easy culture.

T. acaulis.—A dwarf species, only growing some 6 to 8 inches high. Golden-yellow-coloured flowers, with brown outside. Very desirable for a damp spot in the rock garden.

T. europaeus.—The common Globe Flower, which is the parent of all the lovely garden varieties. It grows about 18 inches to 2 feet high. Flowers pale yellow.

Amongst the best garden kinds are—" *Citron Queen*," "*Golden Globe*," "*Orange Globe*," "*Prince of Orange*," "*T. Smith*," "*Goldsmith*," all giving shades from citron-yellow to deep orange.

TROPAEOLUM (GERANIACEAE)

Climbing and trailing plants of great beauty.

T. polyphyllum. — Sunny position in light loam. A distinct deciduous plant. It has long trailing stems, with densely crowded glaucous leaves, and is of vigorous habit. The flowers are like Nasturtiums, and of a bright orange-yellow colour, and very freely produced. A very handsome plant for a sunny bank, or to fall over a large rock.

T. speciosum (Flame Nasturtium).—A climbing deciduous plant. It requires to be planted on the north side of some rock or tree, and requires good, deep, moist soil, freely mixed with leaf-mould and sand. The flowers are a most brilliant vermilion colour. A lovely subject for trailing over some bold rock or bank, or through some dark-foliaged tree, such as Holly, which contrasts well with its brilliant flowers. It is not difficult to cultivate, but dislikes disturbance and takes some time to establish itself. Increased by seed or division.

T. tuberosa.—Sunny position in warm loam. Of trailing habit, with large leaves and red and yellow flowers. Is not hardy except in a dry climate.

TULIPA (LILIACEAE), Tulip

A showy genus of bulbous plants, mostly early flowering. The choicer kinds can find a spot in the rock garden. There are a great many species, and a selection should be made from some bulb list.

TUNICA SAXIFRAGA

A pretty little plant of the Pink order for a sunny position in light soil. It has wiry, branching stems and narrow leaves. In the summer it is covered with a profusion of small pink flowers. A very attractive plant, but sows itself about so much that it becomes rather a nuisance. There is, however, a double form which is an improvement on the type.

VACCINIUM VITIS-IDAEA, Red Whortle-berry

This native mountain plant has evergreen box-like foliage and clusters of pretty pale rose-coloured flowers, followed by red acrid

24

berries. It grows about 9 inches high, and is an attractive little plant for a peaty corner. There are a great number of American species, but either too coarse-growing or not of sufficient value for the rock garden.

Veronica (Scrophulariaceae)

A very large genus, very variable in habit. While some are creeping, others form good-sized shrubs. The following are a selection of the best and hardiest :—

V. Autumn Glory.—A shrubby garden hybrid of much beauty and value. Foliage very dark green and handsome. Spikes of deep violet-blue flowers, freely produced in the autumn. A species of much value and beauty, of easy culture, and propagated readily from cuttings.

V. Bidwillii.—A sub-shrubby plant of prostrate habit. Dark green foliage and starry white or pink flowers in great profusion during the whole summer. Any cool, open spot suits it well. One of the prettiest and best.

V. canescens.—A very minute, creeping species, with tiny, whitish, hairy leaves, and comparatively large pale blue flowers. A most dainty little plant for a choice spot on a level with the eye. Any light soil suits it well.

V. Chamaedrys (Germander Speedwell).—The well-known native species. Has heart-shaped, hairy leaves, and bright blue flowers in the greatest profusion. Creeping habit.

V. chathamica. — A prostrate shrubby species, making long, rambling growths and box-like leaves, and spikes of purple flowers. A very choice plant, and should be grown in a sheltered spot, to hang over the face of some rock.

V. cupressoides.—A shrubby species, growing 2 to 3 feet high. The foliage is attractive, being like a cypress. Violet-coloured flowers. Comes from New Zealand, and is fairly hardy in this country.

V. Hulkeana.—A shrubby species. Bright green, rather leathery leaves. Flowers a very beautiful shade of pale lilac, freely produced in May and June. Rather straggling habit, and growing 2 to 3 feet high, but needs support. It looks very well in a semi-decumbent position on some bank. One of the most lovely of all the Veronicas, but not very hardy, and should be planted in a sheltered and sunny position in good sandy loam. Easily propagated by cuttings.

V. Lavaudiana.—Sheltered position in sandy loam and leaf-mould. Stems decumbent, branches erect. Compact habit, growing about 9 to 12 inches high. Leaves dark green, margined with dark brownish-crimson. Flowers white, and buds red, borne in spreading heads. The effect of the red unopened buds and white flowers is most beautiful. This species is rare, and one of the most beautiful of the Veronicas. It is unfortunately supposed not to be hardy, but with me it has stood 18 degrees of frost without the least protection. The flowers appear in May in the utmost profusion. It can also be propagated from cuttings.

V. pyrolaeformis.—Spreading habit ; foliage light green. Small arching spikes of pale lilac similar in shade to *V. Hulkeana.* This dainty little " Speed-well " is well worth growing.

V. Teucrium prostrata.—A trailing species, with bright blue flowers in racemes, in the utmost profusion. A variable species.

Other good varieties of the dwarf and trailing type are *V. incana, V. saxatilis* and its varieties, *V. Teucrium* and its varieties, "*Royal Blue,*" " *Trehane.*"

Of the shrubby species *V. Lilacina, V. loganoides, V. Lyallii, V. Balfouriana, V. Gauntletti, V. La Sediusante, V. Redruth,* and *V. salicifolia* are among the best of the newer kinds.

Vesicaria (Cruciferae)

A genus of bushy plants of the easiest culture in any light loam. They are not of much value for the rock garden.

V. graeca.—Grows 9 to 18 inches high. Flowers yellow.

V. utriculata. — Grows about 12 inches high, with yellow flowers, very like a Wallflower.

Vicia (Leguminosae)

Pretty perennial species of the Vetch tribe. They are all of the easiest culture in any soil, and can be propagated by seed.

V. argentea.—Prostrate habit. Silvery-coloured leaves. Large whitish flowers veined and spotted purple. Useful trailer on account of its foliage.

V. Cracca.—Trailing habit and purple flowers. A pretty plant for a wild corner.

V. sylvatica.—Beautiful white and blue flowers in June and July. Of trailing habit, and useful for growing over some rock.

Vinca (Apocynaceae), Periwinkle

These well-known trailing plants may be useful for clothing some bare bank under trees, where little else would grow.

V. herbacea.—Is a deciduous species, with deep blue flowers, and not nearly as rampant in habit as the type, and may be used for covering some rocks in the choicer parts.

Viola (Violaceae), Pansy Violet

This genus has given us some of the most beautiful flowers that deck the hedgerows at home, or the alpine slopes abroad. The garden Pansy is but a hybrid Viola, and the well-known garden Viola, so near akin to the Pansy, is but a cross between the Pansy and other Violas. Of this large genus the following is a selection :—

V. biflora (Two-flowered Yellow Violet).—Half-shady position in moist loam. Flowers yellow, and generally two borne on each stalk. Increased by division. Flowers in May and June.

V. calcarata (Spurred Violet). — Half-shady position in loam. Flowers purple or white, borne in great profusion. A variable species. Propagated by seed and division.

V. cornuta (Horned Pansy).—Half-shady position in moist loam. Pale blue or mauve-coloured flowers. Seed, cuttings, or division.

V. gracilis.—Of the Wild Pansy type. Open position in light soil. Deep purple flowers in great abundance in spring. A very pretty species.

V. hirta.—Of the Violet type. Forms compact tufts, with blue, white, or reddish-purple flowers. Grows anywhere, even on hot, dry banks.

V. odorata (Sweet Violet). — Same as above, except that the flowers are sweet-scented. The parent of the well-known garden Violets.

V. pedata.—Of the Violet type. Half shade in good, well-drained light soil. Dwarf and compact habit. Leaves deeply divided. Flowers bright blue, but very variable. One of the most beautiful, and, at the same time, hardest to cultivate of the genus. Propagated by seed and division.

V. tricolor (Heart's-ease).—This is the species from which all the garden Pansies are supposed to have descended. Some of the choicer varieties may be included in the rock garden.

Besides the species just described, the following are worthy of cultivation :—*V. cenisia, V. canadensis, V. lutea, V. pinnata, V. heterophylla, V. sorora, V. striata.*

Vittadenia Triloba (*see* Erigeron Mucronatus)

Wahlenbergia (Campanulaceae)

A very attractive genus of essentially Alpine plants, which are closely allied to the Harebells. They are all hardy and free-flowering, requiring full exposure to the sun in light gritty soil;

they do best when planted in a position slightly raised from the surrounding ground, so as to ensure perfect drainage. Propagation is best by seed, as they do not readily divide.

W. Dalmatica.—Tufted habit with narrow leaves. Deep violet-blue flowers in July and August. A very pretty plant.

W. gentianoides.—Well-drained soil in open position. Pale blue flowers on stems 6 to 8 inches high. Well worth growing and quite hardy.

W. gracilis.—Narrow hairy leaves. Stems square and branched. Blue terminal flowers in May and August. This is a variable species of which the best known are, *Capillaris, Littoralis,* and *Strieta.*

W. graminifolia.—Forms close tufts of long grass-like leaves. Large purple flowers in bunches. Quite easy to grow and readily raised from seed.

W. hederacea (see *Campanula hederacea*).

W. pumilio.—Forms dwarf compact tufts of narrow leaves of a bluish-grey-green tint. Large lilac-blue, bell-shaped flowers in May and June.

W. pumiliorum.—Very similar to the last, but of a somewhat more straggling habit. A good hardy plant.

W. saxicola.—Of quite a distinct habit. Requires a sunny position in light loam, in which it spreads freely, throwing up tufts of narrow leaves. Flowers white veined with purple, borne on slender stems 3 inches high. Blooms during the whole summer. A beautiful and attractive plant and well worth growing.

W. serpyllifolia.—Forms tufts of small narrow leaves. Flowers purple. An attractive plant, doing well on rocky ledges. One of the best of the genus. The variety *major* has larger flowers, and, if possible, more brilliant than the type.

W. tenuifolia.—Dwarf and compact in habit. Heads of small deep purple flowers on stems 3 to 4 inches high.

W. vincaeflora.—Grows about 12 inches high, forming loose tufts of narrow wiry leaves. Lavender-blue flowers, freely produced.

WALDSTEINIA (ROSACEAE)

Pretty plants nearly allied to the Strawberry.

W. fragarioides.—Trailing habit, with bright red stems and large bright yellow flowers. Of easiest culture in ordinary soil.

W. trifolia.—A trailing species of vigorous habit and bright yellow flowers. A pretty evergreen plant for covering any bare spot. Is indifferent to position or soil.

Wulfenia carinthiaca

Dwarf evergreen plant for a half-shady position in deep, rather rich soil. Purplish-blue spikes of flowers. Not difficult to cultivate. A very pretty and attractive plant. Increased by seed or division.

Xerophyllum asphodeloides

A tuberous-rooted plant, forming tufts of grassy leaves and spikes of white flowers. A nice plant for a moist, peaty spot.

Zauschneria californica

A deciduous shrubby plant. Requires a warm position in very sandy soil. Grows about 18 inches high. Small, rather hairy leaves, and bright vermilion flowers in the autumn. A pretty and hardy plant, but requires shelter, as the branches are very brittle and easily broken by the wind. The varieties *Mexicana* and *Splendens* are very similar to the type.

Zenobia (*see* Andromeda)

A SELECTION OF PLANTS FOR DRY AND SUNNY POSITIONS, AND TIME OF FLOWERING

Antirrhinum	.	.	. Summer.
Calandrinia .	.	.	. „
Callirhoë .	.	.	. „
Cheiranthus	.	.	. Early summer.
Erinus	.	.	. „
Geranium .	.	.	. Summer.
Gerberia .	.	.	. „
Gypsophila .	.	.	. „
Helianthemum	.	.	. „
Hieracium .	.	.	. „
Leontopodium	.	.	. „
Malvastrum	.	.	. „
Mathiola .	.	.	. „

Mesembryanthemum .   .   Summer.
Ononis   .   .   .   .   „
Onosma   .   .   .   .   „
Opuntia   .   .   .   .   „
Origanum .   .   .   .   „
Rosmarinus .   .   .   .   Early summer.
Sedum   .   .   .   .   Summer.
Sempervivum .   .   .   „
Thymus   .   .   .   „
Tunica   .   .   .   „
Zauschneria .   .   .   Autumn.

A SELECTION OF PLANTS FOR FULL SUN OR PARTIAL SUNNY POSITIONS, AND TIME OF FLOWERING

Acantholimon   .   .   Summer.
Achillea   .   .   .   Early summer.
Æthionema .   .   Spring and summer.
Alyssum   .   .   .   Spring.
Androsace .   .   Most species, spring and early summer.
Antennaria .   .   Summer.
Anthemis .   .   .   Early summer.
Arabis   .   .   .   Spring.
Arenaria   .   .   .   Spring and early summer.
Astragalus   .   .   Autumn.
Aubrietia   .   .   Spring.
Campanula   .   .   These like rather more shade. Most species, spring and summer.
Cerastium .   .   .   Summer.
Cistus   .   .   .   Early summer.
Convolvulus .   .   Summer and autumn.
Cytisus   .   .   .   Early summer.
Delphinium   .   .   Summer.
Dianthus .   .   .   „
Draba   .   .   .   Spring.
Dryas   .   .   .   Summer.
Epilobium   .   .   „
Gentiana .   .   .   Some species, early summer. Most Gentians prefer shade.
Globularia   .   .   Summer.

Hypericum . .	Early summer.
Iberis . . .	"
Inula . . .	Summer.
Jasione . .	"
Linum . . .	"
Lithospermum .	Spring to autumn.
Lychnis .	Early summer.
Nepeta . .	Summer and autumn.
Noccaea . .	Early summer.
Pentstemon . .	"
Phlox , .	Spring and summer.
Phyteuma .	Summer.
Polygonum .	Summer and autumn.
Potentilla . .	Summer.
Primula . .	Some species, spring and summer.
Rubus . .	Summer.
Saponaria . .	Spring to autumn.
Saxifraga . .	Most species, spring and summer.
Scabiosa . .	Summer.
Silene . .	Spring.
Statice . .	Summer and autumn.
Thalictrum .	Summer.
Tropaeolum .	Summer and autumn.
Veronica . .	Spring to autumn.
Vciia . .	Summer and autumn.
Vinca . .	Summer.
Wahlenbergia .	Early summer.

A SELECTION OF PLANTS FOR POSITIONS IN DEEP SHADE

(Most of these will also do in partial shade.)

Arenaria balearica . .	Summer.
Epigaea repens . .	Spring.
Ferns	Many species.
Haberlea rhodopensis and virginalis .	Early summer.
Houstonia . .	Summer.
Jankaea Heldreichii . .	"
Mitchella repens . .	Early summer
Ourisia coccinea . .	Summer.
Primula . .	Some species, spring and summer.
Ramondia . .	All species, early summer.

A SELECTION OF PLANTS FOR PARTIAL SHADY POSITIONS

Acaena	. . .	Summer.
Adonis	. . .	Early spring.
Ajuga	. . .	Summer.
Allium	. . .	,,
Androsace	. .	Some species, spring and summer.
Anemone	. .	Spring and summer.
Aquilegia	. .	,, ,,
Asperula	. .	Spring.
Aster	. .	Spring and summer.
Campanulas	.	Some species, early summer.
Celmisia	. .	Summer.
Coronilla	. .	Early summer.
Cyclamen	. .	Autumn.
Cypripedium	.	Summer.
Daphne	. .	Spring and summer.
Epimedium	.	Spring.
Erigeron	. .	Early summer.
Erodium	. .	,,
Hepatica	. .	Early spring.
Incarvillea	.	Summer.
Iris	. .	Some species, summer.
Lysimachia	.	Summer and autumn.
Meconopsis	.	Summer.
Morisia	. .	Early spring.
Œnothera	.	Summer and autumn.
Omphalodes	.	Early spring.
Oxalis	. .	Summer and autumn.
Parochetus	.	Summer.
Platycodon	.	,,
Primula	. .	Most species, spring and summer.
Saxifraga	.	A few species, spring and summer.
Soldanella	.	Early spring.
Spiraea	.	Some species require moisture. Summer.
Symphyandra	.	Autumn.
Tanakaea	.	Summer.
Tiarella	. .	Spring.
Tricyrtis	. .	Autumn.
Trillium	. .	Spring.
Viola	. .	Summer.

A SELECTION OF PLANTS FOR MOIST POSITIONS IN SUN OR SHADE

Anagallis	Summer.
Caltha	Spring.
Cornus	Summer.
Cortusa	Early summer.
Cypripedium	Some species, summer.
Dodecatheon	Early summer.
Galax	Spring.
Gaultheria	Summer.
Gentiana	Some species, spring and summer.
Gunnera	Summer.
Iris	Some species, summer.
Meconopsis	,, ,,
Mertensia	Spring and summer.
Mimulus	,, ,,
Mitchella	Summer.
Myosotis	Spring and summer.
Orchids	Some species, spring and summer.
Ourisia	Summer.
Primula	Some species, spring and summer.
Ranunculus	Spring and summer.
Rodgersia	Summer.
Saxifraga	Some species, spring and autumn.
Shortia	Spring.
Spiraea	Many species, spring to autumn.
Trollius	Spring and summer.

A SELECTION OF PLANTS SUITABLE FOR TRAILING OVER ROCKS

Acaena.
Æthionema, most species.
Alyssum, most species.
Androsace lanuginosa, A. l. Leichtlini.
Antirrhinum : A. asarina, A. glutinosum, and A. sempervirens.
Arabis, all species except A. androsace.
Arenaria, most species, especially A. montana.
Aubrietia, all species.
Callirhoë involucrata.
Calystegia, all species.

Campanulas : C. Elatines, C. garganica and varieties, C. isophylla, C. muralis, C. portenschlagiana.

Cerastium, most species.

Cistus florentinus and some other species.

Clematis, all species except C. recta.

Convolvulus, all species.

Coronilla iberica.

Cotoneaster adspressa, C. humifusa, C. microphylla.

Cydonia japonica and varieties.

Cytisus ardoini, C. decumbens, C. Kewensis.

Daphne cneorum.

Dianthus caesius, D. deltoides, D. deltoides alba, D. fimbriatus, D. plumarius and hybrids, D. suavis.

Dryas octopetala.

Epilobium obcordatum.

Erica carnea and varieties.

Genista prostrata.

Gypsophila prostrata, G. repens and varieties.

Helianthemum, all varieties.

Hippocrepis comosa.

Hypericum fragile, H. repens, and H. reptans.

Iberis, all varieties.

Lippia nodiflora.

Lithospermum prostratum, L. purpureo-coeruleum.

Lysimachia Nummularia and L. N. var. aurea.

Mesembryanthemum Muchlenbeckia and all species.

Nepeta Mussini.

Œnothera, most varieties.

Othonnopsis (syn. Othonna) cheirifolia and O. crassifolia.

Parochetus communis.

Phlox procumbens, P. reptans, P. Stellaria and varieties, P. subulata and varieties.

Polygonum vaccinifolium.

Ribes prostrata.

Rose, all of the Wichuriana type.

Rubus, many species.

Salix herbacea, S. repens, S. sericea pendula.

Saponaria ocymoides and varieties.

Saxifraga, the mossy type.

Sedum spurium.

Silene alpestris, S. Schafta.

Sphaeralcea Munroana.

Symphyandra pendula.

Thymus Serpyllum and varieties.

Tropaeolum polyphyllum.

Tunica Saxifraga.
Veronica Chathamica, V. repens, V. Teucrium, and other varieties.
Vinca, all species.
Waldsteina fragarioides and W. trifolia.

LIST OF PLANTS SUITABLE FOR THE MORAINE

Achillea rupestris.
Androsace carnea.
    „   ciliata.
    „   villosa.
Armeria caespitosa.
Asperula hirta.
Campanula Allionii.
    „   carnica.
    „   waldsteiniana.
Dianthus Freynii.
    „   neglectus.
Douglasia vitaliana.
Erodium corsicum.
    „   guttatum.
Geranium cinerium.
Hypericum Coris.
Inula acaulis.
Œnothera caespitosa.
Omphalodes Luciliae.
Penstemon Davidsoni.
Potentilla nitida.
    „   „   alba.

Saxifraga Boryi.
    „   Boydii.
    „   „   alba.
    „   burseriana and varieties.
    „   caesa.
    „   Elizabethae.
    „   lilacina.
    „   oppositifolia and varieties.
    „   Paulinae.
    „   retusa.
    „   rocheliana.
    „   Salomoni.
Sedums in variety.
Sempervivums in variety.
Silene acaulis.
    „   „   Bernarti.
    „   Elizabethae.
    „   Hookeri.
Wahlenbergias in variety.

A SELECTION OF DWARF SHRUBS, PINES, AND CONIFERS

Abies (syn. Picea) excelsa Clanbrasiliana, 4 feet, A. e. pygmea, A. e. Remonti, A. e. procumbens, A. e. parviformis, A. e. pumila and pumila glauca.

Amydalus Nana, 2 feet.

Andromeda polifolia, 1 foot.

Arctostaphylos uva-ursi and varieties, Californica and Nevadensis.

Azalea amoena and varieties (see p. 244), A. procumbens (syn. Loiseleuria procumbens).

Berberis Darwinii nana, 1 foot, B. Stenophylla Irwinii, B. Thunbergii minor.

Betula, var. crenata nana.

Cassiope (syn. Andromeda) fastigata, C. hypnoides, and C. tetragona (see p. 228).

Cassinia Fulvida, 3 feet (syn. Diplopappus chrysophylla).

Cedrus Comte de Dijon.

Cistus (see p. 258).

Cotoneaster (see p. 264).

Cryptomeria japonica nana.

Cupressus Lawsoniana nana, and minima glauca.

Cydonia (syn. Pyrus) japonica Simonii, prostrate habit.

Cytisus (see p. 266).

Daphne (see p. 267).

Erica (see p. 277).

Euonymus Kewensis, E. nana.

Fuchsia (see p. 281).

Gaultheria (see p. 282).

Genista (see p. 283).

Helianthemum (see p. 291).

Hypericum calycinum, 1 foot; H. coris, 1 foot; H. empetrifolium, 1 foot. For other varieties see p. 294.

Juniperus communis aurea, 1 to 2 feet; J. Hibernica compressa, J. prostrata, J. recurva densa, J. Sabina tamariscifolia. Prostrate habit.

Kalmia (see p. 298).

Ledum (see p. 300).

Ligustrum Delavayanum, 2 feet.

Lonicera depressa and L. rupicola.

Menziesia (see p. 309).

Pernettya (see p. 323).

Philadelphus candelabra, P. Manteau-d'Hermine.
Pinus sylvestris Beuvronensis, P. s. globosa, and P. s. g. viridis,
    P. s. pygmaea.
Polygala (see p. 327).
Potentilla fruticosa, P. Friedrichseni and other varieties.
Prunas prostrata (syn. Amydalus incana).
Pyrus Cydonia japonica pygmaea, P. jap. Simonii, P. jap. Sargenti.
Retinospora (syn. Chamaecyparis) obtusa nana, R. o. aurea, and
    R. o. pygmaea, R. pisifera nana, R. Sanderi.
Rhododendron (see p. 343).
Ribes prostrata.
Rosa (see p. 344).
Rosmarinus prostrata.
Rubus nutans, 1 to 2 feet ; R. pedatus (see p. 345).
Salix ambigua, 1 to 3 feet ; S. herbacea, S. repens, S. retusa,
    S. r. serpyllifolia (see p. 345).
Senecio Grayii, 2 feet.
Skimmia japonica, 2 feet.
Spiraea arguta multiflora, S. bullata, S. decumbens, S. Hacquetii,
    S. japonica rubra, S. tomentosa, S. trilobata.
Teucrium latifolium.
Thuya nana aurea, T. plicata nana, T. umbraculifera, T. minima
    glauca, T. occidentalis, " Little Gem," T. recurva nana.
Thuyopsis nana.
Ulex nana.
Vaccinium (see p. 369).
Veronica (see p. 370).

A SELECTION OF HARDY FERNS SUIT-
ABLE FOR ROCK GARDEN IN SUN
OR HALF SHADE.

Allosorus crispus (Parsley Fern).
Aspidium (syn. Polystichum) acrostichoides, A. aculeatum, A. angu-
    lare.
Asplenium fontanum, A. adiantum-nigrum, A. viride, A. angusti-
    folium, A. Ruta-muraria, A. Trichomanes, A. Ceterach.
Athyrium felix-foemina and varieties.
Cystopteris alpina, C. fragilis, C. montana.
Nephrodium (syn. Lastrea) Cristatum, Felix-max and varieties
    N. marginales, N. rigidium, N. recurva, N. spinulosum. All
    the Nephrodiums like half shade.

Onoclea (syn. Struthiopteris) germanica (Ostrich Fern).

Osmunda Claytoniana, O. gracilis, O. Regalis and var. cristata. The last two like moist, peaty soil.

Polypodium Cambricum, P. Dryopteris (Oak Fern), P. Phegopteris (Beech Fern), P. vulgare and varieties.

Woodwardia aspera, W. japonica.

A SELECTION OF HARDY FERNS FOR SHADY POSITION

Adiantum Capillus Veneris, A. pedatum.

Aspidium aculeatum, A. cristatum, A. munitum.

Asplenium marinum, A. adiantum nigrum, A. Trichomanes, A. thelypteroides.

Botrychium Lunaria.

Hymenophyllum tunbridgense.

Nephrodium (syn. Lastrea) marginale, N. aemulum, N. recurva, N. noveboracense.

Woodsia ilvensis, W. oregana, W. obtusa, W. polystichoides.

Woodwardia aspera, W. virginica, W. japonica.

All the above like a moist soil.

A SELECTION OF BULBOUS PLANTS

Allium (see p. 225).

Anomatheca cruenta; sunny position in sandy loam; rosy-crimson flowers, August to October; seed.

Anthericum (see p. 236).

Brodiaea gracilis; deep yellow flowers. B. uniflora.

Calochortus Benthami; 6 to 8 inches; rich yellow flowers in July and August. C. caeruleus; grows 3 to 6 inches high; lilac-coloured flowers in July. C. lilacinus; grows 6 inches high; large purple flowers. C. Maweanus; grows 6 inches high; purplish-white flowers in June and July. C. pulchellus; grows 10 to 12 inches high; bright yellow flowers in the summer. Other species are also well worth growing. They all like a sunny position in light sandy soil.

Chionodoxa Luciliae; grows about 6 inches high; flowers deep blue, shading to white in the centre; blooms in early spring; very pretty. There are several varieties which are also good.

Colchicum (see p. 261).

Chionodoxa Luciliae ; grows about 6 inches high ; flowers deep blue, shading to white in the centre ; blooms in early spring ; very pretty. There are several varieties which are also good.

Colchicum (see p. 261).

Crocus (see p. 265).

Erythronium (see p. 281).

Fritillaria armena ; dull purple flowers in spring. F. aurea ; bright yellow flowers ; grows 6 to 8 inches high. F. coccinea ; scarlet-coloured flowers. F. Meleagris (Common Fritillary) ; colours various. F. pallidiflora ; grows 1 foot high ; flowers yellow. F. pudica ; dark yellow flowers in May ; grows 6 inches high. F. tulipifolia ; purple-coloured flowers. And other varieties.

Galanthus (Snowdrops).

Habranthus (see p. 291).

Iris (see p. 297).

Lapeyrousia anceps ; grows 9 inches high ; bluish-purple flowers in September. L. corymbosa ; grows 6 inches high ; blue flowers in May.

Leucojum (see p. 220).

Lilium (see p. 302).

Muscari (see p. 313).

Narcissus (see p. 314).

Orchids (see p. 318).

Puschkinia scilloides ("Striped Squill") ; grows 6 inches high ; flowers white, striped blue ; blooms in spring.

Scilla (Squill), various species.

Sternbergia (see p. 365).

Trillium (see p. 368). T. aurea ; flowers yellow, in April.

Triteleia (syn. Brodiaea) uniflora ; pale blue-coloured flowers in April and May.

Tulipa (see p. 369).

Zephyranthes rosea ; flowers pink, in May. Z. versicolor ; grows about 12 inches high ; rose-coloured flowers in the winter.

PLANTS FOR MASSING

Besides the plants which can usually be grouped together because they belong to the same family, the following are particularly useful for massing on account of the positions they like, their colours, and time of flowering :—

Silene alpestris.
Campanula pulla.
    „   pulloides.

Arabis albida.
Aubrietia, in variety.
Alyssum saxatile.

Campanula turbinata.
Armeria cephalotes.

Lithospermum prostratum.
Saxifraga, encrusted species.

Dianthus neglectus.
Hutchinsia alpina.
Noccea alpina.

Ourisia coccinea.
Tiarella cordifolia.

Androsace Chumbyi.
Saxifrages, encrusted species.

Nepeta Mussini.
Cerastium tomentosum.

Shortia galaxifolia.
Galax aphylla.

Omphalodes verna.
Ourisia coccinea.

Veronica repens.
Thymus serpyllum alba.

Cortusa Matthiolo.
Primula luteola.

Primula sikkimensis.
Anemone rivularis.

Gentiana acaulis.
Lychnis Viscaria alba.

Hieracium villosum.
Campanula turbinata Isabel.

Æthionema, gd. fl.
Campanula muralis.

Dryas octopetala.
Thymus serpyllum coccinea.

Ramondia, in variety.
Haberlea rhodopensis.
Ferns in variety.

Caltha palustris.
Primula rosea.

Wahlenbergia serpyllifolia.
Saxifrages, encrusted species.

Hypericum fragilis.
Campanula portenschlagiana.

Gypsophila prostrata.
Genista prostrata.

Saxifraga umbrosa.
Anthericum Liliastrum.
Trilliums.

Cheiranthus alpinus.
Erysimum ochroleucum.
Lithospermum prostratum.

Tunica saxifraga.
Dianthus deltoides.
Mossy Saxifrages.

25

INDEX

Printed in the United Kingdom
by Lightning Source UK Ltd.
123322UK00001B/34/A